Communication and Awareness

COMMUNICATION

and

AWARENESS

Gary Cronkhite

University of California, Davis

Cummings Publishing Company

Menlo Park, California • Reading, Massachusetts
London • Amsterdam • Don Mills, Ontario • Sydney

To Charles, Irene, Rick, and Ty

Cover design and book design by Design Office/Bruce Kortebein

Cover photographs: upper left and lower right by Marshall Berman; upper right by Earl Dotter/BBM; lower left by Nacio Jan Brown/BBM

Drawings by John Johnson

Acknowledgments

For the photographs that are not accompanied by credit lines, the publisher would like to acknowledge the following sources:

Charles Arnhold for the photographs on pp. 19, 49, 89, 147, 175, 203, 219, 225, 262, 293, 345, and 375 (which were taken expressly for this book), and also for the photographs on pp. 3, 307, 321, 347, 350, and 387.

Jeffrey Blankfort/BBM for the photograph on p. 300.

Elihu Blotnick/BBM for the photographs on pp. 23 and 101.

Nacio Jan Brown/BBM for the photograph on p. 83.

Earl Dotter/BBM for the photographs on pp. 77 and 158.

Troubador Press for supplying the photograph on p. 139.

Contents

Preface

Introducing people to the study of communication is an exciting and challenging task. I find it exciting because I see communication as a crucial and pervasive aspect of our lives, but one which most of us practice almost as a reflex until we realize that what we have been doing all our lives is in fact an art, a science, and a field of study in its own right. Learning about communication is largely a process of becoming *aware* of something we have been doing all our lives and then, on the basis of this awareness, learning to do it more effectively.

Perspective

The basic approach of this book developed rather directly as a response to the analysis of education voiced by Postman and Weingartner in their book *Teaching as a Subversive Activity.* They called for a new education devoted to cultivating "crap detectors"—people who can recognize propaganda and deal with it effectively.

I am sympathetic with their analysis, but I believe it needs some modification. Taken at face value it might appear they are calling for the encouragement of "cynical listening": listening with prejudice, on the assumption that all communication is designed to take advantage of the listener. In fact, communication can serve at least three important functions for an individual, as I note in the opening chapters: it can be a means of gathering information, it can facilitate cooperation, and it can facilitate self-actualization, improving one's social relationships. Thus what we need to develop is a generation of people who are *aware* of what is happening in communication encounters, who are capable of listening *critically, cooperatively,* and *sensitively,* and capable of doing all three simultaneously. Further, it is important that we learn to listen critically, cooperatively, and sensitively not only to others, *but also to ourselves.*

Plan of the Book

To accomplish those goals, this book has been divided into four major parts, each designed to develop awareness of some crucial aspect of communication.

The first part, "Becoming Aware of Communication," begins with a chapter which places communication in a broad perspective, outlining

its role in the evolution of ideas and thus its contribution to the survival of humanity, arguing that we must be aware of the bases for the
decisions we make in response to communication in order for the
evolution of ideas to proceed in a way which maximizes our chances
of survival. In a sense it provides an "ethical" basis for communication without ever mentioning the word: Communication which reduces
the listener's awareness of the bases for his decisions is to be avoided
not because it is "wrong" according to some moralistic dogma, but
because it is prejudicial to human survival. The second chapter includes
a definition of communication which is moderately restrictive, narrow enough to avoid making our discipline include the study of *all*
human behavior, but broad enough to include that which is *distinctively*
human. That chapter also describes three major functions of communication and develops a model of human perception, cognition,
and message production which is then transplanted into the Barnlund
model of the communication environment. The third chapter reviews
some characteristics of communication and then explains some important communication concepts and models.

The second part, "Becoming Aware of People," can be considered
a call and a plan for the development of empathy, although that concept is alluded to most specifically in the fourth chapter. This part
includes chapters dealing with interpersonal differences in demographic characteristics; with some personality characteristics which
seem especially relevant to communication; with theories of how opinions and policies develop and change to serve the functions of consistency, social learning, and ego-maintenance; and with the functions
of reference persons and groups under the headings of commitment,
consensus, and credibility.

The third part, "Becoming Aware of Messages," deals with what I
consider the central focus of communication: the means by which
human cognitive systems are linked. It includes chapters on the ways
in which messages appeal to human motives or values, the reasoning
used in such appeals and how such reasoning can be evaluated, the
human language system and its effects upon those who use it, and the
extraverbal means of communication.

Finally, "Becoming Aware of Contexts" deals with some specialized
situations and formats in which communication occurs. That requires
some explanation.

First, the informal face-to-face interpersonal encounter in which most human communication occurs is not treated as a special context. The reason is that the rest of the book deals predominantly with such encounters: the theory described in the first twelve chapters is most easily applicable to interpersonal encounters; the examples used to explicate that theory are usually interpersonal; the exercises recommended usually require interpersonal communication; the cartoons usually picture interpersonal contexts, as do the photographs; and I assume the predominant classroom activity in communication courses will be interpersonal.

Second, there are several *very* specialized communication formats which I have omitted—interviews and public debates, for example. Because only so many contexts can be covered in an introductory textbook, I was simply forced to omit some of those which are encountered relatively infrequently. Professors and students who are especially interested in some of those contexts will find that most of the general communication principles surveyed here are applicable, and they can then supplement this book with others which treat the unique considerations and constraints which those contexts impose.

Thus the contexts I have chosen to treat in this last section are those which occur less frequently than informal face-to-face interpersonal encounters, but more frequently than interviews, public debates, and courtroom communication. Further, those I have treated are ones which pose special problems. Writing and public speaking, because they usually involve extended monologues with limited audience feedback, require special attention to organization which anticipates questions the audience will not be able to ask. Small groups, formal organizations, and mass society introduce special problems of communication flow in such social structures. And intercultural and interracial communication involve special problems created by encounters with beliefs, values, and behavior patterns which may be completely unfamiliar. I hope that the choices I have made are those which will be useful to you.

Special Concerns

This book is designed to be used as a textbook for an introductory course in general communication theory. As such it reflects my ideas of the sort of book which is needed in such a course. Let me be specific now about what some of those ideas are.

Because the field of communication is rich with a variety of approaches and specific content areas, I believe an introductory textbook should not only provide a broad overview of such approaches and content areas, but should also integrate them in such a way that the student can see what they have in common.

I believe the field of communication is also rich with sound theory based on solid research, and that theory and research should be presented to students in such a way that they will respect the study of communication as an academic discipline.

But I also believe communication theory is intensely practical, so I have tried to provide practical examples and exercises to serve as guides for the student—to illustrate how the theory can be applied in situations he or she is likely to encounter.

Finally, I believe students should enjoy learning about communication. Entertainment is not just a means for reducing student suffering, it is a sound teaching device. Consequently I have tried to inject my own brand of humor as frequently as possible, I have written the book in a very personal style, I have included many original cartoons designed to illustrate specific points in the book, I have included photographs produced especially for this book, and I have imposed on Jo Liska to design end-of-chapter and in-text exercises which students will enjoy, because I believe she is more capable of doing that than I am.

That is what I have tried to do. Since the book is a product of my own biases, I am in no position to judge whether I have succeeded. I hope it meets your needs because, as a teacher of introductory communication courses, I know how difficult it is to find a satisfactory textbook. Now I also know how difficult it is to write one.

Gary Cronkhite

1

Becoming Aware of

COMMUNICATION

What is the role of communication
in society? For that matter, what *is* communication
and what functions does it serve? How does a
person process information and where
does the information come from? What are the important
characteristics and concepts of interpersonal
communication? These are some of the questions
which need to be answered as one begins
to become aware of communication
as a general process.

Chapter One

Communication Awareness
and Human Survival

The psychologist George Miller has written:

> I have the impression that some communication theorists regard
> the human link in communication systems in much the same way
> they regard random noise. Both are unfortunate disturbances in
> an otherwise well-behaved system, and both should be reduced
> until they do as little harm as possible.[1]

Miller objected to that approach for one basic reason, a point this book
is intended to emphasize:

Communication is distinctively human.

The human race has survived and has been able to extend its control
over the environment so successfully for one major reason: the human
brain is distinctively capable of communication. Miller also made that
point when he wrote:

> It is difficult to avoid the impression that infants are little machines
> specially designed by nature to perform this particular task of
> learning language.[2]

This innate human ability to learn language and communication is a
tremendous advantage, of course. But it also poses a problem. Human
beings learn to communicate so easily and so early that they soon forget
what they are doing. A child by the age of four has most of the basic
tools he needs to communicate. For the next few years his parents,
teachers, and peers work to socialize his communication—to teach
him how to use it. But they teach him every day in such subtle ways
that he is barely aware of what he is doing.

Consider yourself as an example. You are now enrolled in a college
course in communication. That means you are probably at least seventeen years of age, and you have been using communication for almost
all of that time. Every day you use an incredibly complex system of
linguistic and social rules to achieve communication. What on earth are
you doing getting college credit for studying something you have been
doing all of your life? You may as well be taking a course in *breathing*.

On the other hand, how often do you think about what you are doing
when you talk to a friend, watch a television program or commercial,
or listen to a political speech? How aware are you of the techniques

you are using for the decisions you make in response to communication? Most people communicate at a very low level of awareness. And the result of this lack of awareness is that most people do not use communication as well as they could. Yet communication is absolutely essential to human survival. All the forms of ecology that get such play in the national media depend primarily upon communication ecology. *That is what this book and this course are all about—communication ecology.*

Survival Value of Communication

Human beings could not begin to deal so effectively with their environment if they weren't able to devise cooperative strategies and coordinate those strategies effectively by means of communication. Communication is mankind's most effective tool. R. Buckminster Fuller has discussed communication as a tool in his book *Operating Manual for Spaceship Earth:*

> All of humanity's tool extensions are divisible into two main groups: the craft and the industrial tools. I define the craft tools as all those tools which could be invented by one man starting all alone, naked in the wilderness, using only his own experience and his own integral facilities. Under these isolated conditions he could and did invent spears, slings, bows, and arrows, etc. By industrial tools I mean all the tools that cannot be produced by one man, as for instance the S.S. *Queen Mary*. With this definition, we find that the spoken word, which took a minimum of two humans to develop, was the first industrial tool. It brought about the progressive integration of all individual generation-to-generation experiences and thoughts of all humanity everywhere and everywhen. The Bible says, "In the beginning was the word"; I say to you, "In the beginning of industrialization was the spoken word."[3]

By this analysis communication is viewed as not only the first "industrial" or cooperative tool, but as the foundation and means for all those which have followed. But more important than the role communication *has* played in the survival of humanity is the role it will have to play in the future. R. Buckminster Fuller again:

> This cushion-for-error of humanity's survival and growth up to now was apparently provided just as a bird inside of the egg is provided with liquid nutriment to develop it to a certain point. But

then by design the nutriment is exhausted at just the time when the chick is large enough to be able to locomote on its own legs. And so as the chick pecks at the shell seeking more nutriment it inadvertently breaks open the shell. Stepping forth from its initial sanctuary, the young bird must now forage on its own legs and wings to discover the next phase of its regenerative sustenance.

My own picture of humanity today finds us just about to step out from amongst the pieces of our just one-second-ago broken eggshell. Our innocent, trial-by-error-sustaining nutriment is exhausted. We are faced with an entirely new relationship to the universe. We are going to have to spread our wings of intellect and fly or perish; that is, we must dare immediately to fly by the generalized principles governing the universe and not by the ground rules of yesterday's superstitious and erroneously conditioned reflexes. And as we attempt competent thinking we immediately begin to reemploy our innate drive for comprehensive understanding.[4]

And now back to Miller:

In order to survive in a fluctuating environment, an organism must have some capacity to collect, process, and use information. This capacity is greatest in man, so that he is able to learn elaborate coding systems and to organize his social behavior by communicating with his fellow men.[5]

(We might add incidentally that, since Miller wrote this passage, communication theorists have been seized by the growing suspicion that women, too, are human, and that they, too, are probably capable of communicating.)

John C. Lilly, the physician who has done much research in communication between humans and dolphins, expressed this idea in more urgent language in his book *The Mind of the Dolphin: A Nonhuman Intelligence:*

In the modern world with the hydrogen bombs and threats of extinction we must, finally, examine our best means of communication with interpersonal man [sic], of group to ever larger group. We must support research that shows promise of giving us new insight into interhuman communication. *For the mental health of each one of us, for the national and international peace of all of us, communication is a paramount and pressing issue.*[6]

Suppose we become more specific about how three major functions of communication contribute to the survival of humanity. It seems almost self-evident that communication has survival value insofar as it makes a person better able to gather information about the environment. That is the function Miller was writing about.

It also seems evident that communication has survival value insofar as it allows people to deal with their environment cooperatively and to avoid destroying one another with the awesome weapons communication has made possible. That is the function Fuller and Lilly were writing about.

It may not be so evident why communication has survival value insofar as it promotes self-actualization. Put simply, one must learn to deal effectively not only with his physical environment but also with his social environment. That, of course, overlaps both of the other functions, but it is an important function in its own right. One must understand himself and his place in his social environment in order to survive as a mentally healthy individual. The survival of mentally healthy individuals is necessary to survival of a mentally healthy society. Lilly also wrote about this function:

> For each one of us this is the most important study that we have ever undertaken: how to communicate with our fellow man is a constant and recurring problem of consuming interest. We want understanding, love, and respect; we receive them through communicating what is in our minds. We want to give understanding, love, and respect; we can give only through communication and only to those who can communicate in turn. . . . If one knows his own basic deep needs, he can communicate in terms of ethics, morals, manners, instincts, the acquisition of new knowledge, the nurturing and teaching of children, the building and maintenance of his own home, the encouragement of his friends, the performance of his work, the participation in the national and international life of his species. If one can realize that he is a unique individual, unrepeated since the beginning of his species, and can also confer this honor on each other human individual, he can then spend the time to learn his own internal language, and the internal language of each other individual, and learn how to translate each into the commonly shared language and thus succeed in communication.[7]

The Evolution of Ideas

Actually this discussion has been a bit simplistic. It may sound as though communication almost automatically assures the survival of the human species, and I don't believe that. Communication has also made it possible for us to destroy ourselves and our planet, either suddenly by an atomic blast or more gradually by cooperative and efficient destruction of the natural resources necessary to keep us alive. Some people believe communication has carried us so far that it is now just a question of which way the world will end—with an atomic bang or an ecological whimper. We have hopes, but our hopes depend on another kind of evolution: the evolution of ideas.

Donald Campbell, the psychologist-philosopher from Northwestern University, has described this process.[8] Evolution, he says, requires three things: variety, selection, and retention.

To see why these three are necessary, suppose we imagine what might happen if atmospheric pollution continues to increase gradually over the next few centuries. First, if there happens to be too little *variety* among human respiratory systems, the human race will soon become extinct. There will have to be enough human beings with large lung capacities, less need for oxygen, and high tolerance for pollutants. If everyone were nearly the same in all these characteristics, they would all die off before evolution had any chance to save the race.

Second, there will have to be a *selection* mechanism. In biological evolution that selection mechanism is very harsh: unfit organisms either die or fail to reproduce. In our example, as atmospheric pollution increases, we will expect more of those with small lung capacities to die at an early age or to spend so much time coughing that they don't have much time for intercourse.

But variety and selection by themselves still wouldn't save the race: people would just die off slowly; although those with large lung capacities would disappear last, the number of human beings would just slowly dwindle toward zero. But that doesn't take into account what Campbell calls the *retention* or *propagation* mechanism. Notice that in each succeeding generation a greater proportion of those with large lung capacity will be reproducing and thus transmitting "large lung capacity" as a genetic characteristic to their offspring. In effect, by continuing to pollute the atmosphere, we will be selectively breeding a new race of human beings with large lungs, reduced need for oxygen, and increased tolerance for pollutants.

It is all a race, of course; atmospheric pollution may increase so rapidly that this evolutionary process can't keep up with it, and we will join the dinosaur, the saber-toothed tiger, and the dodo bird. Millions of years from now the insects' descendants will put our bones in an "interinsect" museum and wonder how we survived as long as we did.

This sounds like a very dim prospect, especially for someone who gets dizzy every time he stands behind a car or passes a smokestack. But fortunately we have more than *biological* evolution on our side. We also have *ideological* evolution, the evolution of ideas. If we can only make public policy evolve fast enough, we can stop pollution before it stops us. The problem is that the evolution of ideas works in ways very much like biological evolution: public policy is overrun with ideological dinosaurs, dodos, and sterile cuckoos.

The evolution of ideas also requires variety, selection, and retention. *If we don't have a variety of ideas and plans available to us, we may suddenly find ourselves facing a time whose idea has not yet come.* The evolution of ideas requires that we encourage free thinking. If we allow censorship of ideas by those in power *now,* we may find ourselves sharing a common tomb *later,* when the ideas that are powerful now are no longer equal to the challenge of a new age. "Freedom of speech" is not just an academic sacred cow; it is a very practical necessity for survival.

But if we have a variety of ideas, we are also going to need a reliable means of *selecting* those we need at any particular time. We can't allow every weird idea that happens along to be put into practice. In biological evolution, many—in fact, most—mutations are ill-adapted and frequently would not survive on their own. The same is probably true of ideological evolution. Without some means of selection, we would soon be overrun with ideological mutations.

By "selection" of ideas I do *not* mean "censorship." There is a vast difference between *killing* an idea and merely refusing to adopt it. An idea that seems today to be a wild mutation may be exactly what we need tomorrow. Death is not the selection mechanism in the evolution of ideas. An idea is "selected" when it is accepted by those who are capable of retaining and propagating it.

Retention, in ideological evolution, is the process of weaving a selected idea into the fabric of society—"institutionalizing" it by expressing it in laws, customs, and conventions, and defending it against attack.

To return to the pollution example, if this process of ideological evolution progresses rapidly enough, we may never have to face the harsher prospect of biological evolution. At the very worst, we may be able to buy time so that humanity can evolve biologically instead of becoming extinct. To do that we need to encourage free-thinking people to produce a variety of ideas, even somewhat radical ideas, for dealing with pollution. We need a gigantic, worldwide "brainstorming" session. At the same time, we need to evaluate critically each of these ideas in order to select those which are likely to succeed, and we need to institutionalize into public policy those which are selected. If this evolution of ideas proceeds rapidly enough, we may find and adopt means of dealing with pollution in time to preserve ourselves.

Communication and Awareness

Now it seems obvious that communication is a necessary part of all three processes. Free, uncensored communication produces the necessary *variety* of ideas; critical public deliberation and debate constitute the means by which ideas are *selected;* and the selected ideas are then publicized, institutionalized, and *retained* using the various communication media. I have written about that before:

> *The functioning of this selector mechanism depends upon the use of communication.* . . . Of course, communication is involved in all three processes: mutant ideas are carried like seeds on the winds of communication; the retention-propagation system uses communication as a selective herbicide to destroy the ideological mutations and as a fertilizer to maintain the health of the ideological strains that have been chosen for preservation. But at the heart of the entire process is the selector mechanism and the discipline which ministers to its health: . . . communication.[9]

That is what this book is about. A wide variety of influences may prevent you from making objective, reliable decisions in response to communication. This is important because each one of us functions day by day as a part of this selection mechanism, making thousands of seemingly trivial decisions each day in response to thousands of seemingly trivial messages. But in the long run, as the years and generations pass, it is those "trivial" decisions which are going to determine the quality of the ideas which survive this evolutionary process. No single dinosaur at any one time ever felt a specific chill which alerted him to the slow advance of the Ice Age, and no one of us is likely to make one *single* decision which will assure the survival of critical thinking, or even noticeably alter the course of ideological evolution.

> *Humanity may well stand or fall, survive or perish, on the overall quality of its communication.*

So far I have been rather vague with the terms "critical," "objective," and "reliable." To be more specific, by a "reliable" decision I mean one which yields the predicted results. If you decide not to touch a bare wire because it might shock you, and if someone else touches it and is shocked, or if you test the wire with an insulated probe and it produces a spark, you have made a *reliable* decision.

However, you have not necessarily made an *objective* one. If your decision was made on the basis of some internal motivation of which you were unaware, such as a pathological fear of copper wires in general, the decision wasn't objective—it was just lucky. Being "right" may be one test of reliability, but it is not a test of objectivity.*

---

* Psychologists dealing with perception frequently talk about perceptions being "veridical" or "autistic." A veridical perception is one which depends on the characteristics of the stimulus being perceived, while an autistic perception depends on the characteristics of the person doing the perceiving. Similarly, one could talk about veridical decisions which depend on the characteristics of the communication and its context, and autistic decisions which depend on the characteristics of the person making the decision. By "objective" I mean "veridical." I prefer the word "objective" because it is more familiar.

It's true that a reliable decision is not necessarily objective, and an objective decision is not necessarily reliable, but we assume objective decisions will be reliable more often than will nonobjective ones. It is not likely to be profitable in the long run to make decisions on the basis of your own idiosyncratic characteristics rather than on the characteristics of the situation.

So objectivity seems to be the key to reliability. How can one assure his own objectivity? Well, one can't *assure* it. But one can promote it by being as aware** as possible of all his own characteristics and all the characteristics of the communication situation, insofar as those characteristics are relevant to the decision. This awareness allows one to decide whether a decision is being made objectively; objective decisions are more likely to be reliable; and decisions which are both objective *and* reliable are critical decisions, which contribute to the quality of ideological evolution.

** *A person is not either aware or unaware. There are many degrees of awareness, ranging from vivid sensations presently commanding one's attention through sensations he vaguely remembers to sensations which he has actively tried to repress. One is more aware of some parts of his mental image than of other parts, at any given time. That is, some parts of his mental image are more* vivid *or salient. For those who don't believe in anything unless it can be measured, awareness can be measured. If awareness is great enough, it can be measured by asking a person to give a verbal account of the reasons for a decision, or to respond on a more or less structured questionnaire. If awareness is low or deliberately repressed, one may have to use autonomic responses to verbal stimuli; projective tests such as the Rorschach or Thematic Apperception Test; or some of the unobtrusive measurement techniques suggested by S.W. Cook and C. Selltiz, "A Multiple-Factor Approach to Attitude Measurement,"* Psychological Bulletin 62 (1964): 36-55, *or by* E.J. Webb et al., Unobtrusive Measures *(Chicago: Rand-McNally, 1966). We all know what awareness is, because we experience it. The difficulty comes when we try to recognize or measure it in others.*

Thus to the point of this chapter and, indeed, the point of the entire book:

> Any communication device which makes the participants in a decision less aware of the bases on which their decision is being made strikes at the heart of the evolution of ideas, because the quality of ideological evolution depends upon a reliable and objective selection mechanism. Since ideological evolution contributes to the survival of humanity, *any communication device which reduces awareness to some extent prejudices humanity's chance for survival.*

That is a strong statement, and it does require some qualification. We generally *presume* any attempt to reduce people's awareness of the bases for their decisions is detrimental to survival, *unless there is good reason for thinking otherwise.* Imagine, however, a packed movie theater in which the projectionist discovers a fire in the projection booth. He has to act quickly or the fire may spread, or someone may smell smoke, yell "fire," and cause a panic. If he tells the audience there is a fire, they may panic and rush for the doors, crushing one another in the melee. He is in both a moral and a legal dilemma, since he and the theater may be both morally and legally responsible for any deaths or injuries. Would the projectionist be justified in shutting off the projector, telling the audience it was broken, assuring them that their ticket stubs would be honored at a later showing of the film, and asking them to leave? Or if that didn't seem believable, would he be justified in telling them there was a fire but that it was minor and there was no danger, and asking them to leave quietly, even though the fire was not minor and there was danger? Either course of action would reduce his listeners' awareness of the situation, but it would certainly contribute to their immediate personal survival.

I believe there are such exceptions to the general rule, but those exceptions are governed by three rules of their own. The Supreme Court of the United States has expressed the first rule well. The Court has generally upheld the principle of free and open discussion, except in cases where free speech constitutes a "clear and present danger" if exercised *at that moment.* The same principle can be applied here: All the participants in a communication situation should be aware of the bases for their decisions unless immediate awareness constitutes a "clear and present danger" to their own safety or to the safety of others.

Second, the communicator who decides to reduce the participants' awareness must be willing to admit to it later, accept the responsibility for it, and accept the judgment of those he or she deceived as to whether the deception was justified.

Third, any deception which contributes to the advantage of the communicator, since it may be adopted as a result of "wishful thinking" on his or her part, should be especially suspect even though it seems to be justified.

These "rules" aren't offered as moral edicts. They are conditions under which communication deception may be justified because it contributes to immediate survival even though deception in general is detrimental to the survival of humanity.

A few years ago Richard Nixon and his host of public relations men raised the art of concealment to new depths. Over a period of years they practiced, as if it were a religion, the "mushroom theory" of cultivating the public: keep them in the dark and cover them with manure. They operated so effectively that there still remains a hard core of Nixon supporters who would not have judged him guilty regardless of the evidence.

This crew has departed, but there will be others—there are others. The defense we have against this assault on our intellects is *awareness*— awareness of how communication operates, of ourselves and others, and of how messages can conceal and deceive. I hope this book will start you on the road to such awareness. And that is the final awareness I hope will be instilled: the awareness that at best this book can do no more than get you started.

> Amid the myths and hysterias of opposing hatreds it is difficult to cause truth to reach the bulk of the people, or to spread the habit of forming opinions on evidence rather than on passion. Yet it is ultimately upon these things, not upon any political panacea, that the hopes of the world must rest.[10] [Bertrand Russell]

Summary

The evolution of ideas is important to the survival of humanity. Communication is the crucial element in the evolution of ideas, since it is absolutely essential in providing a *variety* of ideas, *selecting* among them, and *retaining* those selected. We must all be *aware* of the reasons for decisions we make in response to communication in order for ideological evolution to produce reliable policies which will contribute to the survival of humanity.

Suggestions for Developing Awareness

1. Choose a controversial issue you have recently made a decision about, e.g., to use or not use spray can products or whether to buy a small automobile instead of a big "luxury" model or a van. Trace the steps you followed to make that decision. For example, did you read or listen to evidence for all sides of the argument? What were the sources of your information? Did you critically evaluate the evidence? Having analyzed how you made the decision, how do you feel about it now? Is it a reliable decision?

2. Discuss the question of whether anyone involved in making a decision with respect to a controversial issue has the intellectual, emotional, and moral responsibility to inform himself or herself.

3. How does the idea of "awareness" as presented in this chapter serve to maximize your freedom of choice? For example, consider how limiting the amount of information available to the public limits our ability to make an "educated choice." Has the information available on topics such as nuclear reactor plants and their potential dangers, the unchecked power of the Internal Revenue Service, or CIA activities expanded or limited our knowledge base? How reliable is this information? Have you sought further information from a wide variety of sources or accepted the original information as "fact"? (You might want to turn to Chapter Fourteen for further discussion of dissemination of information through the media.)

References

1. George Miller, *The Psychology of Communication* (Baltimore: Penguin, 1967), p. 45.
2. Miller, *op. cit.,* p. 84.
3. R. Buckminster Fuller, *Operating Manual for Spaceship Earth* (New York: Pocket Books, 1970), p. 105; originally published by Southern Illinois University Press, Carbondale, 1969.
4. Fuller, *op. cit.,* p. 52.
5. Miller, *op. cit.,* p. 46.
6. John C. Lilly, *The Mind of the Dolphin: A Nonhuman Intelligence* (New York: Discus, Avon, 1967), p. 22.
7. Lilly, *op. cit.,* pp. 19-21.
8. Donald T. Campbell, "Ethnocentric and Other Altruistic Motives," in *Nebraska Symposium on Motivation,* ed. D. Levine (Lincoln: University of Nebraska Press, 1965), pp. 306-307.
9. Gary Cronkhite, "Rhetoric, Communication, and Psychoepistemology," in *Rhetoric: A Tradition in Transition,* ed. Walter Fisher (East Lansing: Michigan State University Press, 1974), p. 268.
10. Bertrand Russell, "What Desires Are Politically Important?" in *Nobel Lecturers: Literature 1901-1967,* ed. Horst Frenz (Amsterdam, London, New York: Elsevier, 1969), p. 463.

Chapter Two

The Nature of Human Communication

Human communication occurs when a human being responds to a symbol.

One of the most valuable steps people can take to improve their chances of understanding one another is to be certain at the beginning of a communication exchange that each party understands the way the other is using certain key words. Throughout this book I will use the word "communication," so I would like to describe as clearly as possible what I mean by it.

Not that the way I am going to use the word is "right." Arguing about whose meaning of a word is "right" is one of the silliest and least useful human activities. God doesn't approve certain meanings and disapprove others. There is no way of scientifically verifying the meaning of a word. Even if most people use a word one way, there may still be times when it is useful to use it differently. That about exhausts the possibilities. If one can't use the word of God, Science, or Other People to settle a dispute, what's the use of arguing?

One Definition of Communication

I don't want to argue. I just want to describe the way I am going to use the word "communication" for my purposes in this book. You see, "communication" has been used in the English language to mean almost everything, so one can use it to mean almost anything. The *Oxford English Dictionary,* for example, lists over a dozen different uses of "communication," including "sexual intercourse," "the Holy Communion," and "a semiannual Mason assembly," among others. Now *that* is my idea of a heavy-duty, all-purpose word.

S.S. Stevens has defined communication as "the discriminatory response of an organism to a stimulus."[1] That definition is concise, but it is far too broad for this book. If I thoroughly covered communication by that definition, I would have to write a book dealing with *all* behavior of *all* organisms. I don't plan to do that. Instead, I am going to adopt the following more restricted adaptation of Stevens' definition:

> *Human communication has occurred when a human being responds to a symbol.*

This definition has some implications which may not be immediately obvious. In fact, it limits the focus of this book to (1) human communication which (2) involves symbols, (3) either verbal or nonverbal, (4) produced intentionally or unintentionally (5) by a source who may be aware or unaware of what he is doing, (6) which symbols produce a response on the part of a receiver, (7) which response may be overt or covert, (8) may or may not be intentional, (9) may or may not be performed at a high level of awareness, (10) may or may not match the intent of the source, and (11) may in fact be the person's response to a symbol he himself has produced.

Let me explain those implications one at a time. First, I have arbitrarily decided not to discuss communication among animals. There is good evidence that animals *can* communicate by almost anyone's definition. Chimpanzees who have been taught to use the sign language of the deaf have been able to invent new signs, to use the signs they have learned in new situations and new combinations, and to combine signs in sequences resembling sentences.[2] Dolphins, too, seem to be able to communicate with one another by means of some code which humans have not yet been able to understand.[3] Fascinating as that is, I just don't have space to give this topic the coverage it deserves.

The second implication, that communication involves the use of symbols, is very important and requires explanation. I am making a fairly conventional distinction between two types of signs: signals and symbols. A *sign* is anything that "stands for" something else. A clap of thunder and the word "book" are both signs, because the first stands for the approach of rain and the second stands for the object you are reading. But the thunder and the word "book" are two very different kinds of signs. The thunder is a "natural" sign, or a *signal,* because it bears a natural relationship to the rain it stands for. Nothing any human being has done has made thunder stand for rain, and nothing we can do is likely to end that relationship. On the other hand, the word "book" is an "arbitrary" sign, or a *symbol*; it stands for the object you are reading only because we use it that way. "Book" is "libro" in Spanish, and it could equally well be "noz" in some language we might invent. Its use depends, not upon any natural physical "laws," but upon certain "rules" of the English language.[4] Communication *usually* involves signals, but by this definition it *must* involve symbols.*

However, not all symbols are words. There are nonverbal symbols as well. "Giving the finger" is a symbolic gesture, for example, and it has a rather precise meaning in our culture—precise enough to get you a belt in the mouth in some circumstances. It is symbolic because its meaning is "arbitrary." Some nonverbal behaviors are not so easy to classify, however. Take Roger Klutz, for instance, who belches at a formal dinner. We can assume that the belch has no symbolic meaning; it bears a natural relationship to a gastric disturbance Roger is experiencing. So when I say "Take Roger Klutz," I really mean it. Please take him, the host doesn't want him. The problem is that if Roger were operating in another culture, his belch *might* be symbolic, and it might be a polite gesture as well. In some cultures a belch under such circumstances *does* have an "arbitrary" meaning, loosely translated as "my compliments to the chef." In American culture, Roger would be merely gross; in some other cultures he would be communicating.

It is possible to say that Roger is "communicating" in either case. Certainly the host and the other guests have received information about Roger's table manners, they have interpreted his behavior, and they have probably responded to it, at least covertly. I just don't want to dignify Roger's gastric indiscretions with the label "communication" unless they are *symbolic*. True, *any* human behavior *can* be interpreted by an observer, but that doesn't mean communication has occurred *by my definition*.

---

* *The idea that a symbol "stands for" something else is a little naïve, as explained in Chapter Eleven. A more accurate but more complicated way of stating it is that a symbol has certain rules by which it can be appropriately applied and understood, whereas a signal does not. Thus the word "thunder" is a symbol because speakers of English understand the rules which govern its use. The actual sound of thunder is a signal because there are no such rules which govern its use.*

Of the many signs in this photo, which are symbols and which are signals? That is, which are signs only because they are used that way, and which are signs because they are naturally related to something else? What would you need to know in order to decide whether the girl's bare feet constitute a signal or a symbol?

On the other hand, people do produce symbols unintentionally and may not be aware they have done so. Further, people interpret and respond to symbols unintentionally and without being aware they have done so. As a matter of fact, the major purpose of this book is to make you more aware of some of the ways people communicate unintentionally without being aware of what they are doing.

I am going to assume that communication must involve some sort of response on the part of a receiver. If that response is overt, or observable by someone other than the receiver, the observer can conclude that communication has occurred. But it would be foolish to say that no communication has taken place just because the observer has failed to see or hear any immediate response. Anyone who has played poker knows it is possible to respond to a message internally without showing those responses externally. A really strict behaviorist could lose a lot of money at the poker table. I have done some research in which I measured heart rates and GSR of people while they were listening to messages, and I have watched the recording pen almost go off the paper without any other observable response from the listener. Does that mean no communication would have taken place if the listener hadn't been wearing electrodes? Can a tree fall in the forest if there is no one around to hear it? How should I know? Ask a lumberjack.

Some people would say no "real" communication has taken place unless the listener responds the way the speaker intended. I have trouble taking that position seriously. Listeners almost never respond exactly as the speaker wishes, so there would be precious little communication to talk about if that were one of the requirements. Moreover, the event may be not only communication, but highly successful communication from the listener's point of view, *because* he has enough sense not to do what the speaker wants him to do. "Real" communication is frequently in the ear of the belistener rather than in the mouth of the bespeaker.

Examine the statement, "All communication is persuasion." Do you agree with this statement? Develop a case for your position. If you agree, for example, how does persuasion occur in idle conversation? If you disagree, describe aspects of communication which are beyond persuasion.

Finally, communication can take place when the source and the receiver are the same person. A person can communicate with himself by reading notes, letters, papers, and books he himself has written; by listening to recordings of his own voice; or by watching movies or videotapes he has made. In doing so he is responding to symbols he himself has produced.

This definition of communication excludes some aspects other writers have included and includes some aspects others have excluded. I have adopted it because it suits my purpose in this book. I have used other definitions for other purposes, and I will use still others in the future. I hope you will do the same. The most important point you can learn from this section is that the word "communication," like all words, is there to be *used,* and it has no single, prescribed meaning. Not that the word is completely empty of meaning, so that you can use it any way you please. Like other decisions, the decision about how to use a word such as this should be an *informed* decision arrived at by a process of which you are *aware.* If you are interested in reading about some examples of other definitions of "communication" used for other purposes, Dance has collected and analyzed a large number of such definitions used by other writers.[5]

Functions of Communication

The functions that communication serves are different for each situation, of course, and trying to summarize them is bound to be difficult. In this book, however, we will focus on three general functions which I mentioned in Chapter One: information-gathering, facilitating cooperation, and self-actualization.

Information-Gathering

Postman and Weingartner, in a book titled *Teaching as a Subversive Activity,* report that the writer Hemingway once said, "In order to be a great writer a person must have a built-in, shockproof crap detector." They go on to say: "It seems to us that Hemingway identified an essential survival strategy and the essential function of the schools in today's world. . . . We have in mind a new education that would set out to cultivate just such people—experts at 'crap detecting'."

Yes. And if that should be the essential function of the schools in general, it is an even more essential function of the study of communication. We are bombarded with propaganda almost every minute of every day through every means politicians and businessmen can devise. All too frequently they are assisted by college courses and professors who teach them how to sell themselves, their ideas, and their wares more effectively. More subtly, they are assisted by a system of education which rewards students who learn and accept what is told them by their professors and textbooks. Few professors would grant or even recognize how insidiously the vast majority of perfectly innocuous classroom activities teach uncritical acceptance of "facts," "laws," and "theories."

Yes, most professors *at some time* teach critical thinking, and some professors teach it most of the time. But as Postman and Weingartner point out, the medium is the message in education too, and while students may or may not remember the *content* of a course, the typical classroom *activity*—or *medium*—is absorbing information. And "information" is hard to distinguish from "propaganda." Somewhere, in some course, someone ought to be actively teaching the critical evaluation of propaganda.

But suppose we back up to a more philosophical level and deal with the *information-gathering* function of communication. The infant who confronts this confusion of sense impressions which we call the world must begin very soon to distinguish between reliable and unreliable sense impressions, make reliable inferences, and formulate effective plans for dealing with his world. If he doesn't accomplish that in a fairly short time, he is going to be kidnapped or hit by a truck. Many of those sense impressions are communications from other people. If he uses those communications well, he can prepare to deal with situations before he encounters them, and he can deal with some situations at a distance. As he grows older—*if* he grows older—he will use communication more and more frequently and effectively to gather information about the environment.

Sooner or later, however, he is bound to discover that he can't believe everything he hears, and a little later he will discover that he can't even believe everything he reads. Sometimes other people don't know, and sometimes when they know they don't want to tell what they know. What a cruel discovery when he finds that other people may even use their communication in order to use *him*.

Obviously, it is of considerable advantage to an individual to learn to detect unreliable communication. It is also advantageous to a society for its members to develop that ability. Otherwise, particular individuals or groups can use communication to advance their own interests at the expense of society. Free enterprise is especially dependent upon the consumer's ability to critically evaluate advertising and make practical decisions about what to buy. Democracy is equally dependent upon the voter's ability to critically evaluate political propaganda and make practical decisions about how to vote.

The quality of life in a free society is a rather direct reflection of its members' critical listening abilities. Unfortunately, the present quality of advertising and political propaganda in this country is probably a fairly accurate reflection of the extent to which these critical abilities have been neglected. Not that the decisions being made are necessarily bad, but the extent to which they are good depends on the interests of the society coinciding with the interests of the businessmen and politicians who control those decisions through public communication. What is good for General Motors *may* be good for the U.S.A., but not *necessarily*; consumers and electorates ought to be able to make such decisions on the basis of adequate information and critical evaluation of that information.

This critical listening ability is vital, and it is an ability to which courses in communication can directly contribute.

Facilitation of Cooperation

All of this discussion may sound as if I am arguing that the use of communication to influence others is never justifiable. I don't believe that. The human race probably would not have survived so long and certainly not so well if it had not been for the second function of communication: facilitating cooperation.

The building you live in would never have been built if it had not been for carefully coordinated cooperation. Instead of reading this book, you would be busily scavenging for food if it were not for carefully coordinated cooperation including specialization and division of labor. If you were not busy finding shelter or food you would probably be busy protecting yourself from others, if it were not for carefully coordinated social agreements which make the need for violent defense something of a rarity.

All of this cooperation would be impossible if it were not for communication. We communicate about the need to cooperate and ways to cooperate; we use communication to coordinate the activities of the participants; and we use communication to persuade others to join us. *Everything that makes up what we call "civilization" depends upon cooperation, and cooperation of any complexity and flexibility depends upon communication.*

It is true that certain animals seem to have fairly complex patterns of cooperation, but when one looks at them closely it is easy to see that they have developed to meet specific survival needs and are very inflexible. Ants and bees "cooperate" in the sense that they apparently instinctively perform activities which are so coordinated as to keep them reproducing and supplied with food. But the "cooperation," if it can be called that, is quite inflexible. It doesn't adapt to new needs, and it doesn't improve.

It is no coincidence that *homo sapiens* alone, among all the animals, now seems capable of complex, flexible, adaptive, coordinated cooperation and is also capable of complex, flexible communication.

Self-Actualization

Even if communication had no information-gathering or cooperation-facilitating function, it would be a long time before people stopped talking. A number of studies have demonstrated that people who have all their biological needs cared for still have a strong need for communication—a need that verges on desperation if they are deprived of communication for very long. Communication deprivation can even cause temporary perceptual disturbances, mental disability, and emotional disruption.

Just why that is true is probably a combination of factors. Humans may learn so totally that communication is valuable in gathering information and facilitating cooperation that it becomes rewarding in itself. Or it may be that communication is intrinsically rewarding because it is a species-specific behavior—specific to the human species. "Fish gotta swim, birds gotta fly. . . " and perhaps humans "gotta" communicate because that is their evolutionary essence. Of course, that answer doesn't really *explain* much.

There are a variety of "subfunctions" which communication seems to serve, none of which seems to derive its importance from any effect communication has upon the "real" physical world. Instead, an individual's communication insofar as it serves each of these subfunctions is important largely because it affects the communicator's own self.

One of these is the function of *uncertainty regulation.* Everyone knows that communication is frequently used to *reduce* uncertainty, because uncertainty is generally assumed to be psychologically uncomfortable. But too much certainty or predictability in one's environment is also uncomfortable. As a matter of fact, we call it "boring." So people sometimes use communication to *increase* their uncertainty. Thus they read new books, work puzzles, pose questions that have no ready answers, start arguments for no apparent reason, go to see movies about the bizarre and supernatural, and they gamble on all sorts of symbolic propositions having to do with kings, jacks, snake-eyes, and roulette wheels. This symbolic exploration, while it seems to be designed mainly to reduce boredom, is probably also good because it allows a person to practice dealing with uncertainty.

Identify techniques that you use to regulate the uncertainty in your world. For example, do you have any special "therapies" you find helpful when you are faced with complex decisions or too much information? I have a friend who cuts out recipes from magazines, and I find that I resort to cleaning the house or rearranging my office files when I am overloaded with information. Now, what do you do when you're bored? Do you seek stimulation by watching TV, reading, or socializing?

People use communication to practice *self-disclosure* and learn to *trust* others. Sometimes this serves as therapy for the individual, and sometimes it is socially useful.

Communication may improve one's ability to *empathize* or to understand the feelings and motives of others. It may also improve one's *self-understanding*.

Communication enables one to *share subjective experiences* or feelings with others and to confirm one's own internal feelings, thus gaining self-confidence. It also allows one to anchor one's own feelings, because it provides a means of discovering when they drift too far.

Sometimes it just provides an outlet for the expression or ventilation of emotions before they fester or reach an explosive level.

In short, communication provides a means for social transaction, which improves the individual's mental health, which in turn improves the quality of his or her social transaction.

A View of Communication

There are many ways of looking at the process of communication. In this book I am going to look at it from the inside out. That is, my primary concern is going to be what is happening to a person as he communicates —why he *produces* one message instead of another, and why he *interprets* a message one way instead of another. Consequently, I am going to describe first an "internal" model of human information processing which I will use throughout this book to discuss different aspects of communication. Then I will describe an "external" model of the various types of messages, the ways messages relate to one another, and the ways they relate to the context or environment in which they occur.

Image: Belief-Plan-Value

Kenneth Boulding has described what he calls a person's "image" of his world.[6] He wrote his description during a year he spent at Stanford University, on leave from the University of Michigan. He begins by describing his image of himself in space: surrounded by the Stanford campus, with the Coast Range on one side and the Pacific Ocean beyond; with the Hamilton Range on the other side, the Central Valley of California beyond that, then the Sierras, other mountain ranges and desert, the Rocky Mountains, the Great Plains, the Mississippi . . . ;

the United States as one part of a planet spinning through space. . . .
He then describes his image of himself in time: how he came to be
at Stanford and what he will do in the immediate future; how all that
relates to his life as a whole; how his lifetime is part of the history of
the human race and how the history of the human race is part of a
greater history. . . .

Boulding then turns to a description of his image of himself "in a
field of personal relations": his roles, expectations, and obligations
as a professor, a husband, a father, a friend, and a member of groups
and society. He describes his image of his place in a world of natural
relationships, in which certain events are followed by others in some
fairly stable, predictable sequences, and in which he can predict with
some confidence that certain acts on his part will produce certain consequences. Finally, he describes his image of himself in a world of
feelings, in which he is "sometimes elated, sometimes a little depressed,
sometimes happy, sometimes sad, sometimes inspired, sometimes
pedantic," and "open to subtle intimations of a presence beyond the
world of space and time and sense."

I like Boulding's description of the image, and I hope you will have
a chance to read it. Now, however, I would like to divide his general
description of human cognition into three parts: beliefs, values, and
plans.

Beliefs

*Beliefs are feelings about the probable existence of and relationships among
the objects, people, concepts, events, and ideas which constitute one's image of
the world.* That is, I can believe *in* a thing and I can believe *about* a thing.
I have a very strong belief *in* the existence of automobiles, a weaker
belief in the existence of "black holes" in space, and an infinitely weak
belief in the existence of unicorns. I not only believe in automobiles,
I also believe certain things *about* them: that they have wheels, they
provide transportation, and they can kill, for example. Thus I believe
that automobiles are *related to* other concepts: wheels, transportation,
and death, among other things.

I believe in different types of relationships among concepts; these
types of relationships can be labeled "similarity," "approval," "categorization," and "contingency." Thus I believe that automobiles *are*

similar to trucks in some respects and that Ralph Nader does not *approve of* them. I believe that the concept "automobile" bears relationships of *categorization* to "wheels" and "Porsche," since both are part of the "automobile" category (although in rather different ways). And I believe that there is a *contingency* relationship between automobiles and death: *if* I ride in an automobile, *then* I may be killed.

The strengths of these relationships may vary: I may see automobiles as very similar to trucks but less similar to trains; I may believe Nader strongly disapproves of automobiles or only mildly disapproves; a Porsche necessarily falls in the automobile category (because at this time, at least, Porsche does not build trucks), but a Chevrolet may or may not; and it is less probable that I will be killed if I ride in a train than if I ride in an automobile.

To push this mind trip one step closer to insanity, the strengths of my beliefs in these relationships may vary: I may have a strong belief that Nader disapproves of automobiles, or my belief may be quite weak, or I may in fact *dis*believe.

Finally, my beliefs are related to one another. Obviously, it is going to be difficult for me to believe that God created the universe if I do not believe in the existence of God. I say "it is difficult" instead of "it is impossible" because, as I will note in a later chapter, people *do* maintain beliefs which are logically contradictory. Nevertheless they seem to work toward eliminating such contradictions when they become aware of them.

Values

Values are feelings of liking or disliking for the objects, people, concepts, events, and ideas which constitute one's image of the world. If asked to do so, I can make lists of things I like and dislike. Moreover, I can to some extent rank-order these things in terms of how much I like them. Thus I like eating ice cream more than I like rolling in ground glass. But these value orderings may change from time to time, just as my beliefs may change. As a matter of fact, my values usually change *because* my beliefs change. To understand that, we will consider how values relate to beliefs.

Generally speaking, one's values *depend upon* one's beliefs. For example, I drive a Datsun 240Z. I *value* it because I *believe* it corners well, has quick acceleration, gets good gas mileage, and does not require many repairs. I also value cornering, quick acceleration, and good gas mileage, but I do not value repairs. Unfortunately, I have some other beliefs which detract from my evaluation of the Z. I believe that it has very limited interior space, bumper strength, and ground clearance. The values I place on those concepts depend in turn upon other beliefs: I believe I own a bicycle and a Saint Bernard; I believe I am going to have to move in a few weeks; and I believe there are many times when I will want to drive on dirt roads in the Sierras and the Rockies.

On the whole I value my Z, but that could change if I come to believe less strongly in its cornering, acceleration, and gas mileage, or if I come to value cornering, acceleration, and gas mileage less, or if I come to place more value on carrying my bicycle and my Saint Bernard, pulling a trailer, and driving on dirt roads. In short, the value one places on something depends upon the values he places on other things to which he believes it is related.

Sometimes, however, the opposite is true; to a certain extent one's beliefs depend upon one's values. Because I value the Z *in general,* I find myself talking about how much luggage I can cram into it, how my Saint Bernard doesn't like to ride anyway, and how surprisingly well it negotiates back roads (even though I hit a rock last summer and knocked a hole in the floor).

Plans

Plans are feelings about the sequences in which behaviors must be performed in order to achieve certain outcomes. Miller, Galanter, and Pribram, who also spent a year at Stanford sometime after Boulding was there, found a copy of his book in the library and were inspired to elaborate on his concept of the image by describing how plans form a part of that image.[7] Plans can be thought of as a special type of belief in a contingency relationship: "*If* I perform this sequence of behaviors, *then* these outcomes will occur."

Three important characteristics of plans are: (1) they range from very specific to very general; (2) they are hierarchically related to one another; and (3) the plans one chooses depend upon one's beliefs and values.

You may have a very specific plan for writing, which consists of moving a pencil in an organized fashion across a piece of paper, and a more general plan for completing a degree at the college or university in which you are now enrolled. The specific plan for writing is related hierarchically to the general plan for completing your degree because you will use the more specific plan many times in executing the more general one. Your plan for completing your degree includes subordinate plans for taking a certain number of courses which are generally required. That plan may be quite formal; it may actually be written and filed somewhere as a "plan of study."

Your plan for passing this course is part of this more general plan of study. You probably haven't written it down, but you have some idea of the sequence of behaviors you are going to perform to accomplish it. That sequence of behaviors may have been given some shape by a syllabus your professor gave you the first day of class, or by his description of the course requirements.

Among those requirements may be the writing of a paper. You may not have given that much thought yet, but when the time comes you will put together a plan for doing the paper. That plan will consist of a number of subordinate plans which you already have stored and should be able to recall when they are needed: plans for talking to your professor about a topic, finding books in the library, making an outline, and actually putting the words on paper. At the bottom of the hierarchy are a number of plans which were stored so long ago and learned so thoroughly that you won't even have to think about them when you do them. And among those very specific plans is the one I mentioned several paragraphs ago: moving a pencil in an organized fashion across a piece of paper. Obviously, you didn't have to plan the physical act of writing when you planned to complete your degree, because the writing plan was stored and ready to become part of the more general plan to which it is hierarchically related.

Your choice of the general plan of completing a college degree was made because of certain beliefs and values you have. You believe certain outcomes will occur as a result of executing that plan. On the whole you apparently value those outcomes more than those of alternative plans such as getting a full-time job immediately after high school or hiking into the wilderness and living off the land. *Some* of the outcomes of the degree plan are undesirable, of course: having to read books like this, take exams, write papers, and live in poverty, among other things. But in light of what you believe will be the outcomes and how much you value those outcomes, the degree plan seems to have the advantage at the moment.

Stop for a moment and reflect upon your image as belief, plan, and value. Begin by thinking of your immediate location in space: where you are now, what is within touching distance, within 50 feet, a mile, and work your way out to the universe, then backwards toward a nuclear particle. How do you use space and what values do you place on proximity, open space, arrangements in space, movement in space, spatial relations, environment, personal space?

Think next of your location in time starting with now, what happened in the last hour, yesterday, last week, last month, a year ago, five years ago, thinking over the events of your life and from where your life came; then go forward to the next minutes, tomorrow, next week, six months, a year, and beyond. How do you use your time and what values do you place on punctuality, schedules, speed, long- and short-term commitments, goals, and planning?

Then place yourself in the field of personal relations and examine who you are in relation to those around you. Again, start with your closest friends and family, and move outward to the many people you know, and further to people you don't know, then to people from distant cultures. What do you value in your relationships with your parents, brothers, sisters, friends, peers, bosses, professors? What are the various roles (plans) you play as, for example, brother or sister, student, athlete, citizen, intellectual?

Continue by seeing yourself in the objective physical world of nature—the forces that operate on and in your body and other living things, the sensations you receive from this world, and the laws which govern the operation of machines and orbital paths. How do you use natural laws and what values do you have in regard to communion with nature, animals, physics and biology, forces of the universe?

   Finally, locate yourself in the world of emotions
and feelings; in what state of mind are you now, what
have been your strongest emotions, and what range
of emotions have you experienced? What emotions
do you value most and in what way do the following
feelings play a role in your everyday living: anger,
self-concern, pleasure, comfort, openness, excitement,
humor, confidence, sadness, remoteness, anxiety,
sexuality, aggressiveness, well-being, suspicion, trust,
power, alertness, helplessness, control.

   These are things you know about yourself, and they
are elements in your image and your subjective knowledge. Can you see a hierarchy in how your most important images relate to the lesser ones? It would be
appropriate to jot down these images and retain them, as
the author will continue to refer to Image: Belief-Plan-
Value throughout this book. To become aware of your
own image is the start of high quality communication.

Sensation and Perception

A "sensation" is just an item of data which comes to you through one
of your senses. A "perception" occurs when a number of sensations
are organized into a pattern and find a place in the image. Sometimes
the sensations don't fit into the image very well. In that case two things
can be done: one can see, hear, or feel the sensations in such a way
that they *do* fit, or one can change the image so it will absorb the new
sensations more easily.

Perception of Messages

A communication message which one receives is initially a sensation,
and it must be integrated into the image. Messages have to conform
to certain "rules" or "expectations," which are part of the image. Otherwise they may be judged as unintelligible or meaningless. For example,
messages which are presumed to be spoken English have to conform
to certain rules for English sound combinations or they will be perceived as gibberish, and they have to conform to rules for English
sentence structure or they will be perceived as nonsensical. They have
to conform to rules of English meaning or they will be perceived as

meaningless. And they have to conform to rules for appropriate use, or they will be perceived as tactless, crude, or inappropriate.

Now suppose an incoming message is one which really doesn't fit well into the listener's image. Take as an example the utterance Richard Nixon made to John Dean in one of their conversations: "Jesus Christ, get it!" If that message was an instruction to Dean to get the "hush money" to pay the Watergate burglars, it would not fit very well into the image of someone who believed Nixon was innocent. Such a person would have at least four chances to "misperceive" the utterance: (1) He could perceive it as unintelligible if it were garbled or if the volume were too low. Then he could avoid having to fit it into his image at all. (2) He could perceive it as nonsensical if it didn't seem to be acceptable English. That would be difficult with this utterance, but if it were more complex that would be a second possible way to avoid fitting it into the image. (3) He could perceive it as meaningless since there is no clear meaning for "it." That, in fact, is what many people who favored Nixon actually did. (4) He could perceive it as inappropriate in the context if interpreted as a serious instruction to get the "hush money," so he could view it as ironic or joking, in which case it would fit easily into his image of Nixon as an innocent man.

But suppose he failed to perceive it as unintelligible, nonsensical, meaningless, or inappropriate as generally interpreted. Then he would have to *change his image* of Nixon. He might change his *beliefs,* for example, by viewing Nixon as somewhat less honest but a lot more practical. Then to compensate he might change his *values* by coming to value honesty in a president less and practicality more, thus keeping the value of Nixon about the same.

However, these belief and value changes would have some implications for this person's subsequent message *plans.* His new message plans would no doubt involve talking more about Nixon's practical nature and less about his honesty when arguing with Democrats.

Notice, however, that this person's perceptions have also been *planned*; he has devised strategies or plans for perceiving incoming sensations and organizing them into the image. One attempt to diagram all of this is represented in Figure 1. The outside ring, labeled "plans," is the only one which has any contact with the external world. But there are two types of plans represented here: "sensory" and

FIGURE 1
The Image: Belief-Plan-Value model.

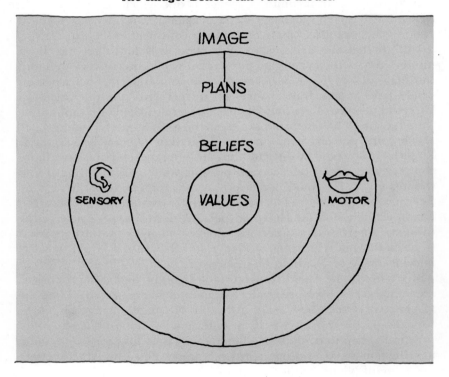

"motor." Sensory plans are those for receiving and organizing incoming stimuli into the image; motor plans are those for acting on the external environment in some way.

The ring labeled "beliefs" has contact with both plans and values, but its only contact with the external world is through plans: Beliefs are affected by incoming stimuli filtered through sensory (perceptual) plans, and they in turn affect the plans which the individual chooses.

The inside circle, labeled "values," is affected by the individual's beliefs and can, in turn, affect those beliefs. But values have no *direct* contact with either plans or the external world.

Message Transaction

The Image: Belief-Plan-Value model provides a way of looking at what goes on *inside* an individual as he or she processes information and makes plans to respond to it. But I have not yet said much about what is happening *outside* the individual: where the information is coming from or what kinds of responses he has available. A model developed by Barnlund does that well.[8] Barnlund's model is reproduced in Figure 2. I have transplanted the Image: Belief-Plan-Value model into the circles representing Person One (P_1) and Person Two (P_2) in Barnlund's model.

For the sake of simplicity let's look first at what is happening to P_1. Notice that there are dotted arrows leading out from P_1's sensory plans. These are *perceptions*. The solid arrows leading out from P_1's motor plans are *messages*. (By my definition of communication there could be other solid arrows representing P_1's nonmessage or signal responses. They are not drawn here, because they would really complicate the diagram.)

Consider the perceptions (dotted arrows) first. Some of these are perceptions of *private* cues (C_{pr}) available only to P_1. Others are perceptions of *public* cues (C_{pu}) available to both P_1 and P_2. The idea is that when I am talking to you there are some things I can observe but you cannot, some things you can observe but I cannot, and some things we can both observe.

In addition to these perceptions of the environment, P_1 also perceives the messages produced by P_2, some of which are verbal (C_{beh_v}) and some of which are nonverbal ($C_{beh_{nv}}$). Further, one of the dotted arrows indicates that P_1 is observing his own nonverbal messages. For some reason, Barnlund has not provided any arrow to indicate that P_1 is also observing his own *verbal* messages, but we will just imagine that arrow.

Once the diagram is understood from P_1's point of view, it is easy to see that the diagram for P_2 is simply the mirror image of that for P_1.

We need an example to put this in more familiar terms. Each semester I ask the students in my beginning communication course to analyze communication events from their own experience in terms of communication theories and models. One student used Barnlund's model to analyze her experience selling Avon products in one particular

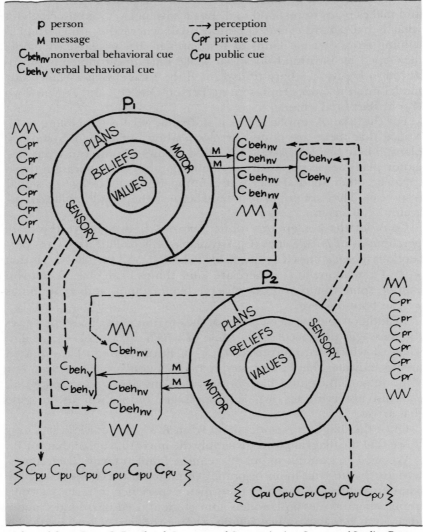

FIGURE 2
An illustration of the relationship between the Image: Belief-Plan-Value model and the Barnlund model.

p person $\dashrightarrow$ perception
M message C_{pr} private cue
$C_{beh_{nv}}$ nonverbal behavioral cue C_{pu} public cue
C_{beh_v} verbal behavioral cue

(Adapted from Dean C. Barnlund, *Interpersonal Communication: Survey and Studies,* Boston: Houghton Mifflin, 1968, p. 26.)

home. The student, Linnea Kline, has agreed to let me use her example. Linnea will take the place of P_1 in the diagram, and the Customer will take the place of P_2.

Linnea had a number of private cues (C_{pr}) available to her but not to the Customer. She knew many things about herself, whereas the Customer knew nothing about her until they met. She also knew some things about the products she was selling which the Customer did not share.

The Customer, on the other hand, also knew many things about herself which Linnea did not know: her need for Avon products, her past experiences with them, how much money she had to spend on such products, and so forth.

But there were public cues (C_{pu}) available to both, certainly including the general neighborhood in which both lived, TV programs they both watched, magazines they both read, but more relevantly including past Avon advertising both had encountered.

Linnea described how she observed the house before she entered: how large it was, how well it was kept, how large the property was, and how it was landscaped. Sometimes these observations are a little difficult to classify. They might be considered public cues, but since they were to some extent produced by or at least chosen by the Customer, they probably better represent nonverbal behavior cues ($C_{beh_{nv}}$) indicative of the Customer's personality and status. Linnea herself was producing similar cues in the way she dressed, the way she entered the house, and the way she smiled. Linnea, of course, observed the Customer's dress and manner as well.

Because she was a salesperson trying to make a good impression, Linnea was especially conscious of her own nonverbal cues, of course. Since Linnea did the reporting, it is impossible to know for certain to what extent the Customer was aware of *her* own nonverbal cues, but I think we can assume she *was* aware, since both her house and her personal appearance were neat and orderly, and she observed such social amenities as offering Linnea a cup of coffee.

Describing the verbal cues (C_{beh_v}) would require too much space, but Linnea does say the conversation gave her the chance to tell the Customer she lived in the same neighborhood and was a college student, and the Customer responded well to that information.

If we knew more about the Customer we could go deeper into the model and talk about her beliefs, values, and plans. We could make a fairly complete list of the alternative plans available to her, including refusing to open the door, talking to Linnea but not buying (with a variety of verbal justifications for not buying), or talking to Linnea at length *and* buying, which was the alternative she actually chose. Knowing what Linnea said and did and knowing that it was successful, we can speculate about the Customer's beliefs and values with respect to college students, neat dress, good manners, people who lived in the neighborhood, and Avon products. When Linnea approached the house she had already made many assumptions about the beliefs and values of the Customer before she ever saw her, and she had chosen her own sales plan accordingly.

And so do we all: *We observe the nonverbal and verbal cues of others, filter them through our own beliefs and values, draw conclusions about the beliefs, values, and plans of the others, and on that basis choose communication plans which we believe will lead to outcomes we value.* And this book is devoted to making you more aware of some of the considerations involved in that process.

Summary

Communication occurs when a human being responds to a symbol, according to the definition used in this book. This definition limits the focus of this book to (1) human communication which (2) involves symbols, (3) either verbal or nonverbal, (4) produced intentionally or unintentionally (5) by a source who may be aware or unaware of what he is doing, (6) which symbols produce a response on the part of the receiver, (7) which response may be overt or covert, (8) may or may not be intentional, (9) may or may not be performed at a high level of awareness, (10) may or may not match the intent of the source, and (11) may in fact be the response of the person to a symbol he himself has produced.

A *symbol*, as used in this definition, is a sign which stands for something else only because it is *used* to stand for something else, whereas a *signal* is a sign of something else because of a natural physical relationship.

The major functions of communication are *information-gathering, facilitation of cooperation,* and *self-actualization.*

A person's cognitive image consists of *beliefs, plans,* and *values.* One's experiences, including communications from others, are filtered through his perceptual plans so as to be made consistent with his beliefs and values; one's behavioral plans, including those for communication, are made on the basis of his beliefs and values. Those perceptual and behavioral plans which are chosen are those the individual believes will produce outcomes he values.

Communication occurs in a context of *public* and *private cues.* In communicating, one produces verbal and nonverbal symbols which serve as cues to others and to himself as well, since he is frequently aware of the symbols he himself is producing.

Suggestions for Developing Awareness

1. "Speech is civilization itself. The word, even the most contradictory word, preserves contact . . . it is silence which isolates."

   Do you agree with this statement? Is silence communication? Identify instances in which silence is meaningful or when you use silence to express your feelings or a mood.

2. Examine some other definitions of "communication" (in the article by Dance, for instance), and analyze how those other definitions would fit some types of communication and communication situations better than the one given in this book.

   You might want to form small groups in your class and have each group write their own definition of communication. Each group would then present their definition to the class and explain why they chose it. Does each definition deal with the definitional issues mentioned in this chapter? Do different group definitions fit different kinds of communication? What different topics would books cover if they were based on these different definitions of communication?

3. Examine the statement, "You cannot not communicate." Does the fact that someone can observe you mean that everything you do is communication? To what extent does your answer to that question depend upon your definition of communication?

4. In the book *Zen and the Art of Motorcycle Maintenance* by Pirsig, the author
    describes two images of the world as being romantic (intuitional and
    impressionistic) and classic (rational and structured). He proceeds to
    show how a person from each perspective might view a motorcycle.
    If you viewed a motorcycle from the romantic perception, how do you
    think you would perceive it? What about from the classical perception? As
    a start, a classical perspective might value the bike as a marvelous struc-
    tured system of interlocking and interrelated parts that are individual
    creations of the mind. The romantic might see the motorcycle as a beau-
    tiful hunk of metal that has power to carry one forth in the wind to
    interesting places. Can you expand each of these perspectives and show
    that each is an equally valuable insight into what a motorcycle is? How
    would a romantic or classical person view the uses of this machine, the
    repairs of the machine, the ultimate value of the machine? Describe some
    of the difficulties you might encounter if you were communicating about
    a motorcycle with a friend who had the "other" perspective.

References

1. S.S. Stevens, "A Definition of Communication," *Journal of the Acoustical
    Society of America* 22 (1950): 689-690.

2. R.A. Gardner and B.T. Gardner, "Teaching Sign Language to a
    Chimpanzee," *Science* 165 (1969): 664-672.

3. John C. Lilly, *The Mind of the Dolphin: A Nonhuman Intelligence* (New York:
    Discus, Avon, 1967).

4. Richards made this distinction, characterizing symbols as "arbitrary"
    signs. See C.K. Ogden and I.A. Richards, *The Meaning of Meaning*
    (London: Kegan Paul, Trench, Trubner, 1936). I prefer Peirce's state-
    ment that a symbol is a sign which is a sign only because it is used as one.
    See C.S. Peirce, *Collected Papers,* vol. II (Cambridge, Mass.: Harvard
    University Press, 1932), paragraph 307.

5. Frank E.X. Dance, "The 'Concept' of Communication," *Journal of
    Communication* 20 (1970): 201-210.

6. Kenneth E. Boulding, *The Image* (Ann Arbor: University of Michigan
    Press, Ann Arbor Paperbacks, 1956).

7. George Miller, Eugene Galanter, and Karl Pribram, *Plans and the Structure of Behavior* (New York: Holt, Rinehart and Winston, 1960).

8. Dean C. Barnlund, *Interpersonal Communication: Survey and Studies* (Boston: Houghton Mifflin, 1968), p. 26.

Some Assumptions about Communication

Communication Is a Process
Communication Is Transactive
Communication Is Multidimensional
Communication Is Multipurposeful

Some Communication Concepts and Models

Sources, Messages, Channels, Receivers (Berlo)
Noise: Signal and Semantic (Shannon-Weaver, Smith)
Information and Redundancy
Feedback (Westley-MacLean)
Decoding and Encoding
Communication Networks (Bavelas)
Interaction (Bales)
Transaction (Stewart)
Information-Gathering (Becker)
Uses of Theories and Models

Summary

Chapter Three

Communication Characteristics, Models, and Concepts

The purpose of this chapter is to introduce you to some of the assumptions and concepts in general communication theory before I become
more specific.

Some Assumptions About Communication

Most communication theorists make some basic assumptions about
the nature of communication. Some of their lists are longer than others.
I have chosen a few which I believe are the most defensible and which
most theorists would accept. They are important to someone trying
to understand communication because they influence the way one
looks at what happens in a real social event, what he reports, and what
he concludes about it.

Communication Is a Process

Communication does not consist of a single message fired by a source
at a target audience, to be evaluated in terms of how far it misses that
target. Communication has no beginning and no end. A communication "event" has only an arbitrary beginning and end, chosen by the
observer. Everyone involved in the communication process functions
as *both* a source and a receiver, sometimes changing functions in rapid
sequence and sometimes operating in both capacities simultaneously.
Even CBS and the *New York Times,* while they appear on the surface
to be sending one-way messages to passive audiences, are in fact quite
affected by the messages they receive from the audience. They *must*
respond to the messages they receive from their audiences or have
their circulation cut off, whereas the audiences are free to ignore their
messages if they wish. The point is even more obvious in interpersonal
or face-to-face communication. Thus those models which picture communication as beginning with a source and proceeding until it collides
with an audience are woefully inadequate as representations of the
actual communication process.

   But communication is a process in an even stronger sense.

> *Communication is a process because when it stops it no longer exists.*

A machine can be stopped and studied at rest. If something is wrong with an automobile engine it can be disassembled so as to locate the problem. Sometimes, in fact, that is the *only* way to find out what is wrong. Of course, one never really knows if the engine is going to run right until it has been reassembled and is started again, and some problems require that an electronic gadget be used to diagnose the difficulty while the engine is operating.

The point is that insofar as something is a machine, it can be studied at rest. Communication is not a machine. Sometimes it makes use of machines and physical structure, and sometimes when it stops there are artifacts left behind—marks on paper, filmstrips, and the like. But those are not communication itself.

What does that say about the analysis of communication? It says that one should do his best to observe the actual event. Whenever that is impractical (or whenever he needs a record of what he has observed), he should try to simulate (mimic or reproduce) the event as accurately as possible. Videotape and even audiotape or sound film are very useful tools for such simulation. Some parts of some events just can't be recorded in that way, of course, in which case one will have to rely on carefully written notes.

The battle over the tape recordings Richard Nixon made of his conversations in his White House office made one thing perfectly clear. A typed transcript of those conversations provided a very inadequate simulation of the actual events, because vocal inflections and timing were omitted. Even audiotapes omit facial expressions and movements which are sometimes essential to understanding what is happening.

Communication Is Transactive

Second, the communication process involves *multiple causality, interaction,* and *transaction.* Messages do not have a single effect; they have many effects. Some of those effects are visited upon the intended receivers, some upon unintended receivers, and some upon the source of the message. Further, messages are also *caused,* and they have multiple causes. Usually they are responses to other messages which their sources have encountered, sometimes quite recently and sometimes in the distant past. They are caused by personal characteristics of their sources; they are caused by audiences, immediate, potential, and past; and they are caused by the circumstances, immediate and remote, under which they are delivered.

Finally, sources, messages, and audiences interact in very complex ways. Assuming sources produce many messages, as they obviously do, the effect of one message is going to be altered by the source's previous messages. A speaker who says something stupid or untrue on one topic at one time will have to cover his tracks carefully if he expects to maintain credibility when speaking on another topic at another time. Sources also interact through messages: a speaker may considerably damage his own credibility by attacking something which another well-respected speaker has previously praised. Messages may also interact with each other, as they provide audiences with new information and alert them to defend themselves against subsequent messages. And audiences interact with messages, sources, and with each other as they exert feedback influences upon sources, causing those sources to modify subsequent messages to other audiences. In order to picture the communication process adequately, communication models must take into account the multiple causality and complex interaction which is inherent in that process.

But all this is true of processes which are merely *interactive.* When I say communication is *transactive* I mean a little more:

> *A communication event is a unique combination of people, messages, and situation such that if any one of those elements changes it creates a different communication event.*

You may have observed conversations in which there was one person who said absolutely nothing, merely listening to the others talk. But when that person left, the conversation changed entirely. Perhaps the others also left, or changed topics drastically, or suddenly became much quieter or noisier, or expressed very different opinions—but you knew it was a different conversation.

You may also have noticed that people change radically when they move from one communication situation to another, becoming more or less talkative, more or less rational, expressing different opinions, or seemingly undergoing complete personality changes.

Change one element in a communication event and one may completely change the event—this is what I mean when I say communication is transactive.

Communication Is Multidimensional

Third, the characteristics of sources, channels, messages, audiences, and the effects of messages are all *multidimensional.* Sources, for example, are not merely believable or unbelievable; they are to some degree trustworthy, authoritative, likeable, dynamic, and similar to the listener, among other things. Further, some of those characteristics may be relevant to the communicative process at one time and irrelevant at another, depending upon the speaker's purposes, the listeners' expectations, the circumstances in which the message is presented, and the medium through which it is transmitted. Channels differ in the amounts and kinds of information they are capable of transmitting; they differ in immediacy; and they differ in the extent to which the listener can review at his own will the information transmitted, among other things. Audiences differ in personal and personality characteristics, motives, attitudes, beliefs, values, past behaviors, characteristic behavior patterns, reference groups, and a host of others. Messages may differentially affect both audience and source beliefs, values, personalities, motives, or characteristic behavior patterns and specific behaviors, including future listening, reading, speaking, writing, and choices among potential reference groups. Models which treat any of these components of the communication process as if they were unidimensional do not do justice to the process.

Communication Is Multipurposeful

Finally, communication is *multipurposeful.* To the extent that the participants act as sources, they have purposes which they wish to accomplish. To the extent that the participants act as receivers, they have purposes they wish to accomplish: to become more informed, to evaluate their own opinions, to prepare to refute what is being said, or to assure that whoever is speaking will listen when it comes his turn to speak, for example. The person or agency responsible for bringing the participants together, if such a person or agency exists, must also have purposes for doing so. Persons or agencies not even aware that a particular communication episode is occurring may have stakes in the outcomes, although one might not term those stakes "purposes." In short, a complete communication theory or model cannot refer to *the* "purpose" of any given communication event, *since the purposes are probably far more numerous than the persons who brought the event to pass.*

Think of the communication which takes place in one of your classes. What is "the" purpose of it? Is *the* purpose *your* purpose—to become better educated in general, to learn about something you are especially interested in, to fulfill a requirement, to earn credit toward a degree. . . ? Which? Probably more than one of those and possibly all. Or is *the* purpose the instructor's purpose—to excite you, to educate you, to earn his or her pay. . . ? Or is the purpose that of the chairman of the department in which the course is offered, or of the dean, or of the university president, or of the board of regents, or of your parents, or of your employer. . . ?

Do not check one. Check "all or most of the above."

Assumptions, Models, and Theories

Throughout this chapter I will discuss various models and theories which illustrate key concepts in communication. These models will be useful for more than illustration, however, since a person who is trying to understand a given communication event needs some sort of framework which suggests what he should look for. Generally, we ought to expect a satisfactory model to be based on these basic assumptions that communication is a transactive, multidimensional, multipurposeful process.

Obviously, no theory or model is going to do all we ask of it. All the models to be surveyed, at least, fail one or more of the criteria. It is the purpose of a theory or model to reduce "reality" to a manageable number of elements and relationships among those elements. If the model becomes so simple as to ignore important parts of "reality," it becomes useless because it does not accurately represent communicative events. If the model includes everything the communicative process includes, it becomes useless because it is as unmanageable as the "reality."

What we are looking for is a model which represents accurately enough for our purposes those communicative events in which we are interested at a particular time. Just as a mechanic carries many tools in his tool kit, the competent student of communication will be familiar with a variety of communication theories and models so that he or she can use that one which is appropriate for the analysis of a given situation.

Some Communication Concepts and Models

Since a number of concepts are of such general use in communication theory, you should be familiar with them. Some have turned out to be useful, while others seem to be unnecessary jargon. I will deal briefly with those I perceive to be most widely used, illustrating them with models which have emphasized them.

Sources, Messages, Channels, and Receivers

Berlo's "SMCR" model illustrates how these four concepts have been treated by communication theorists.[1] The model is shown in Figure 1. I have frequently referred to "sources" and "receivers," and will continue to do so throughout this book, but the terms can be misleading. They suggest that one person acts as a source while others act as receivers, whereas in fact *everyone* acts as *both,* usually simultaneously, almost all the time.

Separating the message from the channel in which it is sent can be very misleading, too. It is impossible to think of a message without a channel or medium; it is even difficult to think of them separately. A message may be coded into one medium or channel such as a written English radio script, and then recoded into another when it is read into the microphone, and recoded into another when it is transmitted,

FIGURE 1
Berlo's SMCR model of communication.

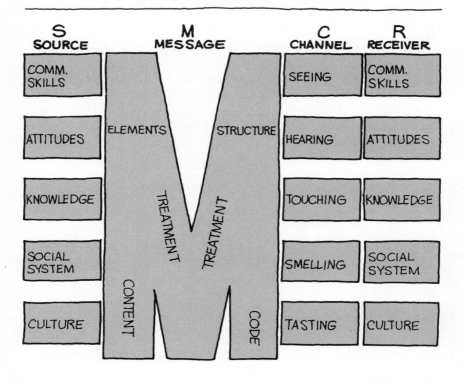

(Adapted from David K. Berlo, *The Process of Communication,* New York: Holt, Rinehart and Winston, 1960, p. 72.)

and recoded into another when it is received. But all of this isn't very useful in human communication. A wink and the words "I love you" are not just the same message in different channels; they are different messages.

FIGURE 2
The Shannon-Weaver communication model.

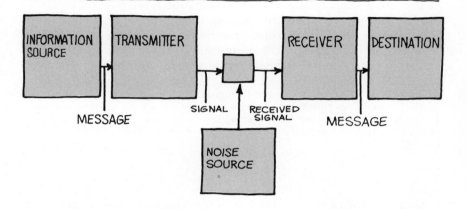

FIGURE 2
The Shannon-Weaver communication model.

(From Claude E. Shannon and Warren Weaver, *The Mathematical Theory of Communication,* Urbana: The University of Illinois Press, 1949, p. 98.)

Noise

The Shannon-Weaver model[2] actually preceded the Berlo model, and it introduced the same concepts. The model, which is shown in Figure 2, also shows "noise" interfering with the message in the channel. That sort of noise is what Smith[3] calls "signal" noise, because it is physical interference with the physical signal. As a matter of fact, the term "interference" would probably be better, since "noise" in the communication theory sense is not necessarily sound.

The other kind of noise, which Smith calls "semantic" noise, is not shown in this model. If it were, it would be diagrammed as an arrow striking the message between the information source and the transmitter, or between the receiver and the destination. The concept refers to the fact that what is meant is frequently not what is said, and what is heard is frequently not what is understood. *I know you believe you understand what you think I said, but I am not sure you realize that what you heard is not what I meant.*

The varieties of semantic noise are too many to enumerate, but they are represented by such confusions as "sane" and "seine," and such reports as "The queen broke the bottle of champagne across her bow as she slid gracefully into the sea." Semantic noise is also caused by the fact that we often perceive what we want to perceive, and we often produce very revealing messages quite inadvertently, e.g., the dreaded "Freudian slip." It is especially important to notice that *semantic* noise can occur even when transmission within the *physical* channel is perfect.

A "noiseless" or "errorless" communication event is highly improbable. Discuss examples that illustrate semantic and signal noise. What plans might you construct to reduce the semantic or signal noise in your examples?

Kirk and Talbot refer to three different types of noise or "distortion of information": (1) systematic or stretch distortion, (2) fog distortion, and (3) mirage distortion.[4] *Stretch* distortion is that in which information is systematically altered, and it can be corrected if one knows the rules by which it is altered. If one knows that an acquaintance *always* lies in certain circumstances, he can easily correct for the distortion. *Fog* distortion is that in which part of the message is lost or obliterated by random or "white" noise. This is more difficult to correct. "White noise" is what your air conditioner and shower sound like. It is very effective, which is why we have the expression, "you know I can't hear you when the water's running." *Mirage* distortion is that in which the message appears to be something it is not. One can wreak all manner of havoc by mistaking the sentence "I really hate to be going" for "I really have to be going." The antidote, again, is redundancy, as well as information garnered through another channel, which is really a sort of redundancy.

These concepts apply somewhat differently to the "signal channel" as opposed to the "semantic channel." Signal channel capacity is limited by the number of possible variations in the physical medium through which the signal is transmitted. The number of possible variations in human speech limit the capacity of the vocal auditory channel, for example. The amount of information which can be transmitted is further limited by the presence of noise in the channel and by the need to increase redundancy to overcome the effects of that noise. Consider, for example, the problem of a couple attending a noisy party. They suspect that sometime during the evening one or the other or both of them are going to want to leave. They also know that communication may be difficult because when that time comes the noise level may be high, they may be across the room from each other, and they do not want to offend their host. To combat this noise in the channel they prearrange two signals, one to indicate "go" and the other "stay." By doing so they limit the maximum amount of information to the smallest unit possible, increasing redundancy tremendously, but they have effectively overcome the noise in the channel.

Information and Redundancy

These terms are used a little differently in communication theory, and they should be explained.

"Information" is used by Shannon and Weaver in a very special sense. The amount of information transmitted by a given symbol does not depend upon that symbol itself, but rather upon the number of alternative symbols from which it was chosen. *A symbol carries information to the extent that it reduces uncertainty.* If the number of available symbols is great and they are all equally likely to be selected and transmitted, then the selection and transmission of any one symbol considerably reduces the uncertainty and transmits a great deal of information. If a symbol transmitted is one of only two possible symbols, then it reduces much less uncertainty and transmits much less information. If one of two possible symbols is much more probable than the other, its transmission reduces uncertainty even less and provides even less information. If one symbol is 100 percent probable, its transmission provides no information at all. It is said to be totally "redundant." Redundancy is the mirror image of information. *A symbol is redundant to the extent that it is predictable.*

Suppose someone asks you to guess: (1) which card has been drawn from a deck of 52; (2) which side of a flipped coin has come up; and (3) which side has come up on a flipped coin when you know the coin is so loaded that heads will show nine times out of ten. Now suppose you are lucky enough to get a look at the card and the coins. Your uncertainty is reduced a great deal, and you receive a great deal of information by seeing the five of clubs, not to mention the amount of money you can probably win if your opponent is willing to bet with you. Your uncertainty is reduced much less when you see the first coin, since the odds were only 50-50, and you receive much less information. Your uncertainty is reduced much less when you see that heads is showing on the second coin, since the odds were nine out of ten anyway; you have received very little information, since the outcome was highly predictable and redundant.

This theory can be applied to language, although philosophers are still arguing over the extent to which such application is legitimate. The appearance of the letter "u" after "q" in English is totally predictable, totally redundant, and carries no information value whatever. Other letters are "informative" to the extent to which they are probable given the letters preceding them; an "a" is extremely probable after the sequence "zebr," for example (although rumor has it that there is such an animal as a "zebrula"). Words also vary in probability, especially when they occur in sequence, given the constraints of grammar. We depend upon that fact when we omit high-probability, low-information, highly redundant words in telegrams and newspaper ads. The recipient of a telegram reading "Streets water-filled—please advise"* would have no difficulty responding appropriately if he knew the telegram came from a New York streetwalker who had recently transferred to Venice to practice her trade.

One might suppose from all of this that redundancy is useless and should be avoided in interpersonal communication. To the contrary, it is quite useful at times. One major purpose of grammatical rules is to *provide* redundancy. Then, in case some words are missed, it is easier to guess what they were. A good lip-reader with a good knowledge of English grammar can get along reasonably well at a noisy cocktail party without ever hearing a word his partner says. However,

---

* *A telegram reportedly sent to his agent by Robert Benchley*
upon his arrival in Venice.

FIGURE 3
The Westley-MacLean model of communication.

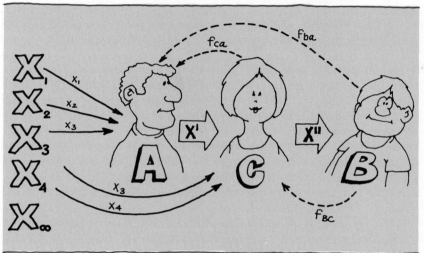

[Adapted from Bruce Westley and Malcolm MacLean, Jr., "A Conceptual Model for Communication Research," *Journalism Quarterly* 34 (1957):34.]

unnecessary redundancy should be avoided since it does reduce efficiency and effectively reduces channel capacity, limiting the amount of information that can be transmitted in a given amount of time.

Feedback

Feedback is another way of dealing with noise. The receiver can give the source return messages which indicate whether he is understanding and, if not, how and why he is misunderstanding. There is a danger in this concept. Just as it is usually difficult to tell who is source and who is receiver, it is frequently difficult and useless to tell the difference between message and feedback.

Westley and MacLean suggest a model which demonstrates the various functions of feedback in communication.[5] Their model is diagrammed in Figure 3. A communicator represented by "A" selects and abstracts from his own sensory perceptions a message which he transmits to "C." Communicator "C" then selects and abstracts from his own sensory environment data which includes "A's" message and also includes other sensory data, some of which may also be perceived by "A." On the basis of this sensory input, he composes and transmits a message to "B" and also transmits a "feedback" message to "A," probably indicating the extent to which his perception of "A's" message coincides with his own perceptions of their environment. Communicator "B," in turn, decodes "C's" message and may provide feedback to both "A" and "C." Although it is not represented in the diagram, he may encode further messages of his own, and he is probably privy to environmental data of his own, some of which he shares with "A," some with "C," some with both, and some with neither. This model certainly gives a better picture of the roles of feedback and sensory environmental data in the communicative process. This model is also effective in representing the "two-step flow" of information from the mass media to the public.

That "A, B, and C" was a little difficult to follow. Suppose we give them names. Ann hears on her car radio on the way to school that peace has once again broken out in the Middle East. When she arrives in class she reports to Chris (A to C message) that the president has again demonstrated his leadership in international affairs. Chris responds with an inappropriately obscene expression of disbelief (C to A feedback), and she passes the word on to Bob (C to B message). Bob guffaws and writes a note which he lets Chris read (B to C feedback) before sending it on to Ann (B to A feedback).

Decoding and Encoding

These two terms seem to me to be prime examples of the invention of jargon for the sake of jargon, but they are frequently used, and they can be confusing. Briefly, "decoding" is what you are doing now, and "encoding" is what I did when I wrote this chapter. "Decoding" is what one does when he listens or reads; "encoding" is what he does when he writes or speaks. "E" is for Expert, who speaks amid cheers; "D" is for Dummy who believes what he hears. Bad. But what can you expect at one o'clock in the morning?

Communication Networks

Some of the models of small group processes are adaptable to communication in general, and they have an advantage over the models surveyed to this point: they introduce additional persons into the picture, so that we can consider communications among a number of individuals.

For example, a number of research studies have investigated the flow of information among people in groups in which different channels were available through which they could communicate, forming different networks. Bavelas described four kinds of communication patterns, for example, which can be established among five people by selectively closing certain channels.[6] Some types of networks are diagrammed in Figure 4, including an all-channel communication network in which each member of the group is free to communicate with every other member.

Consider the differences in these types of communication patterns. The all-channel network appears to be the most "democratic," but it is also likely to be the most chaotic since messages can flow in all directions. Participants generally seem more satisfied with this pattern. The wheel, on the other hand, appears quite autocratic, but it is also more likely to be disciplined and organized. However, communication in the wheel network is entirely dependent upon the ability, motivation, and benevolence of the person occupying the center position since all communication must flow through that person. If he is incapable, uninterested, or if he wants to sabotage communication for some reason, the entire process can break down very quickly. Further, the demands on his communicative abilities are considerable. If information flow is heavy, since it all must pass through this person, information overload can occur very quickly.

While network diagrams developed from research with communication in small groups, they really seem more useful in analyzing communication in organizations. Figure 5 contains two diagrams of a small business organization, one of which represents the formal or prescribed communication network, while the other represents the informal "grapevine." Arrows have been used not only to indicate the open channels but also the direction of communication in those channels.

FIGURE 4
Some types of group networks.

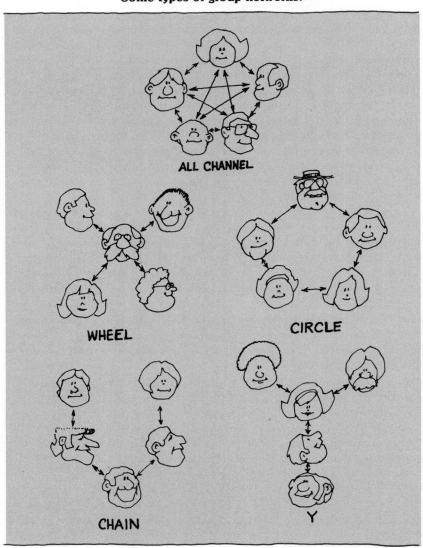

FIGURE 5
Communication networks in an organization.

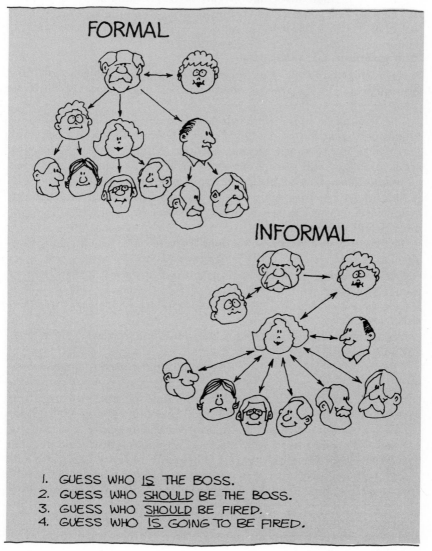

Studying these two diagrams side-by-side gives an interesting picture of the organization and even of the personalities of the people in the organization. Such information can be very valuable to executives and hence very valuable to communication consultants. When I say "valuable" I am talking about money.

Interaction and Transaction

Early in this chapter I referred to the concepts of "interaction" and "transaction." There are two models which might serve to illustrate the difference.

The first of these is Bales' Interaction Process Analysis.[7] Bales has suggested a method of categorizing the communication acts people perform in interacting with one another. While it was developed for application to small groups involved in problem-solving discussions, its potential application seems much broader than that.

Bales describes four main categories into which types of communication interactions can be classified, and each of these categories contains three subcategories.

The category of **positive reactions** includes acts which *show solidarity, show tension release,* and *show agreement.*

Problem-solving attempts include *giving suggestions, giving opinions,* and *giving information.*

Questions include *asking for information, asking for opinions,* and *asking for suggestions.*

Negative reactions are those which *show disagreement, show tension,* and *show antagonism.*

There are a number of ways this model can be used to analyze communication. One can, for example, identify the types of communication acts which characterize different time periods during group formation and interaction. In the small problem-solving group Bales worked with, for example, both positive and negative reactions increased over time until a solution was chosen, at which time negative reactions generally disappeared. Positive reactions generally outnumbered negative reactions throughout the session. Even more specifically, within the general category of problem-solving attempts, giving information seemed to occur most frequently early in the session, giving opinions occurred most frequently in the middle portion, and giving suggestions occurred most frequently toward the end.

The approach has also been used to study the sequences in which communication acts occur. A given speaker shows an overwhelming tendency to react in his first statement to the preceding speaker, usually by agreeing, secondarily by stating his own opinion, and if neither of these, by disagreeing. His second statement, however, is almost always either a case of giving information or opinion.

Thus Bales' Interaction Process Analysis seems quite useful and versatile in the analysis of communication beyond the small group setting. Note that, even if Bales' specific categories are not used, one might still use the *method,* which is a sort of content analysis of ongoing communication exchanges, by forming other categories more appropriate for one's purpose. For example, a very different set of categories might be used to analyze communication in an informal social group.

Stewart, on the other hand, provides a very useful model which is clearly *trans*actional. He analyzes a "dyadic" (two-person) situation in terms of interpersonal perception.[8] His model is "transactional" in the sense that he assumes an individual changes as a function of the communication situation in which he is involved. His "transactional paradigm" specifies the perceptual relationships involved in a two-person communication.

In Stewart's terms "my → me" represents my self-image, and "my → you" represents my perception of you. The perceptual relationships involved in the dyad can be represented:

my → me

my → you

your → you

your → me

In addition, I have some perception of your perception of me, and you have a perception of my perception of you, etc.; thus:

my − → your − → me

my − → your − → you

your − → my − → me

your − → my − → you

It is possible to extend Stewart's basic paradigm to include other elements. It has been suggested, for example, that each of us has a different perception of our relationship, so we can add the following perceptual relationships:

my $-\rightarrow$ us

your $-\rightarrow$ us

my $-\rightarrow$ your $-\rightarrow$ us

your $-\rightarrow$ my $-\rightarrow$ us

We can extend the paradigm beyond a two-person situation by adding "him_1, him_2, . . . ," and "her_1, her_2, . . . ," and we can add other objects, events, concepts, and ideas as "it_1, it_2, . . . " This makes it possible to represent an infinite variety of relationships, and it serves to remind us of the incredible complexity of the perceptions involved in a communication exchange.

Consider what problems we could cause if we complicated the model further by representing *messages* as perceptual relations enclosed in parentheses, so that

my (my $-\rightarrow$ your $-\rightarrow$ me) you

represents my attempt to describe to you my perception of your perception of me.

Besides being fun to play with, this model seems useful in that it serves as a reminder of the tremendous complexity of the simplest perceptions we try to communicate. Too much contemplation of such matters could also be hazardous to one's ability to talk, since I suspect it would soon lead to a spreading paralysis of the brain beginning with the speech center and moving out, much like the old story of the centipede who thought too much about how he walked.

A number of other writers have proposed transactional models. Those of Berne, Buber, Goffman, and Rogers in particular are discussed in the next chapter.

Information-Gathering

Some of these models are especially useful in analyzing communication in its cooperation-facilitating function, and others in analyzing the social-transaction or self-regulation function. None of those sur-

FIGURE 6
Becker's mosaic model of communication.

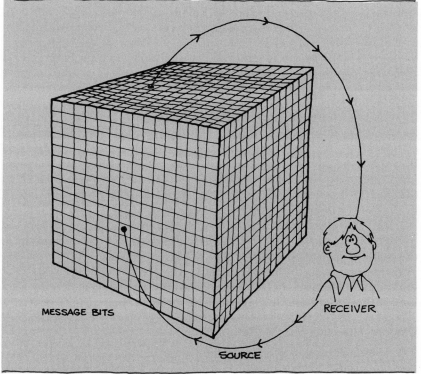

MESSAGE BITS

RECEIVER

SOURCE

(Adapted from Samuel Becker, "Rhetorical Studies for the Contemporary World," in *The Prospect of Rhetoric*, eds. Lloyd F. Bitzer and Edwin Black, Englewood Cliffs, N.J.: Prentice-Hall, 1971, p. 34.)

veyed so far have been *specifically* useful in the analysis of communication in its information-gathering function. The last model is one of the few which take that approach.

Becker[9] envisions the communication process as analogous to a receiver passing through a mosaic cube of information, as pictured in Figure 6. The blocks comprising the cubes represent items of information which he encounters. The picture of the process does not (because it *cannot*) represent Becker's stipulation that the cube is constantly changing, so that new items of information become available and others become unavailable. Another way of thinking of this stipulation is to think of the mosaic as having no boundaries at all; it is, instead, a never-ending succession of layers of information through which an individual passes from birth to death and, for that matter, through which countless generations of human beings have passed and will continue to pass until the human species becomes extinct and/or evolves into some other form. Not only are the layers of information limitless in *number,* but they are also limitless in *expanse* in that there is an infinite variety of information to which an individual might theoretically attend at any given point in time. However, the items of information which he can encounter at any given time are limited by his *position* (in physical, psychological, and social senses) at that time. His position at that time is "determined" by the path he has taken in the past in the trip through this information-universe, and his path in the future depends upon the "choices" he makes now.

I find that this model has one considerable advantage: It concentrates on the *listener* as an active *gatherer of information* rather than upon the speaker as a manipulator with the listener pictured as a passive information-sponge or a totally reactive amoeba-like creature responding only to light and shock administered by the speaker (often with a minimum of light and a maximum of shock).

Uses of Theories and Models

Theories and models seem useful to achieve at least four goals. First, they are useful in teaching in that each one seems to suggest one or more communication variables which the others have neglected, so that the student is encouraged to think about communication in a variety of ways. Second, they are useful in that they can usually be applied in one way or another to practical communication situations so as to suggest potential problems which might develop in such situations, or to identify possible reasons for problems which have already developed. Third, theories and models are theoretically useful in that they can be manipulated more easily than the "reality" they represent. Finally, they can be used to generate specific, testable research hypotheses. Obviously, some are more useful than others *in general* and some serve one of these *specific* functions better than others.

Models will probably be most useful to you at this point to help you understand and analyze what is happening in real communication situations, whether those situations involve face-to-face interpersonal communication, a speaker addressing an audience, or communication about public policy through the mass media.

Different models are useful for different purposes. The linear models of Berlo and Shannon-Weaver will be most useful if you are analyzing a situation in which information is being transmitted from a designated source to a designated receiver. The model from information theory is useful when the messages transmitted are being chosen from a set of known alternatives. Actually, none of these three models are very useful very often in analyzing interpersonal communication, although the concepts they include are useful.

Because it more effectively deals with feedback, the Westley-MacLean model is generally a better one for analyzing situations in which several people are involved, and it is especially useful in analyzing the flow of communication in a group of people. Communication networks are most useful in analyzing communication flow in more or less established social groups and organizations. Bales' Interaction Process Analysis can be used whenever one is interested in the *types* of communication occurring among people over a period of time. Stewart's model is most useful in describing the development of close interpersonal communication, usually between two people. Finally, Becker's model is designed to describe how people become informed, how they gather information, and how they make decisions.

It is possible that some combination of these models will be most appropriate in understanding a given communication event. *Your choice of models will depend upon what you want to look at, and what you see will be determined by the model you choose.*

The preceding several paragraphs have identified general considerations for applying the models discussed in this chapter. Describe specific communication events that would lend themselves to analysis by one or more of these models. For example, the Shannon-Weaver model is most useful for "analyzing a situation in which information is being transmitted from a designated source to a designated receiver." What specific communication event would exemplify this kind of situation?

Summary

Human communication is a *transactive, multidimensional, multipurposeful* process. It involves sources, messages, channels, and receivers, and it may be described in terms of encoding and decoding.

Successful communication must overcome *noise* (or interference) of both signal and semantic types. Such interference can be characterized as fog distortion, mirage distortion, and stretch distortion. To the extent that a message reduces uncertainty it is said to contain *information;* to the extent that it is predictable it is said to be *redundant.* Redundancy is useful in overcoming the effects of noise, and so is *feedback,* which consists of messages returning to the source which let him know the effects of his own messages.

Communication can be described in terms of *networks,* which give the observer some indication of who is communicating with whom. It can also be described in terms of the types of *interactions* which are occurring among the communicators. Further, it can be described in terms of *message transactions,* which indicate how the elements of communication combine to produce a unique, unrepeatable event. Finally, it can be viewed from the point of view of an individual gathering information as he passes through his environment.

Models which embody these concepts are useful in learning about communication, in analyzing practical communication problems, in developing theory, and in generating research hypothesis. Different models are useful for different purposes. Your choice of models will depend upon what you want to look at, and what you see will depend upon the models you choose.

Suggestions for Developing Awareness

1. Discuss what it means to say that a communication event was "successful." Does your view of "successful" communication depend upon the persons involved, the topic, and the situation? How?

2. Analyze changes in your own behavior as you go through a typical day. Are you more talkative in some classes than in others? Why? Now

consider the different groups of people you associate with. Do your opinions change from group to group? Are you more willing to voice your opinions in one group than in others? Why are you more inclined to talk openly with some people and not others?

3. Redundancy in a message reduces the chances of error and misinterpretation. To illustrate this point, choose a page from this text and identify the different ways the author restated his point in order to reduce the chances of misinterpretation. Look for cues such as "in other words," "for example," or "let me put that another way."

4. Use one or more communication models to analyze a communication event you have observed. Explain why you chose the model(s) for that specific event. After the analysis, do you think your choice was the best you could have made, or would some other model have given you a better "picture" of the event?

References

1. David K. Berlo, *The Process of Communication* (New York: Holt, Rinehart and Winston, 1960).

2. Claude Shannon and Warren Weaver, *The Mathematical Theory of Communication* (Urbana: University of Illinois Press, 1949).

3. Alfred G. Smith, *Communication and Culture* (New York: Holt, Rinehart and Winston, 1966), p. 275.

4. John R. Kirk and George D. Talbot, "The Distortion of Information," *ETC* 17 (1959): 5-27.

5. Bruce Westley and Malcolm MacLean, Jr., "A Conceptual Model for Communication Research," *Journalism Quarterly* 34 (1957): 31-38.

6. Alex Bavelas, "A Mathematical Model for Group Structures," *Applied Anthropology* 7 (1948): 16-30.

7. Robert F. Bales, "How People Interact in Conferences," *Scientific American* 192 (1955): 31-55.

8. John Stewart, ed., *Bridges Not Walls* (Reading, Mass.: Addison-Wesley, 1973), editor's introduction.

9. Samuel Becker, "Rhetorical Studies for the Contemporary World," in *The Prospect of Rhetoric*, eds. Lloyd F. Bitzer and Edwin Black (Englewood Cliffs, N.J.: Prentice-Hall, 1971), pp. 21-43.

2

Becoming Aware of

PEOPLE

Communication serves as the bridge over the
sometimes troubled waters which separate one person
from another. To understand why communication
is necessary, why it is sometimes so difficult, and
how it can be made more effective, it is important to
become aware of the many ways people differ: in
personal characteristics, in personality, in opinions and
policies, and in the reference persons and groups
to whom they commit themselves, with whom
they try to achieve consensus, and to
whom they attribute credibility.

The "General Persuasibility" Approach

Empathy: Identification, Needs, and Goals

Need for Empathy (Burke and Byrne)
Developing Empathy: Some Theories
   Stewart
   Buber
   Rogers
   Goffman
   Berne
   Maslow, Jourard, Fromm

Some Barriers to Empathy

Age
Sex
Race
Educational Level
Socioeconomic Status
Etcetera

Summary

Chapter Four

Interpersonal Differences
and Empathy

I suppose if there were no differences among people there would be no need for communication. But that would be a very boring world. Much of the excitement in life consists of using communication to bridge those differences.

Certain differences resist this communication bridge most stubbornly and are also most difficult to change. There is a technical term for them: "demographic" differences. Demographic characteristics are the sort that the U.S. Census Bureau uses to classify people — characteristics such as age, sex, race, educational level, intelligence, and socioeconomic status.

It is especially ironic that demographic differences *are* so difficult to bridge when there is no objective reason why they *should* be. True, communication can't *change* your age, your sex, or your race. Communication can change your personality, your opinions and policies, your commitments and reference groups — all things we will consider in later chapters — so why deal with demographic variables which are difficult or impossible to change? For two reasons: (1) because people *assume* that those who differ demographically also have different personalities, opinions, policies, reference groups, and motives, and (2) because people who differ demographically have different experiences which affect their personalities, opinions, policies, reference groups, and motives.

So we will give some thought to demographic characteristics with the goal of eliminating those differences which are imagined and minimizing or at least understanding those which are real.

Consider age, sex, race, geography, and socioeconomic status.

1. What assumptions do we often make about the opinions and policies of young people, of middle-aged people, and of elderly people? about their motives? about their personalities? about their reference groups?
2. What assumptions do we often make about the opinions and policies of women and of men (or girls and boys)? about their motives, personalities, and reference groups?
3. What assumptions do we often make about the opinions and policies of blacks, of chicanos, and of

caucasians? about their motives, personalities, and reference groups?

4. What assumptions do we often make about the opinions and policies of southerners, of mid-westerners, and of easterners? about their motives, personalities, and reference groups?

5. What assumptions do we often make about the opinions and policies of rich people, of middle-income people, and of poor people? about their motives, personalities, and reference groups?

How do these assumptions often become barriers to communication? Are there specific instances in your own life or that you have witnessed where such assumptions have worked against successful communication?

The "General Persuasibility" Approach

Much of the research in communication which has focused on demo-graphic characteristics has tried to relate them to something called "general persuasibility." The term "general persuasibility" refers to the extent to which a person responds to persuasive messages *in general,* regardless of the topic, the evidence, the types of motive appeals, the language, the speaker, and all the other communication variables discussed in later chapters. It refers to the extent to which a person is generally susceptible to the influence of others. A book by Hovland and Janis titled *Personality and Persuasibility* covers the concept in detail.[1] A better and more recent discussion is that of McGuire.[2]

General persuasibility seems closely related to "conformity," which is the tendency of a person to agree with the opinions of groups of others. He keeps one ear to the ground and listens for the sound of "the Galluping herd," to paraphrase Gore Vidal. The person who is highly persuasible probably also conforms.

It also seems to be related to "general attitude instability"—the tendency of a person to change his or her mind even in the absence of communication.[3]

So what relation does general persuasibility have with age, sex, and educational level? Most of the research has been done to find out what kinds of people are most easily persuaded.

The biggest problem with that line of research is that it leads to forming stereotypes. Some of the conclusions, for example, have been that, on the average, older people are more difficult to persuade,[4] women are easier to persuade except when the speaker is a woman,[5] and there seems to be little relation between intelligence and persuasibility,[6] although better educated people may be slightly more persuaded by "logical" arguments and less persuaded by crude "emotional" propaganda,[7] whatever those may be. In every case the differences due to age, sex, intelligence, and education have been so small that they would be swamped by other considerations. That is, the differences among individuals, topics, and situations are so much more important as to make consideration of age and sex *in these terms* hardly worth one's time. From this research one might expect an older man to be very resistant to persuasion and a young woman to be a pushover, so to speak. Anyone who has been observing people long enough to be reading this book knows that those are wild overgeneralizations.

Empathy: Identification, Needs, and Goals

Besides, once one knows another person is going to be difficult to persuade, what does he do with that information? It seems much more useful to think of demography in terms of *interpersonal differences* and the difficulties such differences create when one is trying to empathize with another.

Empathy, the ability to feel and understand what another person is feeling and thinking, is probably the most valuable asset a communicator can acquire.

> *Empathy is both a cause and an effect of successful communication; in fact, cause and effect in this case blend so completely that in a broad sense we can say that empathy is communication.*

If one is able to empathize with another, they are better able to communicate; if they are better able to communicate, they are better able to empathize.

This facilitates *all three* functions of communication: (1) The *informa-tion* one receives from empathic communication is likely to be more reliable. If the information is not reliable, empathy makes it easier for one to detect deception on the part of another. (2) Empathic communication facilitates *cooperation* since it helps the people involved to be more aware of one another's needs, goals, and intentions. (3) Empathic communication facilitates *self-regulation* since it promotes mutual understanding. Most of the subfunctions of self-regulation require that an individual reflect his or her self off someone else in order to define that self and be confident his or her own feelings and emotions don't become too eccentric. Such reflection or social trans-action requires the interpersonal understanding which empathic communication facilitates.

Kenneth Burke calls this "identification through consubstantiality."[8] He says there is a "natural divisiveness" among people promoted by differences such as those we are discussing. Identification, communi-cation, and persuasion, which all seem to blend into one in Burke's description, help to bridge this natural divisiveness. One person per-suades another by talking the other's language and by identifying one's own needs and goals with those of the other, so the two become "consubstantial," which means, literally, a part of the same substance.

Byrne has made a career of demonstrating experimentally that one person likes another better to the extent that he sees the other as similar in attitudes toward a variety of things.[9] Brock has demonstrated that a communication approach based on similarity is remarkably effective even when compared with communication based on expertise.[10]

Now to the real importance of demography in communication: When you differ from another person in age, sex, intelligence, edu-cational level, race, socioeconomic status, and so forth, it is more dif-ficult for the two of you to achieve empathy or identification. It can still be done, but you will both have to work at it. You will have more difficulty really feeling and understanding each other's feelings and thoughts. You will be more likely to suspect one another of having different beliefs, values, needs, and goals, which may lead you to dis-trust and dislike one another.

Think of a close friend. How similar are your opinions
about education, work habits, marriage, personal appearance, religion, politics, sports, books, hobbies, self-
disclosure, and in other areas? On which of these subjects
do large differences occur? What is the source of these
differences? Do these differences of opinion result from
differences in age, sex, race, socioeconomic status, or
from different experiences? Do you minimize these
differences in your relationship with this friend?

Unfortunately, empathy doesn't just happen because you want it to
happen. The ability to empathize has to be developed. *Ideally, the development of empathy will be a transactive process in which the two people involved
share their experiences, perceptions, beliefs, values, and plans through mutual
trust and self-disclosure.* Suppose we consider first how empathy can be
developed in that kind of relationship.

One way to begin is by recalling the relationships pictured in the discussion of Stewart's transactional model in the previous chapter. If
I had the opportunity to know you and were trying to empathize with
you, my relevant perceptions would include my perceptions of myself,
my perceptions of you, my perceptions of your perceptions of yourself, my perceptions of your perceptions of me, my perceptions of our
relationship, and my perceptions of your perceptions of our relationship. Then, if we were to add some mutual acquaintances and some
mutual experiences to the picture, we could introduce incredible complexity. It is important to realize first that a "simple" relationship
between two people *is* incredibly complex, which makes empathy both
difficult and important.

Actually, Stewart's model seems to have been derived from or inspired
by the philosopher Martin Buber, who writes about "dialogic" as the
study of the kinds of relationships which are possible between "I" and
"Thou." Buber emphasizes the transactive nature of communication
and empathy in pointing out that two people entering into face-to-face
communication not only necessarily change one another, but create
a "We" that is something different from the mere combination of the
two people involved. Buber is difficult to read, but his insights make

it worthwhile if you are really interested in learning to practice and practicing to learn empathy. I cannot begin to do him justice here.[11]

Carl Rogers also writes about empathy when he deals with therapeutic communication.[12] He describes how we come to perceive the world in such a way as to enhance and protect our own self-concepts. That idea will be developed more fully in Chapter Seven. What is important for the moment, however, is to realize that my perceptions of you and my perceptions of the ways you perceive me are likely to be those which will enhance my own self-concept. For example, I am more likely to perceive you as intelligent *because you are reading my book,* and I am likely to believe that you perceive me to be intelligent as a result of your reading it. Those perceptions may or may not be accurate, but they enhance my own self-concept, so I am more likely to adopt them. Further, to the extent that we believe one another to be intelligent, sensitive, and the like, we will each expect the other to agree with our own perceptions of the world. Thus we will be likely to exaggerate our agreements and minimize our disagreements. If two people see one another as basically different, they are more likely to *dislike* one another, exaggerating their disagreements and minimizing their similarities (see Chapter Six for discussion of the consistency motive).

All of that can hinder real empathy, because it can cause us to misperceive one another. Real empathy consists of recognizing and understanding our actual similarities and differences, realizing that they need not threaten our respective self-concepts.

Goffman, too, is writing about similar problems when he describes how people present themselves in interpersonal encounters—how they choose their clothes, their friends, the books they read, the opinions they express, their "interests," the ways they behave, and the ways they communicate so as to enhance not only the images they present to others but also the ways they conceive of themselves.[13] Again, such contrived images can interfere with our perceptions of ourselves and others, which is the essence of empathy.

Berne has expressed it in terms of the "games" people play in their interpersonal relationships, as they alternatively adopt the postures or strategies of the immature Child, the authoritarian Parent, or the mature Adult.[14] He describes such "games" as "Man Talk," "Morning After," "Ain't It Awful," and "Rapo," among a host of others. Each is a transactional strategy for dealing with reality and other people, much like Goffman's "interaction rituals."

All of these writers deal basically with the ways in which we protect and conceal our self-concepts from one another and from ourselves, sabotaging self-actualization, empathy, and social transaction in the process. And they all recommend the development of mutual trust and self-disclosure in some form or another, to a greater or lesser degree, as an antidote. They are joined by many other writers, including Maslow,[15] Jourard,[16] and Fromm.[17] The idea is that we must learn to recognize and accept interpersonal differences and then learn to trust one another to the point that we can use communication to disclose our true selves.

All of these recommendations are fine for the development of empathy in a fairly intimate long-term communication situation which allows two people to practice mutual trust and self-disclosure, but what about empathy in those situations in which you know little about the other person and have little opportunity for learning more?

I believe that practicing trust and self-disclosure when it *is* possible produces an ability to empathize which generalizes to situations in which self-disclosure, at least, is *not* possible.

But something more is needed. It is related to the demographic differences I mentioned earlier. Specifically, we need to think about such differences as they relate to the motives we may expect of others. We will be considering motives in detail in Chapters Four through Nine, at least. But suppose we begin now with Maslow's hierarchy of needs.[18] He has argued that human needs can be listed in a hierarchy from those which are most basic and must be satisfied first to those which will be dealt with once the more basic ones are satisfied. Listed from the most basic to the least, they are: (1) physiological needs, (2) safety needs, (3) love needs, (4) esteem needs, and (5) need for self-actualization.

Demographic differences have implications for need fulfilment: people low in socioeconomic status are likely to be more concerned about basic needs, for example, and people at high educational levels are at least more publicly concerned with self-actualization. But demographic differences have other implications as well.

Let me be a little more specific.

Age

The commencement speaker who wants to do more than fill his time and collect his fee is undoubtedly at a disadvantage simply because he is older than his listeners; the student leader negotiating with a faculty group to gain support for greater student freedom and responsibility is similarly disadvantaged because he is younger. If such people indicate that they *expect* their listeners to be fair and open-minded, they are more likely to be. Further, a person in such a situation should do everything he can to emphasize the ways in which he and his listeners are *similar,* and he should make much of the interests, concerns, and motives they have in common. The student asking that the college administration give students a greater voice in student affairs, if he distrusts everyone over thirty and shows it, is likely to get about the reception he expects, especially if he shows no understanding of the problems of the administrators. The college administrator trying to quiet a protest rally, if he comes on as a gigantic father image concerned only with placating alumni and state legislators by punishing students, will be fortunate to be hanged only in effigy. This is not to suggest that one should compromise principles for the sake of effect; it is to suggest that, when the age difference is great, one must make the most of those similarities and common concerns which do exist.

It is also important to consider the motives which characterize those of different ages. Generally the older a person is, the greater stake he or she has in maintaining the *status quo.* In proposing change to an older person, one should be prepared to demonstrate with good evidence and reasoning that the changes will enhance rather than threaten that person's security. That is usually not as difficult as it sounds. In the previous example, the administrators might be reminded that students who are given responsibility tend to act responsibly; they can be reminded that student government will require fewer faculty committees, leaving more time for teaching and research. A student using such an argument need fear only one thing: he might be elected president of the university by unanimous acclamation. Whatever the function the communication is designed to serve, one will help his cause if he chooses examples and illustrations which are interesting and familiar to persons of the age of his listeners.

Do you have a close relationship with an elderly person? If you do, what areas in your relationship have been emphasized and what areas play little or no role in your communication? If you do not have such a relationship, have you made any assumptions about elderly people which tend to hinder empathy or lines of communication? Think also of your relationship with a child and ask similar questions about the communication between you.

Sex
Communication between the sexes has some natural built-in advantages which hardly need to be elaborated. In spite of that, there are a number of sex-related communication problems, most of which have

been imposed by society. After all, there is not that much difference between the actual physical needs and goals of men and women. Most of these social differences are "vestigial" in the sense that they are left over from less civilized days when the generally greater physical aggressiveness and strength of the male was more of an advantage than a disadvantage. These social differences seem now to be about as useful as other vestigial characteristics such as the tailbone and the appendix, but they still exist and they still hamper communication, so we still have to deal with them.

What seems to have developed is the extension or transformation of the physical strength of the male into a general social and economic dominance as well, without any rational grounds for the extension. All of that has been discussed and is being discussed at length elsewhere. What is important for our purposes is that communicators of opposite sex may unwittingly adopt socially stereotyped roles which hinder their communication. Sometimes both communicators play the game, so that they "act out" socially prescribed communication roles without ever really coming to terms with their respective needs and goals, feigning a divisiveness which need not exist. Sometimes one communicator assumes that the social roles are in effect while the other will reject the roles. That can be very destructive to communication.

The man may be so accustomed to playing the dominant role in such encounters that even when he tries to shed it his communication reveals his assumption of superiority. The woman who rejects that assumption will be offended, and the man may never know what went wrong. Similarly, the woman may be so accustomed to assuming that the man is going to take care of her that her communication projects helplessness quite unintentionally, even while she protests her equality at a conscious level. The liberated man may then decide (1) that this woman is *really* a helpless ninny, or (2) that she is using her helplessness when *that* is to her advantage and using her equality when *that* seems more beneficial. Neither interpretation is very flattering, and either one is going to sabotage communication. A third problem is a rather pervasive tendency on the part of both men and women to give a man more credit for knowing what he is talking about unless there is some reason to believe otherwise. That is simply irrational and has led to all manner of foolish decisions, but this low credibility of women among both men and women is consistently reaffirmed.[19]

Race
This analysis of communication between the sexes can be transferred almost directly to communication between the races, with two exceptions: (1) there are none of the "natural built-in advantages" for interracial communication, since there is no biological motivation for successful communication; and (2) the social status differences do not seem to be extensions of physical differences. Rather, the physical differences seem to be used as cues for racial stereotype formation.

   Different races form stereotypes of one another for a variety of reasons. Certain personality types are especially likely to stereotype, as pointed out in the next chapter. Sometimes racial stereotypes are socially learned and sometimes they serve ego needs, as discussed in Chapters Six and Seven. They may serve as or be served by different reference groups, treated in Chapter Eight; they may be represented in language differences, as mentioned in Chapter Eleven; and they may be the result of the actual intercultural differences described in the last chapter. Whatever its causes, interracial stereotyping is the sworn enemy of communication and empathy. But the *racist* is himself a stereotype, an object of understanding and empathy. A more detailed treatment of interracial communication appears in the last chapter of this book.

Educational Level
It is probably most useful to consider the kinds of experiences which may conspire to make the formally educated person different from the person who has less formal education.

   First, the vocabulary of the person who chooses to remain in school is likely to differ from that of the person who leaves school. The educated vocabulary may or may not be more extensive; it will, however, be different. The college professor talking with a group of longshoremen will have at least as much difficulty with vocabulary as the longshoreman in the opposite situation. The misguided notion that the academic vocabulary is more extensive or "correct" is probably due to the fact that college professors teach speech and English but long-shoremen generally do not. Until educators abandon the provincial conviction that their vocabularies are somehow superior, their brand of communication will continue to be uniquely well adapted to the academic community and uniquely poorly adapted to other communities.

Second, much of the experience provided by education is experience in dealing with abstractions. Thus the educated person is probably better equipped to deal with involved, abstract arguments, and that is often what is meant by "logical" argument. However, an involved, abstract argument can be less logical than one that is simple and concrete, and it is certainly more difficult to evaluate. This may make the educated person unusually susceptible to erroneous reasoning; that person may be a pushover for any argument that sounds complicated. *Further, the more education a person has, the more pressure he feels to have an opinion on any subject, and he may be too inclined to adopt neat packages of opinions and justifications for them.* Consider, for example, a person arguing that the members of a craft union should admit more blacks to membership. His reasoning and evidence will have to be unimpeach-able; it will probably have to be less impeachable, in fact, than if he were arguing the same proposition with members of the American Association of University Professors (which, by the way, might be no less segregated).

Third, it should be obvious that the educated person will have areas of specific knowledgeability which differ from those of the less educated person. His or her *general* knowledgeability may be greater or less than that of the person having less formal education; certainly, education alone does not guarantee general knowledge. There will be certain areas in which an educated person has greater knowledge, depending upon the direction his or her formal education has taken; similarly, the less educated person will have certain areas of greater knowledge, depending upon the direction his or her nonacademic experience has taken. One had best know what his listeners know, whether their knowledge is academic or nonacademic. If their knowledge is extensive in the area, he will have an easier job in that he can assume much of what would otherwise have to be explained, but the job will also be more difficult in that the information must be completely accurate and documented, and the inferences must be carefully reasoned. This person will also run a greater risk of boring listeners by telling them things they already know.

Fourth, it may be expected that the educated person will be more committed to and interested in anything academic, while the uneducated person may have some degree of anti-intellectual bias. Certainly, research and theory in choice behavior would lead one to that prediction. If a person has made a choice as significant as that between leaving school or remaining and has committed time and money as completely as one usually must to either of those alternatives, that person will be likely to seek justification for the choice, becoming more favorable toward the alternative chosen and less favorable toward the alternative rejected. However, some reservations are in order. Teachers, for example, will probably agree strongly that there is a need for more educational television programs. Persuading them to watch such programs, however, may be about as easy as persuading a bus driver to take a vacation trip. Uneducated people, too, often have a strangely ambivalent attitude toward education; they may make tremendous sacrifices to send their offspring to college, on the assumption that "you have to have a college education to get ahead," but they may remain very suspicious, even antagonistic, toward what is taught.

Finally, the different experiences of educated and less educated persons create a much greater gap to be bridged when the educated person talks with those who are less educated, or vice versa.

The educated person talking with less educated persons has at least two problems to overcome: they will be watching closely for indications that the educated person considers himself or herself superior to them, and they will be suspicious that education may have produced motives which they do not share and which may not be in their own best interests. If one can satisfy others on those two points, they will probably respect his or her education and be more likely to believe the person because of it.

Such a person would be well advised to avoid any suggestion of deliberately choosing simple language and oversimplifying explanations as a condescension to the stupidity of the listeners. He will avoid technical jargon, of course, but can still use Standard American English; he may simplify the explanation, but can do so by using illustrations with which the listeners are familiar rather than by treating them as if they were children. If he can handle it, some humorous deprecation of himself, of his educational experiences, or of education in general may be very helpful. Above all, he should try to be relaxed, natural, and friendly. Second, such a person will take the time to remind his listeners of motives, interests, and opinions they have in common in order to assure them that he is interested in their welfare.

The less educated person conversing with those who are educated has two somewhat different problems: to overcome his own insecurity and to convince the listeners that he is well informed. To overcome insecurity, one should remember that, while he may be less educated in general, if the topic has been narrowed adequately and researched carefully he should be the leading expert on that topic. To assure the listeners of his credibility, it may be best to tell them just that: while you feel somewhat overwhelmed at the prospect of speaking to such a distinguished audience you also feel that, because you have done some careful research on this topic, you believe you have some specific information which will be useful to them.

Socioeconomic Status
Again, when a person has a much higher or much lower socioeconomic status than that of others, there may be a serious lack of identification between them. The person of high status talking with those of low status will have problems very similar to those of the educated person talking with those who are less educated. Such people will be quick to see that one is trying to adopt their slang or dialect and will probably interpret this as condescension. They will also suspect him or her of trying to exploit them, unless one can give good evidence of being interested in their welfare.

The person of low status talking with those of high status has less critical problems. There may be some tendency on the part of the listeners to think "if you're so smart why ain't you rich?" but that problem will probably not be too serious unless his or her socioeconomic status is extremely low. In that case there may be an additional problem: one may also be suspected of being lazy. A person in such a position should be aware of such tendencies and should subtly introduce evidence that he or she is neither stupid nor lazy. There may be a further tendency under certain circumstances for such people to suspect that the poor person is trying to exploit them, to "get something for nothing." Again this person will need to emphasize whatever motives and interests he or she shares with others in order to minimize the differences which exist.

It may also be useful to consider the different concerns and opinions which may be created by the different experiences of those in the lower, middle, and upper classes. The young person, for example, should be especially aware that there are many older persons in the middle and upper classes who have risen from the poverty and insecurity of the Depression to present positions of relative affluence and security. It is easy for such persons to attribute the increase in their personal fortunes to their own industry and ingenuity, and to become quite impatient with the poor. One should be aware of this rather pervasive economic viewpoint, for it is relevant to a wide variety of topics and one is likely to encounter it often.

This may also account to some extent for the preeminence of the economic security motive among the middle class. It is interesting that economic security has become such a god-term for the middle class, while it seems somewhat less important to the upper and lower classes. The security motive generally is not high in the hierarchy for an upper-class audience because they have achieved security; security is simply lower in the hierarchy for a lower-class audience because matters of mere survival are of more immediate concern.

Etcetera

Obviously, it would be possible to continue this discussion at some length by dealing with matters such as religion and geographic location. However, with an understanding of the general approach, you should be prepared to continue the analysis to whatever extent seems profitable. Ultimately, the individual must use his or her own judgment to discern the characteristics which predominate among those with whom one is conversing, and to devise means for adapting to those characteristics. Generally, one should ask at least the following questions and add others of his or her own: (1) What general characteristics of these people can interfere with our communication, and how can I overcome the effect of those characteristics? (2) What characteristics and motives of these people make our communication on *this* topic especially difficult, and what can I do to overcome the effect of those

characteristics and motives? (3) In what ways do I differ from these
people which might make them feel a lack of identification with me
or a dislike for me, or might make them doubt my credibility or distrust my motives, and what can I do to overcome these differences?
With careful study, observation, and practice, one can develop the
sensitivity and imagination to answer these questions in ways which
will enhance communication.

Summary

Interpersonal differences frequently serve as unnecessary barriers to
communication. *Empathy*—the ability to feel what another person is
feeling even when the two people are quite different from one another
—is the key to overcoming such barriers. One can develop empathy
by becoming aware of the ways his own perceptions are distorted to
enhance his own self-concept, by learning to practice interpersonal
trust and self-disclosure, and by learning how differences in age, sex,
race, educational level, and socioeconomic status operate to reduce
interpersonal trust and understanding.

Suggestions for Developing Awareness

1. What is empathy? There is probably no definitive answer. One might
    think of empathy as the process of getting inside someone else's image and
    acting on the beliefs, plans, and values of that image with awareness
    and respect. Consider the seriousness of such an enterprise; the time
    required; the movement between your image and his or hers; the
    similarities and differences in images; and consider how the following
    acts play a positive or negative role in empathizing:

judging	moralizing	moving	laughing
analyzing	touching	interrupting	sharing
listening	asking	hugging	joking
suggesting	emoting	philosophizing	advising

2. What are some important aspects of empathic listening? Consider the effects on listening of predisposition (assumptions), attentiveness, physical and nonverbal elements, spacial distances, fluency of speaker, image interference or image enhancement, relationship of listener to speaker, emotions and feelings, ego, topicality, and sex.

3. "When I was a boy of fourteen, my father was so ignorant I could hardly stand to have the old man around. But when I got to be twenty-one, I was astonished at how much he had learned in seven years." (Mark Twain)

   Obviously, Twain's relationship with his father lacked empathy. Have you ever experienced such a relationship? What plans could bring more empathy into that relationship?

4. Create your own product and advertising campaign. Choose a specific audience for selling your product to. What personal characteristics will you emphasize in order to create empathy with this audience? How can these characteristics be changed for different audiences?

5. Write an essay or make a collage describing yourself. Include anything you wish about your background, interests, goals, etc., in order to give as complete a description as possible of *who you are*. For example, I would include a Ph.D as one goal; books, dogs, cats, water skis, and antiques as some of my interests; and the Hancock building, the ocean, Pier 66, variety stores, horses, and a country club as my background.

   Now, following the same format as just described, prepare an essay or collage describing your image of an "ideal" friend. Share this description with other members of the class. Who is most similar to you? Most different from you? How do you feel about these persons?

   Compare the description of yourself with the description of your "ideal" friend. How are they similar and/or different? Are your real friends similar to this "ideal" friend? Is your "ideal" friend male or female? If, for example, your "ideal" friend is female, would your description differ for a male "ideal" friend?

References

1. Carl I. Hovland and Irving L. Janis, *Personality and Persuasibility* (New Haven, Conn.: Yale University Press, 1959).

2. William J. McGuire, "Personality and Susceptibility to Social Influence," in *Handbook of Personality Theory and Research,* eds. Edgar F. Borgatta and William W. Lambert (Chicago: Rand-McNally, 1968), pp. 1130-1187.

3. Gary Cronkhite and Emily Goetz, "Dogmatism, Persuasibility, and Attitude Instability," *Journal of Communication* 21 (1971).

4. Clare Marple, "The Comparative Susceptibility of Three Age Levels to the Suggestion of Group versus Expert Opinion," *Journal of Social Psychology* 4 (1933): 176-186; Irving L. Janis and D. Rife, "Persuasibility and Emotional Disorder," in Hovland and Janis, *op. cit.,* pp. 121-137.

5. Franklin H. Knower, "Experimental Studies of Changes in Attitudes: I. A Study of the Effect of Oral Argument on Changes of Attitude," *Journal of Social Psychology* 6 (1935): 315-344; Thomas M. Scheidel, "Sex and Persuasibility," *Speech Monographs* 30 (1963): 353-358.

6. Janis and Field, in Hovland and Janis, *op. cit.;* Orville M. Pence and Thomas M. Scheidel, "The Effects of Critical Thinking Ability and Certain Other Variables on Persuasibility" (Paper delivered at the convention of the Speech Association of America, Chicago, December, 1956).

7. Carl I. Hovland, A.A. Lumsdaine, and F.D. Sheffield, "The Effects of Presenting 'One Side' versus 'Both Sides' in Changing Opinions on a Controversial Subject," in *Experiments on Mass Communication,* vol. 3 of *Studies on Social Psychology in World War II* (Princeton: Princeton University Press, 1949), pp. 201-227; H.J. Wegrocki, "The Effect of Prestige Suggestibility on Emotional Attitude," *Journal of Social Psychology* 5 (1934): 384-394.

8. Kenneth Burke, *A Rhetoric of Motives,* 1950, available in paperback in combination with *A Grammar of Motives* (Cleveland and New York: Meridian, World, 1962).

9. Donn Byrne, "The Influence of Propinquity and Opportunity for Interaction on Classroom Relations," *Human Relations* 14 (1961): 63-69; "Interpersonal Attraction and Attitude Similarity," *Journal of Abnormal and Social Psychology* 62 (1961): 713-715; "Interpersonal Attraction as a Function of Affiliation Need and Attitude Similarity," *Human Relations* 14 (1961): 281; "Response to Attitude Similarity-Dissimilarity as a Function of Affiliation Need," *Journal of Personality* 30 (1962): 164-177; with William Griffitt and Carole Golightly, "Prestige as a Factor in Determining the Effect of Attitude Similarity-Dissimilarity on Attraction," *Journal of Personality* 34 (1966): 441-442; with Don

Nelson, "Attraction as a Function of Topic Importance," *Psychonomic Science* 1 (1964): 93-94; "Attraction as a Linear Function of Positive Reinforcement," *Journal of Personality and Social Psychology* 1 (1965): 659-663; with Ray Rhamey, "Magnitude of Positive and Negative Reinforcements as a Determinant of Attraction," *Journal of Personality and Social Psychology* 2 (1965): 884-889; with Terry Wong, "Racial Prejudice, Interpersonal Attraction, and Assumed Dissimilarity of Attitudes," *Journal of Abnormal and Social Psychology* 65 (1962): 246-253.

10. Timothy C. Brock, "Communicator-Recipient Similarity and Decision Change," *Journal of Personality and Social Psychology* 1 (1965): 650-654.

11. Martin Buber, *I and Thou,* trans. Ronald Gregor Smith (New York: Charles Scribner's Sons, 1958).

12. Carl R. Rogers, *Client-Centered Therapy* (Boston: Houghton Mifflin, 1951); and *On Becoming a Person* (Boston: Houghton Mifflin, 1961).

13. Erving Goffman, *The Presentation of Self in Everyday Life* (New York: Doubleday, 1959).

14. Eric Berne, *Games People Play: The Psychology of Human Relationships* (New York: Grove Press, 1964).

15. Abraham Maslow, *Toward a Psychology of Being* (Princeton, N.J.: Van Nostrand-Reinhold, 1962).

16. Sidney M. Jourard, *The Transparent Self* (Princeton, N.J.: Van Nostrand-Reinhold, 1964).

17. Eric Fromm, *The Sane Society* (New York: Rinehart, 1955).

18. Abraham H. Maslow, *Motivation and Personality* (New York: Harper and Row, 1954).

19. Lawrence B. Rosenfeld and Vickie R. Christie, "Sex and Persuasibility Revisited," *Western Speech* 38 (1974): 244-253. These writers cite a variety of studies dealing with the credibility and persuasibility of women, arguing that both are more culturally than biologically determined and analyzing the cultural pressures which produce both phenomena.

Authoritarianism and Dogmatism

Self-Esteem and Security

Achievement and Affiliation

Aggressiveness and Aggression

Anxiety and Alertness

Dominance, Leadership, Need to Influence, and Mach IV

Cognitive Style

Interpersonal Trust, Anomie, and Mach IV

Summary

Chapter Five

The Role of
Personality

People differ, too, in the ways they characteristically operate in communication situations. In understanding what is happening in a communication situation, it is very helpful to know about some of these characteristic modes that people use. If you are part of the situation, it is helpful to know about some of your own personality characteristics and the reasons for them. Understanding others and understanding yourself won't *guarantee* successful communication, but it should certainly help.

Actually, Chapter Four has already dealt with one such characteristic: general persuasibility. Some people are pushovers for every sales pitch that comes along, and others are downright stubborn. I pointed out that there really isn't too much one can do with that information. But there are other personality characteristics that are more interesting, and some of them are useful in understanding general persuasibility itself.

Those who are authoritarian or dogmatic, for example, communicate and respond to communication in ways quite different from those who are open-minded. People also communicate differently when they differ in self-esteem, security, aggressiveness, need for achievement, need for affiliation, cognitive style, interpersonal trust, anomie, and need to influence (or "Machiavellianism"). Those are some of the personality differences that I will consider in this chapter.

There are many theories about *why* people differ in personality, about the ways learning modifies genetic differences. Hall and Lindzey describe twelve different theories of personality in their book by that name.[1] Unfortunately, if I were to write about those theories, there wouldn't be much space in the chapter to treat communication, but if you are interested most textbooks in general psychology discuss them. Also, if you are interested in the research findings which support the generalizations I am about to make, many of those can be found in *Personality and Persuasibility,* Chapter 7 of *Persuasion: Speech and Behavioral Change,* and *Handbook of Personality Theory and Research,* especially Chapter 24.[2]

Authoritarianism and Dogmatism

These two characteristics are discussed together because dogmatism appears to be a more general extension of authoritarianism. Both characteristics seem to be collections of symptoms, which makes them rather difficult to define. An authoritarian individual, as described by Adorno, is one who tends to use beliefs for the purpose of ego-defense and is especially likely to be influenced by what that individual considers to be an authority.[3] Rokeach objected to the F-scale, the test of authoritarianism, on the grounds that it measured authoritarianism only among those on the extreme right of the political spectrum, whereas the symptoms it is supposed to measure may be equally characteristic of the left-wing radical. He defined open-mindedness, the opposite of dogmatism, as "the extent to which the person can receive, evaluate, and act on relevant information received from outside on its own intrinsic merits, unencumbered by irrelevant factors in the situation arising from within the person or from the outside."[4] Obviously that should be of interest to communicators. Suppose we consider, then, some of the symptoms of the dogmatic individual which are especially relevant to communication.

For one thing, dogmatic persons tend to maintain strong central beliefs which are highly resistant to change. These are generally religious, political, or philosophical values; beliefs about the nature of personal worth; and beliefs about the nature of authority. The dogmatic individual, for example, is expected to agree strongly with statements such as: "It is better to be a dead hero than a live coward"; "The main thing in life is for a person to want to do something important"; and "Man on his own is a helpless and miserable creature." It is interesting that most studies have found that dogmatic persons are especially easy to persuade. This is probably because these studies have used messages designed to change what Rokeach has termed "peripheral" beliefs; the dogmatic person seems to be willing to sacrifice these peripheral beliefs in order to maintain those beliefs which are more central.

A second characteristic of dogmatic persons is that they tend to overlook the relevance of one of their beliefs to another, which allows them to maintain two contradictory beliefs simultaneously. Two test items with which the dogmatic person will agree are: "Even though freedom of speech for all groups is a worthwhile goal, it is unfortunately necessary to restrict the freedom of certain political groups"; and "The highest form of government is a democracy, and the highest form of democracy is a government run by those who are most intelligent."

Rokeach has reported remarkable belief change when people are made aware of such inconsistencies in a subtle way, so that they do not feel the need to defend the contradictions.

A third characteristic of dogmatic persons is their tendency to organize the world into two primary categories: things they accept and things they reject. This is evidenced by their tendency to agree with statements such as: "Of all the different philosophies which exist in this world, there is probably only one which is correct"; "To compromise with our political opponents is dangerous because it usually leads to the betrayal of our own side"; and "There are two kinds of people in this world—those who are for the truth and those who are against the truth."

Further, it is especially difficult for the dogmatic listener to accept a person but reject something that person says, or vice versa. The dogmatic person relies heavily on the opinions of those that person considers to be authorities. Such a person agrees, for instance, that "It is often desirable to reserve judgment about what's going on until one has had a chance to hear the opinions of those one respects," and "In this complicated world of ours the only way we can know what's going on is to rely on leaders or experts who can be trusted." The dogmatic person would like to find someone who would tell him or her how to solve personal problems. On the other hand, the dogmatic listener is quick to reject someone who disagrees with him or her on an important issue; one test item with which such a person will be likely to agree is the statement, "My blood boils whenever a person stubbornly refuses to admit he's wrong."

I worked one summer as one of a crew of four men charged with the job of building a road through a mountain pass in which the snow had only recently melted. With concerted and collective ingenuity the crew succeeded in miring the only available truck and the only available bulldozer in one of the many available mudholes. Trying to pull one with the other made both sink deeper. After the winch cable was fastened to a very sturdy tree, the bulldozer pulled itself onto solid ground using its own power and was then used to pull the truck free. This is mentioned not because it was an unusually brilliant or original solution, but rather because a person talking to those who are highly dogmatic is in a very similar situation. If the person and the proposition are both somewhat suspect, the person coming out in favor of that proposition will only reaffirm the listeners' suspicion of both. Instead, one must find stable central beliefs of the listeners with which he agrees and use those common beliefs to gain firmer terra for himself; once he is on solid ground, he is in a better position to advance the proposition. Dogmatic listeners will be especially likely to accept a person who agrees with some of their strong central beliefs, and once they have accepted that person they will be especially likely to accept the arguments. Open-minded listeners may not respond as favorably to such treatment, but neither will they take offense as long as the approach is not obvious and insincere. As suggested elsewhere, a person is well advised, both ethically and pragmatically, to choose central beliefs with which he or she actually agrees. The listener is well advised to consider what effect his or her own dogmatism may have on *response* to communication.

Three words of caution seem appropriate. First, there is a tendency to think of the dogmatic person as less intelligent than the open-minded person. There is no research evidence that intelligence provides any guard against dogmatism. Second, *it is tempting to consider those who agree with us to be open-minded.* The reverse is more likely, since dogmatic individuals seem to be generally more easily persuaded. Finally, the fact that an individual takes an extreme position on any one issue does not necessarily indicate that the person is dogmatic as defined here; he may simply believe that he is right. An individual may be suspected of being dogmatic if that person takes extreme positions on *many* issues; changes many of his or her less consequential opinions often and especially in response to the influence of persons believed to be authorities; refuses to consider the possibility of being wrong in certain central beliefs; fails to see how his or her beliefs relate to one another; and rejects other persons to the extent that he or she rejects what they say.

The terms "dogmatic" and "open-minded" carry immediate connotations with which we all identify. We generally identify positively with open-mindedness and negatively with dogmatism. Dogmatism still exists, however, and it probably is more a part of our own lives than we realize. Have you ever admired a particular professor to the point that he or she becomes an idol?

Or have you ever felt this way about a person of the
opposite sex or a minister or a political leader? What
dangers are inherent in such situations? How often
have you supported a cause, only to find later that you
changed your mind about it (or never changed your
mind)? Have you ever rejected a person simply on
the basis of what he or she has said? Have you ever
unknowingly held conflicting views only to be embarrassed when you discovered they were at odds with
each other?

Self-Esteem and Security

Research in this area seems to lead to the conclusion that the person
low in self-esteem is especially easy to persuade. Of course, one will
not often know which of the listeners are low in self-esteem. That information would not be very useful anyway; one could then predict which
of the listeners would be most responsive, but could seldom base his
appeal on such knowledge. However, it is sometimes used when one
has limited time or resources and has a choice of directing appeals to
different groups. Politicians, for example, who have a limited number
of speaking engagements, might consider which constituents are
likely to be lowest in self-esteem and direct the majority of their appeals
to those persons. If there are groups in the district who have been consistently exposed to experiences likely to reduce their self-esteem, the
cunning politician may choose to appeal primarily to those groups. If,
as I believe, awareness is the basis of ethical communication, such tactics should be exposed.

Sometimes people use such information to decide *when* to advance
an appeal. They may wait until the group to be persuaded has some
reason for being low in self-esteem. For example, national confidence
probably reached a low point about the time President Kennedy took
office in 1961. Russia had put the first Sputnik in orbit and followed
that with a man in space. It was a propitious time for persuasion.

Sometimes people try to manipulate the esteem of others. Listeners
may be reminded of facts and experiences which threaten their self-
esteem. Obviously, the threat to esteem will probably come from a

source other than the person speaking, and the speaker will probably assure the listeners that he or she does not hold them in low esteem; they may also be assured that the person has confidence in their ability to meet the threat and that he or she has a plan by which they may restore any esteem they have lost.

The self-esteem of listeners may also interact in strange ways with the esteem of the person they are listening to. A speaker will generally try to increase his or her own prestige and convince listeners that they have much in common. Sometimes this backfires. If the person speaking is high in prestige, those who see themselves as having a great deal in common with him or her will also be high in self-esteem and thus difficult to persuade. On the other hand, if the listeners are low in self-esteem, the communicator who is really sophisticated may try simultaneously to convince the listeners of their similarity without lowering his or her own esteem. That is a tricky proposition. It is in part the plight of a black college professor speaking to a group of young blacks in a ghetto high school, trying to convince them to continue their education. The job is to persuade his or her listeners that they have a great deal in common, that they can achieve the same sort of position he or she has reached, and avoid any suggestion of being overly impressed with his or her own accomplishments.

Achievement and Affiliation

The person low in self-esteem is likely to have some needs that differ from those of people high in self-esteem. Two which appear at first most obvious are need for *achievement* and need for *affiliation*.

As with many personality characteristics, we need to distinguish between chronic and acute lack of self-esteem. It may be that the person who is chronically (consistently) lacking in self-esteem eventually abandons the *expectation* of achievement or affiliation and rationalizes, sublimates, or somehow reduces his or her dependence on achievement and affiliation as sources of need satisfaction. If this is true, it may be that the person who is usually *high* in self-esteem, when that self-esteem is temporarily (acutely) threatened, will be the one who reacts by showing the greater need for achievement or affiliation.

Whether that is true or false, it is fairly certain that anyone whose self-esteem is *acutely* threatened will have a *temporarily* greater need for achievement and affiliation. Sometimes a person who perceives others to be suffering from an acute lack of self-esteem for one reason or another will try to persuade them by offering them opportunities for achievement and affiliation. For example, the person may present a plan by which the listeners can regain the confidence they have lost. Or, since people characteristically band together in the face of threat, the listeners may be encouraged to join together to overcome the threat to their confidence. If the listeners are aware of such tactics, they can react consciously in whatever way they believe appropriate.

Aggressiveness and Aggression

Similarly, it is possible to distinguish between chronic aggressiveness, adopted as a life-style, and acute, temporary instigation to aggression induced by circumstances with which one is presently confronted. These appear to be two very different concepts, and they seem to bear different relationships to communication.

Specifically, there is fairly good evidence that the person who is characteristically aggressive is very resistant to persuasion. On the other hand, while the evidence is not as extensive, it appears that those who are *temporarily* induced to aggression are probably *easier* to persuade. To further complicate the picture, acute aggressiveness apparently makes one more willing to accept plans involving punitive or harsh action.[5]

Again it may be difficult to identify a person who is chronically aggressive without knowing that person for some time. However, it is sometimes possible to identify certain persons or groups having a history of aggressive behaviors or beliefs. People who know that their listeners are chronically aggressive sometimes try to state their proposed plans in aggressive terms. For example, consider a person who is trying to convince police that they should not deal harshly with a disturbance. Instead of trying to appeal to their sympathy, the person might point out that the leaders of the disturbance are deliberately trying to provoke harsh police action so they can charge police brutality and advance their cause. He or she might then argue that it is much more sadistic to feed out the rope and hang the protesters at a later date. Those who are trained in communication techniques will recognize such tactics and make their decisions on more rational grounds.

Acute aggressiveness, on the other hand, is generally induced by frustration or threat, and it is quite similar to acute lack of self-esteem. In fact, the same circumstances which induce acute lack of self-esteem may simultaneously induce acute and defensive aggressiveness. Individuals who have been frustrated or threatened are very vulnerable targets for persuasion, and this is especially true if a communicator is urging punitive action. Knowing this, some communicators may wait to advance their propositions until those they wish to persuade have been frustrated or threatened, or may remind them of frustrations or threats they have experienced or are likely to experience. It is to the listener's advantage to know his or her own emotional state and to know how someone else may be using those emotions.

Anxiety and Alertness

Alertness and attention are not synonymous. To say a person is alert implies that the person is ready to respond to external stimulation, but it does not necessarily imply that he or she is ready to pay attention to what someone else has to say. Again, anxiety is the term usually used to refer to a chronic personality characteristic, while alertness and attention are acute states induced by specific situations. That distinction is not perfectly clear, however, for we sometimes speak of acute temporary anxiety.

Alertness, arousal, and activation are used practically synonymously in the literature of psychology. When activation is distinguished from the other terms, it is used to refer more specifically to a state of the central nervous system. Thus psychologists usually speak of *cortical* activation and *autonomic* arousal. Alertness is a more general term, less technical, and thus more acceptable in nontechnical discussions.

There appears to be a continuum of alertness or arousal ranging from sleep through what is generally termed alertness to states of high emotional arousal and outright panic. Further, increasing alertness seems to lead to better task performance up to a point, at which increased arousal begins to interfere with task performance. The point at which arousal begins to interfere with efficiency is very high on the continuum for simple physical tasks, but the interference comes much sooner for complex intellectual tasks such as listening to a complicated explanation or argument.

Obviously, alertness and arousal are closely related to states of aggressiveness and fear. This has been a real problem in research to determine how alertness and arousal are related to communication, since the states of alertness have been induced by introducing some situation in which the listener is threatened or frustrated or complimented. Then it has been difficult to determine whether the effect is produced by the general state of arousal or by the specific *type* of arousal. However, there are some tentative implications for communicators.

Certainly it is desirable that all the participants in a communication encounter be alert. *However, there are times when communicators must be careful to avoid arousal levels so high as to interfere with the task of critical listening.* This is especially true if a discussion is complicated and if the communicators are chronically anxious or have been made acutely anxious by circumstances immediately preceding the communication event. At such times the use of intensely emotional language or highly emotional appeals is likely to interfere with understanding and critical evaluation of communication.

Distraction bears an interesting relationship to alertness. For example, speakers frequently have to deal with distracting stimuli which occur during speeches or which are recalled by listeners. If a person knows that listeners are distracted by something which has occurred, the person may make reference to the event and then use it to capture or recapture the listeners' attention. The same is true if the distracting stimulus occurs unexpectedly while one is talking. On the other hand, some researchers have reported that mildly "distracting" stimuli such as an irrelevant visual presentation may under some circumstances make listeners more susceptible to persuasion. There are competing explanations of this phenomenon and some question as to whether or not it actually occurs.[6] It may be that the "distracting" stimuli, if pleasing, mask the effect of other more distracting stimuli, or listeners may deliberately concentrate more attentively on a message under certain distracting conditions. Some researchers have suggested that the "distraction" prevents listeners from building counterarguments as they listen to propaganda. One thing seems certain: even a mild, pleasant distraction results in less *retention* of material presented in a communication, even if it does not result in less opinion change, so whatever the effects of the distraction, it probably doesn't help the listener. Some persuasive messages, of course, are so bad that any distraction will be welcomed by the listener; if one is distracted, he or she may not react as *negatively* as with no distraction.

Dominance, Leadership, Need to Influence, and Mach IV

The terms, "dominance," "leadership," and "need to influence" seem to be self-explanatory. Mach IV and Mach V are not. They are short for "Machiavellianism," and are two forms of a test designed to determine the extent to which an individual desires to manipulate others.[7] These traits are considered together not because they are identical but because people who are dominant, often leaders, high in need to influence others, or "Machiavellian" pose special problems in communication situations.

Such persons are easier to identify than some of those previously discussed. Persons who are in positions of leadership are likely to be there because their need to influence is unusually strong, and the need to influence is likely to be unusually strong because they are in positions of leadership. Further, persons in professions which require close interpersonal relationships, such as psychiatry and sales, have been demonstrated to have especially high scores on Mach IV and V. Finally, men on the average seem to be more Machiavellian than are women; as Christie and Geis put it, "Aside from Lucretia Borgia, most of Machiavelli's observations were of males (his titles suggest this: *The Prince* rather than *The Princess; The Discourses* rather than *The Gossip*)." Forgive them, they were writing several years ago.

It is possible, of course, to fight Machiavelli with Machiavelli. If a person knows that another member of a communication group is more interested in influencing than in being influenced, he or she may use that knowledge by indicating that the other person has, indeed, been influential. This may be done by dwelling upon matters on which both agree or, in a discussion, by demonstrating a willingness to change opinions in response to reasonable arguments. A subtle communicator may allow the other person to take credit for "discovering" the communicator's own arguments and propositions. Thus "inductive" organization leading from data to the formation of conclusions may be more effective with highly manipulative people than is an organizational pattern in which the conclusions are stated and then supported. Manipulative people are especially susceptible to one form of the "bandwagon" device in which the proposed plan is presented as a new one which is likely to be accepted by others. This gives the manipulative person the "opportunity" to be among the early advocates of something which is likely to prove popular. If a communicator is subtle in the use of these methods, Machiavellians may depart congratulating themselves on the ease with which they convinced the communicator and eager to convince others in the same way. Whether such manipulation is justified even as a defense against manipulation is a decision you will have to make. Beware of such techniques if you are a "high Mach" yourself.

Cognitive Style

The characteristic of cognitive style seems primarily relevant to one's understanding of a communication.

Cognitive style has been measured by a variety of tests, and these tests are related to one another in a variety of ways. Basically, however, the theory behind such tests is that some individuals show a high degree of cognitive complexity, perceiving their environments in terms of many categories lying along many dimensions, and responding to a strong need to impose order upon their perceptions of the external world. Other individuals have a low degree of cognitive complexity, maintain few perceptual categories along few dimensions, and are not driven by any obsession to order their perceptions. In short, people's images differ in complexity.

One of the symptoms of dogmatism is a simplistic cognitive structure in which the individual maintains little differentiation among belief

and disbelief subsystems. The highly dogmatic person is one who, to some extent at least, tends to categorize other persons and concepts as either "good" or "bad" and fails to perceive the relevance of his or her beliefs to one another, making it possible to maintain simultaneously contradictory beliefs. Thus cognitive style is one of the components of dogmatism.

Like dogmatism, simplistic cognitive style tends to be more characteristic of those who are less educated and those who are politically, religiously, or philosophically extreme. These relationships are not high enough to be very dependable, however. Consequently, it is difficult to determine the cognitive style of another person.

Still, the characteristic does seem to be important in communication. Communicators high in cognitive complexity are more likely to impose organization upon disorganized communications, more capable of drawing conclusions from data even when other communicators draw no conclusions, and more inclined to perceive relationships between new information and their personal beliefs. For those low in cognitive complexity, on the other hand, communicators will have more effect if they state clearly the intent and organization of their messages, rely heavily upon internal summaries and transitions, draw explicit conclusions, and emphasize the implications of these conclusions for the subsequent behavior of the listeners.

Interpersonal Trust, Anomie, and Mach IV

"Interpersonal trust" seems self-explanatory. It is another component of the conglomerate of symptoms Rokeach has termed "dogmatism." Christie and Geis have been puzzled by the fact that their measurement of desire to manipulate others bears no demonstrable relationship to measures of authoritarianism and dogmatism, but it is significantly related to "anomic disenchantment," a species of interpersonal distrust. They have concluded that there are two types of interpersonal distrust, one of which is characteristic of highly authoritarian and dogmatic persons, includes an apathetic response and moralistic judgment, and amounts to saying "People are no damn good, *but they should be.*" The other, characteristic of the Machiavellian individual, is neither apathetic nor moralistic, and it amounts to saying "People are no damn good, *so why not take advantage of them?*"

The distinction seems to be useful in communication. In either case a communicator may have the problem of convincing people who are characteristically distrustful that he or she is a trustworthy person. The one type of interpersonal distrust, however, seems to be most characteristic of older persons and those of low socioeconomic status, in particular. Such people will probably be more responsive to a communicator who says, in effect, "People are not to be trusted, but one should be able to trust. I trust you and would like you to trust me because I have your interests at heart." The untrusting opportunist, on the other hand, may be more responsive to a communicator who says, "Granted that people in general cannot be trusted, but you can trust me in this specific case because my goals are the same as yours."

In both cases, however, as in most communication situations, the listener's responsiveness depends upon a communicator's ability to demonstrate that their interests, attitudes, and intentions are really similar.

Summary

People who differ in *personality* characteristics also differ in the ways they communicate and respond to communication. Being *sensitive* to one's own personality characteristics and those of others helps one understand communication better. Some of the personality characteristics which relate to communication are: dogmatism, self-esteem, need for security, need for achievement, need for affiliation, aggressiveness, activation level, dominance, leadership, need to influence, Machiavellianism, cognitive style, interpersonal trust, and anomie.

Suggestions for Developing Awareness

1. Consider how affiliations with groups, organizations, and people
   (a) affect your image and (b) become manifestations of your image.
   As examples, you might use social and intellectual groups, schools,
   prominent individuals, leaders, wealthy persons, and poor persons. How
   do some affiliations hamper self-actualization and how do others enhance
   it? How do affiliations sometimes affect the reliability of your information-
   gathering?

2. The ability to understand another person rests, in part, on how much
   information one has about the other person's background, interests,
   goals, etc. Generally, accuracy in predicting another person's behavior
   increases as the amount of information you have about that person
   increases. The following exercise will illustrate this notion.

   Find another person in class, preferably someone you don't know well.
   Each of you should select four things from your wallets that represent
   "frustration," "happiness," "security," and "freedom." Choose one item
   for each feeling. Now, exchange those items and discuss their meaning.

   Then try to predict, based on your information about each other, what
   gift the other person would most like to have. List the following things:
   a puppy, a stuffed teddy bear, a subscription to *Playboy* or *Playgirl,* a
   bottle of Jack Daniels, a "lid," a free dinner, theater tickets, and a book.
   Which gift would the other person most like to have? Are your predictions accurate?

   If you try this exercise again later in the semester/quarter, you'll be
   able to see how much you've learned about each other and how much
   each of you has changed.

3. Find a copy of Rokeach's dogmatism test (it appears in *The Open and
   Closed Mind*). Take the test or, if possible, make copies so that the entire
   class can take it. Score yourself and compare your score to those of others.
   Do the items seem valid? Do you believe that "dogmatic" responses on
   some items are justified? Do others in the class agree with you? If not, why
   do they insist on being so dogmatic? Repeat your position to make it
   clearer to them.

4. Recall times when you have felt especially low in self-esteem or have been
   frustrated in some important way. Were you especially susceptible to
   persuasion when you were low in self-esteem? Did you feel especially
   aggressive when you were frustrated, or did you become apathetic? You
   might want to share these incidents with the class.

References

1. Calvin S. Hall and Gardner Lindzey, *Theories of Personality,* 2nd ed. (New York: Wiley, 1970).

2. Hovland and Janis, cited in ch. four; Gary Cronkhite, *Persuasion: Speech and Behavioral Change* (Indianapolis: Bobbs-Merrill, 1969); Edgar F. Borgatta and William W. Lambert, eds., *Handbook of Personality Theory and Research* (Chicago: Rand-McNally, 1968), especially the chapter by McGuire.

3. T.W. Adorno *et al., The Authoritarian Personality* (New York: Harper, 1950).

4. Milton Rokeach, *The Open and Closed Mind* (New York: Basic Books, 1960).

5. For a more complete discussion of this area, see Carl Carmichael and Gary Cronkhite, "Frustration and Language Intensity," *Speech Monographs* 32 (1965): 107-111; reprinted in Serge Moscovici, ed., *Readings in the Psychology of Language* (Chicago: Markham, 1971), pp. 454-462.

6. See: Leon Festinger and Nathan Maccoby, "On Resistance to Persuasive Communication," *Journal of Abnormal and Social Psychology* 68 (1964): 359-366; and Jonathan I. Freedman and D.O. Sears, "Warning, Distraction, and Resistance to Influence," *Journal of Personality and Social Psychology* 1 (1965): 262-266.

7. Richard Christie and Florence Geis, "Some Consequences of Taking Machiavelli Seriously," in Borgatta and Lambert, *op. cit.,* pp. 959-973.

Attitudes vs. Opinions and Policies

Three Functions of Opinions and Policies
Knowledge and Consistency
Social Reward
Ego-Maintenance

Knowledge and Consistency
Source-Concept-Message Consistency (Heider, Osgood-Tannenbaum)
Choice-Outcome Consistency (Festinger)
Belief-Belief Consistency (McGuire)
Belief-Value Consistency (Fishbein)
Belief-Plan-Value Consistency (Fishbein)
Gestalt Perceptual Consistency (Kofka)

Summary

Chapter Six

Opinions and Policies:
The Consistency Motive

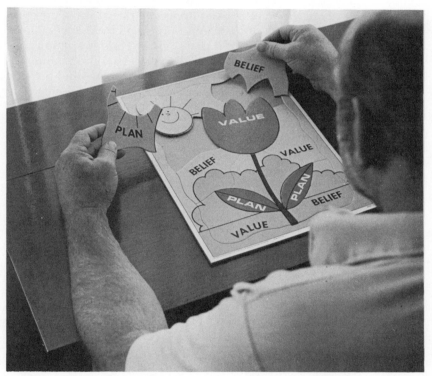

(Kandace Penner)

Personal opinions and policies are important in communication. People communicate about their opinions and policies. They form their opinions and policies as a result of communication. And their opinions and policies determine to some extent the kinds of communication they engage in. Consequently, it is very helpful in understanding communication to be aware of the ways people form their opinions and policies. But before considering that question, it might be useful to discuss what "opinions" and "policies" are, and how they relate to other concepts such as "attitudes" and "behavior."

Some opinions are statements a person makes about his or her belief in the existence of a concept, or its relation to other concepts, or about the probable outcome of certain plans. "That's a stove, and it's hot; if you touch it you're going to get burned," is a collection of such belief opinions. But opinions are not necessarily limited to statements of beliefs. They can also be statements of value. "I think abortion is wrong" is a value opinion, as is "Man, the sun feels good today." Very simply, an opinion is a statement reporting on any part of one's image of the world. It may be expressed overtly but need not be.

A personal policy is a collection of plans for dealing with a particular type of stimulus under different circumstances. Usually we speak of organizations having policies, such as in the expressions, "There's no reason for it, it's just company policy," or "This is our check-cashing policy." I am using the word in the same way, but applying it to people instead of to organizations. One may have an informal personal policy for dealing with panhandlers, for example. Sometimes one may give the panhandler a dime, sometimes a quarter, sometimes buy the person a sandwich, and sometimes refuse to give anything at all, depending on a variety of circumstances. That pattern of behavior constitutes a policy.

Organizations are usually conscious of their policies. People are not, so asking about them is not always helpful. Further, a person's policy in some areas may include making misleading opinion statements and policy statements. A person who is homosexual but afraid of social censure may make a policy of making mildly unfavorable statements about homosexuals and their behavior, for example. Frequently, one must infer another person's opinions and policies from observation of nonverbal behavior.

The reason I am dealing with this issue, and one of the reasons I am using the concepts of "opinions" and "policies" rather than "attitudes," is the hysteria among communication theorists and social psychologists since they discovered that *attitudes frequently don't relate to behavior.* Of course they don't. One of the most frequently used measures of attitude is a set of semantic differential evaluative scales[1] such as this:

Panhandlers

good ___ : ___ : ___ : ___ : ___ : ✓ : ___ bad

dirty ✓ : ___ : ___ : ___ : ___ : ___ : ___ clean

intelligent ___ : ___ : ___ : ___ : ___ : ___ : ✓ stupid

Now suppose the man who made those check marks meets two different people on the street. One is a neat-appearing blond girl wearing a halter top and a jean skirt who says she needs a dime to use the pay phone to call her parents collect in Chicago to tell them where she is. The other is a dirty, disheveled man of about fifty with cheap wine on his breath who says he needs a dime for a cup of coffee. Who will get the dime? Do those check marks on the semantic differential scales help you guess?

The Likert-type scales[2] are a little more useful but more difficult to construct. An example might look like this:

People who ask strangers on the street for
money are probably too lazy to work.

_____	✓	_____	_____	_____
strongly agree	mildly agree	neither agree nor disagree	mildly disagree	strongly disagree

These are probably the two attitude measurement techniques most widely used in communication research. There is another, however, which seems much more promising. That is Triandus' Behavioral Differential.[3] Here is a possible example:

A neat, attractive 18-year-old girl

I would   __: __: __: __: __: __: __: __   would not

give this person money for a phone call.

I would   __: __: __: __: __: __: __: __   would not

give this person money for a glass of wine.

I would   __: __: __: __: __: __: __: __   would not

buy this person a sandwich.

This test is directed toward a person's *policies* rather than attitudes. It should be more useful in predicting what the person will actually do. He still might lie, of course (for instance, if his wife were administering the test).

The difference is really quite simple. Would you give an officer of a bank a test of his attitude toward money and then try to use it to predict whether he would approve a loan to a particular person with a given amount of security to be used for a specific purpose? Of course not. It would be much more useful to know the bank's loan policy.

Now suppose we consider how people decide what their opinions and policies are going to be and what consequences those opinions and policies have. I am going to adopt Katz' "functional approach to the study of attitudes"[4] as the general approach, although I won't always use his language or organization. My basic assumption about opinions and policies is a rephrasing of his basic assumption about attitudes:

> *People plan their opinions and policies to achieve certain outcomes.*

Or, to remain a little closer to Katz' phrasing, opinions and policies perform certain functions for those who have them. The only real reservation about this approach is that it may suggest people "plan" consciously and deliberately. It should be obvious shortly that this is not true.

With this general assumption in mind, suppose we begin to explore what some of those outcomes or functions are which people use their opinions and policies to achieve. I will treat three functions which closely parallel the three functions of communication in general. These three general functions of beliefs and opinions as I see them are to satisfy psychological needs for: (1) knowledge and consistency, (2) social reward, and (3) ego or identity development, maintenance, and regulation.

Knowledge and Consistency

People act as if they not only need to acquire knowledge about their environments, but also as if they need to see and maintain consistency in their knowledge. I have already mentioned this gathering of information as a major function of communication. What hasn't been discussed yet is the apparently overwhelming need for *consistent* information.

Consistency has a great reputation. To some extent the reputation is deserved. Consistency is the basis for logical reasoning. People who are consistent can be depended upon. To the extent that we find consistent, dependable relationships in the world we can make plans to deal with the world. That, after all, is what the image is all about: One's image as described in the first chapter is a set of consistencies one perceives in the world, upon which one bases his or her expectations.

But Ralph Waldo Emerson was so brash as to say in his essay on "Self-Reliance":

> A foolish consistency is the hobgoblin of little minds, adored by little statesmen and philosophers and divines. . . . Speak what you think today in words as hard as cannon-balls, and tomorrow speak what tomorrow thinks in hard words again, though it contradict everything you think today.

What on earth was he thinking? We're accustomed since Einstein to hearing about how parallel lines do eventually meet, about space-time warps, and the like. We've learned to live without knowing whether the universe is exploding or contracting. We've all heard the story of physicists who must one day treat light as if it were composed of particles and the next day as if it were composed of waves. And we've managed to maintain some semblance of sanity. Probably because it doesn't really matter if a sidewalk is a whirling mass of electrons, so long as one can still walk on it.

But Emerson wasn't talking about that sort of inconsistency, which is largely irrelevant to our daily lives. He was arguing that relying too heavily on consistency in everyday reasoning can be irrational.

How can consistency ever be irrational? Well, a variety of types of "consistency" which have been identified by attitude theorists are certainly potentially irrational.[5] We will now consider a few examples.

Source-Concept-Message Consistency

People try to maintain a certain type of consistency between their opinions of other people and their opinions of what those other people say. Heider described this most clearly but also most simplistically.[6] Look at Figure 1 for a moment. This diagram indicates that Person One (P_1) likes (+) Person Two (P_2) and also likes (+) an object, concept, idea, or event (X). However, Person Two does not like (−) the same object, concept, idea, or event. Consequently, according to Heider, the situation is *unbalanced*. It is not *consistent* to like things which one's friends dislike. Person One will try to bring the situation into balance by changing his own opinion of Person Two, by changing his own opinion of X, or by trying to change Person Two's opinion of X. If he succeeds, the new situation can then be diagrammed in one of the four ways shown in Figure 2.

These situations will remain balanced until some new "inconsistency" is introduced. There are other possible unbalanced situations, as shown in Figure 3. The general rule is that it is "inconsistent" (my term, not Heider's) to disagree with a friend's opinion or to agree with the opinion of an enemy.

There are at least two theoretical problems with Heider's model. One is that it considers only two people and one object, concept, event, or idea at a time (X can also be a third person, incidentally), whereas a communication situation frequently involves several people and

FIGURE 1

Diagram of an unbalanced situation in Heider's model.

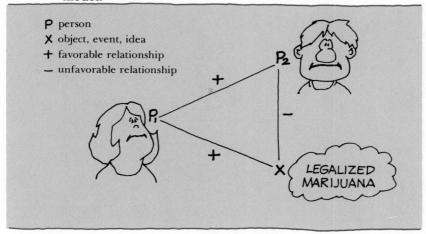

P person
X object, event, idea
+ favorable relationship
— unfavorable relationship

P₂

P₁

+

—

+

X LEGALIZED MARIJUANA

several X's.[7] The other problem is that opinions are represented as either favorable (+) or unfavorable (−), and any opinion change must be from one to the other. In fact, it is clear from both research and personal experience that opinions can vary from extremely favorable through neutral to extremely unfavorable.

Osgood and Tannenbaum have tried to improve upon Heider's balance theory with their "congruity hypothesis."[8] They make their predictions in terms of the "semantic differential" which was discussed at the beginning of this chapter, so they predict not only the *direction* of opinion change but also the *amount*. Their theory rests on the following basic assumptions: (1a) When a listener hears a source make a favorable statement about a concept, the listener's opinion of the source will be congruent (consistent) with his opinion of the concept only if the two opinions are identical. (1b) If the two opinions are not identical they will become more similar to one another after the listener hears the source make the statement. (1c) The less similar the two opinions are before the statement, the more they will change in the direction of similarity.

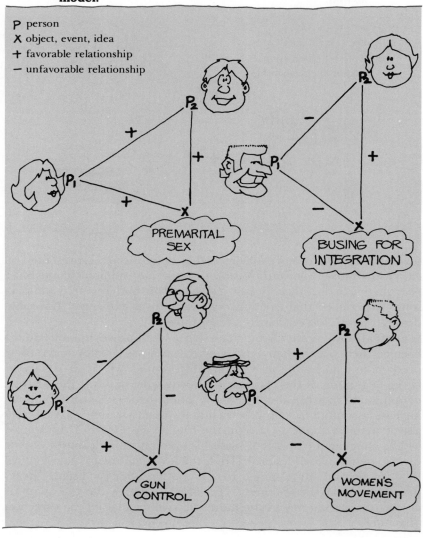

FIGURE 2
The four possible balanced situations in Heider's model.

P person
X object, event, idea
+ favorable relationship
− unfavorable relationship

FIGURE 3

The four possible unbalanced situations in Heider's model.

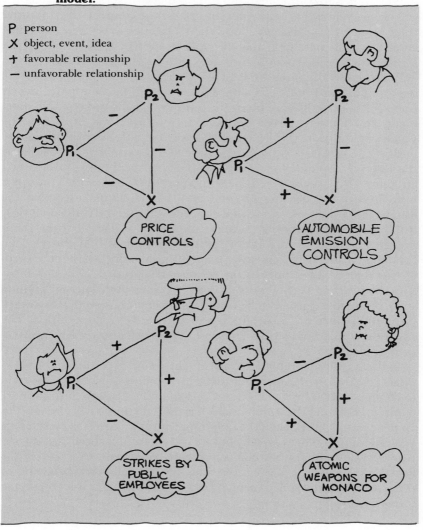

P person
X object, event, idea
+ favorable relationship
— unfavorable relationship

This is all concerned with a situation in which a source says he *favors* a concept. The predictions are basically the same as Heider's, except that Osgood and Tannenbaum try to predict *how much* opinion change will occur. When the source says he *opposes* the concept, the following rules or assumptions apply: (2a) When a listener hears a source make an unfavorable statement about a concept, the listener's opinion of the source will be congruent (consistent) with his opinion of the concept only if the two opinions are exactly opposite one another. (2b) If the two opinions are not exact opposites, they will become more nearly opposite after the listener hears the source make the unfavorable statement. (2c) The less nearly opposite the two opinions are before the statement, the more they will change toward exactly opposite positions.

The case in which the source says he *likes* the concept is fairly clear: the listener's opinions of source and concept will move toward one another. The case in which the source says he dislikes the concept is more confusing, because Osgood and Tannenbaum insist that the listener's opinions of source and concept will then be congruent only if they are *exactly* opposite. Suppose one *mildly* dislikes abortion but is *strongly* favorable toward his or her own church. If that church then condemned abortion, those two opinions would be incongruent, according to Osgood and Tannenbaum, because they would not be *exact* opposites. One would become less favorable toward abortion, as common sense seems to suggest. But he would also become less favorable toward the church, since the two opinions move toward exact opposition. The situation is diagrammed in Figure 4. This prediction seems nonsensical to me.

Actually, these predictions are qualified in two important ways. First, research has shown that extreme opinions are more resistant to change than are neutral ones. Consequently, Osgood and Tannenbaum predict that the opinion which is more extreme will change less. In the example just given, the opinion about the church would change less, since it was more extreme before the communication. Second, the two opinions will not become completely congruent, especially if the initial incongruence is great, because people will resist believing or perceiving that the source actually made the statement if it creates too much incongruity.

FIGURE 4

Direction of change for source and concept when assertion is unfavorable per the congruity hypothesis of Osgood and Tannenbaum.

Note: This is the case only when source and concept are different distances from neutral. Otherwise, with an unfavorable assertion, source and concept will not move apart and with a favorable assertion they will move toward one another.

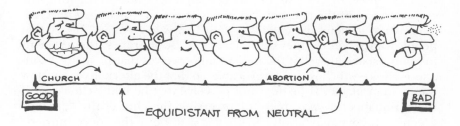

Suppose we leave these complexities for the moment and return to the basic question: Is this type of "consistency" rational or irrational? Even the most likeable people are wrong sometimes. When one is trying to reach a reliable decision, the opinions of those one strongly likes or dislikes can interfere, because of the temptation to agree with friends and disagree with enemies. *Friends are not always right and enemies are not always wrong.* Consequently, their advice and opinions must be evaluated objectively, with special attention to the reasons they are offering the advice or holding the opinions. Trying too hard to maintain consistency between one's opinions of a source and one's opinions of what that source says can destroy that objectivity.

Further, one need not come to like another person less just because he is wrong occasionally. Everyone is. And people who are always right are not necessarily the most enjoyable people to be around. Needless to say, it might be best for one's own mental health to avoid people who are wrong all the time or who give bad advice maliciously and intentionally.

Choice-Outcome Consistency

When people make conscious choices, they frequently try to maintain a curious sort of consistency between the consequences of their choices and the fact that they are responsible for those consequences. This type of consistency is really a special type of ego-defense.

At least since Aesop expounded the theory of sour grapes, if not before, it has been widely recognized that people attempt to justify their behavior by overvaluing its consequences and derogating the consequences of the alternative courses of action which they rejected. That is not to deny the equally potent "grass-is-greener" theory that people want whatever they don't have. The "sour grapes" theory seems to apply especially well if the individual perceives that he made a conscious choice which is now irrevocable, so that the alternatives are now totally unavailable. If he does not perceive that he had a choice, or if there remains any possibility of reversing the choice, the "grass-is-greener" theory may apply. Neither is it to deny the "once-burned" theory. If the individual has made an irrevocable decision with bad consequences, he will probably try to justify it, but if he is ever faced with a similar decision, he will probably choose a different alternative.

Festinger's theory of cognitive dissonance,[9] especially as it has been modified by Brehm and Cohen,[10] is a relatively sophisticated and contemporary development of the "sour grapes" theory. Festinger refers to "cognition," including beliefs, attitudes, opinions, values, and apparently anything else that can be internally experienced. He defines "cognitive dissonance" as the situation in which, considering two cognitive elements alone, the opposite of one follows from the other.

Festinger originally described several different situations which might be considered dissonant, but Brehm and Cohen have argued convincingly on the basis of research that dissonance theory applies best to situations in which *choice* is involved.

Greater dissonance is created in the choice situation to the extent that the choice is important, and it is maximum when the alternatives are nearly equal in desirability and so dissimilar as to make compromise impossible. The individual must perceive that he alone was responsible for making the choice, and he must perceive that the choice is irrevocable. Suppose, for example, a person has just chosen between a Datsun

280Z and a Porsche 914. Such a choice is important in that it represents a considerable cash outlay; it is irrevocable, at least for some time, since most people can't switch cars whenever they change their minds; the alternatives are probably perceived as nearly equal in desirability; and the individual probably perceives that he or she alone made the choice. Consequently, the dissonance created by such a choice would be considerable. What would prevent it from being maximal is the fact that the two cars have very similar advantages and disadvantages. A choice between a sports car and a pickup truck with a camper would create even greater dissonance because of the dissimilarity of the two vehicles.

A speaker attempting to analyze an audience will try to determine whether they have made choices of this sort which might freeze the opinions he is trying to change. People under the influence of choice-produced dissonance will try to reduce that dissonance by perceiving the choice to be less important, the alternatives to be more similar, the choice less voluntary and irrevocable, by seeking information and social support for the decision and, most importantly, by becoming more favorable toward the chosen and less favorable toward the unchosen alternative. If the speaker's arguments are bucking any of those attempts to reduce dissonance, he will have to provide the listener with an alternative means of dissonance reduction or see the proposal rejected. The listener, on the other hand, should be aware that he is especially susceptible to irrational attempts to justify a choice when these conditions are satisfied, *and should be alert to the possibility that he may be misled into making additional unfortunate decisions in order to justify the original one.*

Once again we have a type of consistency which is likely to contribute to unreliable decisions in response to communication.

Belief-Belief Consistency

People seem to maintain certain types of consistency among their beliefs. I am using the term "belief" now in the same sense in which I used it in describing the Image: Belief-Plan-Value model earlier in the book. At that time I said that beliefs *depend* upon one another, or are *related* to one another. Suppose we think a little more about how beliefs are related.

Take the example of a person who is trying to decide whether to buy a fairly expensive imported stereo now or later. Let's assume he has the money to buy now but is trying to decide whether he might get a better deal later. His reasoning could be arranged in a syllogism (although he probably doesn't reason in a syllogism unless he is as organized as he is rich):

> Further dollar devaluation will increase the price of imported stereos.
> Further dollar devaluation will occur.
> Therefore the price of imported stereos will increase.

Obviously he would conclude from such a chain of reasoning that he ought to buy now. Notice, however, that the conclusion that prices are going to increase *depends* upon the first two beliefs.

McGuire has tried to describe how these dependencies work.[11] He has used the notion of "dependent probabilities" in his explanation. To clarify that concept, consider the problem of calculating the probability that you will be able to flip a coin so that it will come up "heads" twice in a row. The probability that "heads" will turn up on the first flip is .50. Stated in terms of probability, your strength of belief in such an outcome would reasonably be .50 also. Now in those cases in which "heads" turns up on the first flip (50 percent of the time), heads will also turn up 50 percent of the time on the second flip. Fifty percent of 50 percent is 25 percent. Thus there is a probability of .25 that you will flip a coin twice in a row and get "heads" both times. The strength of your belief in such an outcome would reasonably be .25 in probability terms.

Now back to the stereo example: If you believe it is .90 (90 percent) probable that further dollar devaluation will increase the price of imported stereos and .50 (50 percent) probable that dollar devaluation will occur, then it would be "logically consistent" to believe there is a .45 (45 percent) probability that the price of imported stereos is going to increase: $.90 \times .50 = .45$. Thus the chance of a price increase, given these beliefs alone, seems to be a little less than fifty-fifty. Of course there may be other reasons to believe the price of imported stereos will increase or decrease, so this analysis is incomplete as it stands. Further, those familiar with the Aristotelian syllogism will protest that it

(Kandace Penner)

Since I believed the gasoline shortage in Colorado during the summer of 1973 was manufactured by the oil companies, I was hard pressed to provide a consistent explanation when a friend and I encountered this gasoline tanker which had run out of fuel between Pueblo and Cañon City. (1) A publicity stunt? (2) A mirage? (3) An absent-minded driver? (4) Evidence that fate is just? (5) Or evidence that the fuel shortage was real? I chose (3) because it was most consistent with my other beliefs at the time. My friend chose (5). Her father is an employee of one of the oil companies.

does not operate in the area of probability. That is certainly true; I can only say that McGuire is modifying (or corrupting, if you wish) the Aristotelian syllogism.

Probably more important is the objection that people don't think in syllogisms. However, McGuire does not argue that they do, only that they tend to maintain this kind of logical consistency insofar as they perceive propositions to be logically related.

The other factor McGuire identifies as operating here is something he terms "wishful thinking." This is the tendency of a person to attach

higher probabilities to conclusions he hopes are true and lower probabilities to those he hopes are false, even though the probabilities are
not logically warranted. Drawing to an inside straight in poker is a
classic example of wishful thinking, which is simply overestimating
the odds in your favor. The moral for the listener is simple: "Wishing
don't make it so." But there are a good many speakers, politicians, ad
writers, and even some of your best friends who will take advantage
of your tendency to believe it does.

To return once again to the stereo example, suppose our friend
really isn't all that rich, but he *wants* that stereo *now*. One way to justify
buying it now is to conclude that the price is going to rise, so it is a "good
investment." He will be very tempted to conclude that there is greater
than a .45 probability of a price increase, so he can justify rushing down
to buy it. The local sound shop may help him reach that conclusion
by running an ad like this:

Yen for a new stereo?

Buy now before dollar devaluation.

Your yen will cost more then.

That is wishful thinking in action.

Thus "logical consistency" as described by McGuire seems to be a
rational and objective type of consistency, but not wishful thinking.
Wishful thinking—the tendency to maintain consistency between what
one perceives to be and what one wishes were the case—seems to be
irrational in anyone's book. Unfortunately, McGuire's research seems
to indicate that his subjects, at least, operated more on the basis of wishful thinking than logical consistency. And that was in the laboratory.
Imagine what must happen in the world outside.

Belief-Value Consistency

Martin Fishbein is the psychologist probably most responsible for
clearly and operationally distinguishing between "attitudes" and
beliefs. His concept of "attitude" is essentially the same as my idea of

value, and my concept of "belief" appears to be identical with his. Fishbein believes that people maintain a specific sort of consistency between their attitudes and beliefs.[12] He speculates and has demonstrated repeatedly that people keep their attitudes about an object (or concept, event, or idea) consistent with their attitudes toward the attributes they believe that object possesses. More simply, if an individual believes Kodak cameras have undesirable attributes he will not have a favorable attitude toward Kodak cameras; if he believes Hasselblad cameras have desirable characteristics, he will like them.

Needless to say, neither the theory nor the reality is that simple. One generally believes that objects possess both desirable and undesirable attributes. The problem is to predict just how favorable one will be toward the object knowing what attributes he believes the object possesses, knowing how strongly he believes each attribute is related to the object, and knowing his attitude toward each of those attributes. Fishbein specifies the relationships in the following formula:

$$A_O = \sum_{i=1}^{N} B_i a_i$$

Don't panic. The formula is fairly easy once it's understood. A represents the attitude toward the object. B represents the strength of the belief that the attitude object possesses attribute i. The a represents the attitude toward attribute i. The "Σ" indicates that once B_i has been multiplied by its corresponding a_i, all the products are added.

Without going any further into the computations involved, note the ways this theory suggests that a communication can change one's attitudes. Consider a hypothetical individual who believes that (1) Hasselblad cameras have many useful features, (2) are expensive, (3) are not easy to use, and (4) do not require frequent repairs. If you want to persuade the person to buy a Hasselblad, you can deal with the *beliefs* by offering evidence to strengthen the first, weaken the second, weaken the third, and strengthen the fourth. You can deal with the *attitudes toward the attributes* by making his attitudes more favorable toward "useful features" and "expense" in cameras, and less favorable toward "ease of use" and "frequency of repair." You can also suggest other favorable attributes of the Hasselblad which he has not considered.

Belief-Plan-Value Consistency

More recently Fishbein has become interested in the problem of predicting behavior, and he has used the same sort of sum-of-products model to deal with that problem.[13] His theory is so similar to the Image: Belief-Plan-Value model of communication that the research he reports and cites in essence supports that model.

The basic idea, stated in my own terms, is that people maintain consistency between the plans they choose to execute and the values they attach to the outcomes they believe those plans will produce. One does not generally choose and execute a plan he believes will produce undesirable consequences, of course. The problem is that there may be a number of alternative plans which might achieve the same outcome. Each general plan consists of subordinate plans, each of which has its own outcomes (or side effects). If all are equally likely to achieve the same desirable outcome, one is most likely to choose that plan which has the fewest undesirable side effects.

This is still another type of consistency. *There is nothing inherently rational or irrational about either belief-value or belief-plan-value consistency.* The reasoning by which one decides that a given plan will produce certain outcomes or consequences, and the evidence on which that reasoning is based, must be evaluated before one can decide whether or not he or she is being logically consistent. Some of the tests of such information and reasoning will be discussed in subsequent chapters.

Gestalt Perceptual Consistency

Boulding's description of the image includes the following passage:

> Sometimes a message hits some sort of nucleus or supporting structure in the image, and the whole thing changes in quite a radical way.

Boulding elaborated this idea a little later:

> The sudden and dramatic nature of these reorganizations is perhaps a result of the fact that our image is itself resistant to change.

> When it receives messages which conflict with it, its first impulse is to reject them as in some sense untrue. Suppose, for instance, that somebody tells us something which is inconsistent with our picture of a certain person. Our first impulse is to reject the proffered information as false. As we continue to receive messages which contradict our image, however, we begin to have doubts, and then one day we receive a message which overthrows our previous image and we revise it completely. The person, for instance, whom we saw as a trusted friend is now seen to be a hypocrite and a deceiver.[14]

One sees such conversions frequently and marvels at them. A straight acquaintance who has always worn short hair, sport shirts, and slacks returns to school at the end of the summer dressed in counterculture garb. A friend who has always spouted antiestablishment rhetoric becomes an insurance salesman. What accounts for such drastic reorganization of an individual's image?

It may seem strange, but the best answer I can offer is that such changes result from a particular sort of need for consistency. When the strain of inconsistent perceptions becomes too overwhelming for a particular part of the image, the whole configuration of that image changes suddenly and drastically. Many beliefs, plans, and values have to be changed in order to produce a new consistency, and opinions and policies change to reflect the cognitive changes.

The psychological theory which best seems to account for such conversions is the Gestalt theory of perception.[15] A "gestalt" is a sudden flash of pattern recognition—the "Oh, now I see it!" response. It may also be a sudden insightful recognition of the solution to a problem, as when one suddenly "sees" how to put a puzzle together after a series of trials and errors.

FIGURE 5 is a popular illustration of two contradictory gestalts. If you concentrate on the white area of the illustration, you will see a white vase as the "figure" on a red "ground." But if you concentrate on the red area you will see two identical red faces confronting one another, forming a red "figure" on a white "ground." With practice you will be able to shift at will from one gestalt (perceptual organization) to the other.

FIGURE 6 is more difficult, but eventually you should be able to see *either* a young woman admiring herself in a mirror *or* a human skull. Can you see both at once?

FIGURE 5

FIGURE 7 is just downright difficult, especially for atheists. As a matter of fact, rumor has it that this figure was once used as a test of the genuineness of religious conversion. Eventually you may be able to see the head of Christ emerge from what first appears to be a Rorschach inkblot. Once you see it you won't be able to see anything else. Keep the faith.

The notions of "gestalt," "figure," and "ground" are not limited to visual perception. At a noisy cocktail party, for example, which voice is meaningful figure and which voices are meaningless background noise depend on which voice one is concentrating on.

The ruling assumption of Gestalt theory is "the law of Prägnanz": perceptual organization moves in the direction of the "good" gestalt. The "good" gestalt is one which conforms to four sublaws.

(1) *The law of similarity:* similar forms, colors, sounds, and the like tend to be grouped together.

(2) *The law of proximity:* elements close to one another tend to be grouped together.

FIGURE 6

FIGURE 7

(3) *The law of closure:* there is a strain toward a satisfactory "explanation," organization, or resolution of disorganized elements,
toward achievement of a "goal" which may be cognitive organization or the solution of a problem.

(4) *The law of good continuation:* missing parts of figures tend to be
supplied by the perceiver. Irregularly broken straight lines,
circles, or other figures will appear to be continuous. Missing
notes of melodies and missing sounds, letters, or words of messages will be filled in, sometimes quite unconsciously.

   In the second chapter I used the example of an individual bombarded
by the "Watergate evidence" during 1973 and 1974. There appeared
to be two gestalts available at that time. If one believed Nixon was innocent, one had to maintain an image of a president too busy with world

affairs to supervise his aides and too devoted to the constitutional role of the presidency to weaken that role by breaching the confidentiality of his taped conversations. One also had to maintain an image of a conspiracy on the part of liberal politicians and press to drive him from office. Any change in that image required a great deal of reorganization to maintain consistency, and was likely to be sudden and drastic.

Similarly, I have heard preachers say that one must believe one of two things about Jesus Christ: either he was and is the Son of God or he was the greatest liar who ever lived. These two beliefs require vastly different gestalts.

Are such radical reorganizations for the sake of consistency rational or irrational? I believe that depends. Ideally one ought to be able to contemplate all the available gestalts and evaluate them critically to see which is most consistent with the available information, rather than switching suddenly from one to the other without any period of critical objectivity between.

Further, while it may be true that there are instances in which there are only two possible gestalts, there is usually some middle ground. Sometimes it is difficult to find that middle ground when one is being pushed from both sides.

Sometimes, too, when one changes gestalts there is a temptation to change more than is logically necessary. In the Watergate case, for example, Lowell Weiker (the Republican senator from Connecticut who clashed with Nixon) was generally considered a turncoat by those who thought Nixon innocent, and he was generally considered a brave man of highest principles by those who thought Nixon guilty. Neither interpretation necessarily followed from Nixon's guilt or innocence.

Finally, there are times when there are only two gestalts available and one seems about as likely as the other. These are the times that try (wo)men's souls. The mature, open-minded person will simply postpone closure, live with the uncertainty, and wait for adequate evidence before making a decision. Any other approach would be too consistent. Or would it be too inconsistent? Being rational is certainly a trial.

Summary

People use communication to maintain certain types of *consistency* among their *opinions and policies.* We usually think of consistency as rational, but it is also frequently irrational, as when we try to agree with those we like and like those with whom we agree; rationalize the consequences of our choices so as to make those choices appear to have been correct; engage in wishful thinking; and fit our opinions and policies into tidy, consistent gestalts whether they fit or not.

Suggestions for Developing Awareness

1. Can you recall a time recently when someone you like expressed an opinion you disagreed with or did something of which you did not approve? How did you respond? Did you begin to like the person less, or did you change your own opinion? Did the two of you discuss the disagreement? Did you try to reach a compromise, or did you agree to disagree?

2. Think about how you have reacted to a recent unexpected news item which contradicted your own opinions or expectations. Did you try to reconcile the news item with your own opinions? If so, how did you do this? Did you look for additional information to reinforce your original opinions, or did you change them?

3. Have you made any major decisions recently, such as made major purchases, changed your major, broken up with a girlfriend or boyfriend, or decided to get married or live with someone? How did you rationalize your decision in order to reduce dissonance? What were the advantages and disadvantages of the alternative you chose and those you rejected? Did the consequences of the decision match your expectations? If not, do you think wishful thinking may have been involved?

References

1. Charles Osgood, George E. Suci, and Percy H. Tannenbaum, *The Measurement of Meaning* (Urbana: University of Illinois Press, 1957).

2. R.A. Likert, "A Technique for the Measurement of Attitudes," *Archives of Psychology* 140 (1932).

3. Harry C. Triandus, "Exploratory Factor Analysis of the Behavior Component of Social Attitudes," *Journal of Abnormal and Social Psychology* 68 (1964): 420-430.

4. Daniel Katz, "The Functional Approach to the Study of Attitudes," *Public Opinion Quarterly* 24 (1960): 163-204.

5. "Theories of cognitive consistency" constitute the majority of attitude theories at the moment. They are treated under that or some similar heading in most textbooks in social psychology and communication. One excellent but difficult book on that specific topic is by Shel Feldman, ed., *Cognitive Consistency* (New York: Academic Press, 1966). An easier and more recent treatment of these and other attitude theories is in Harry C. Triandus, *Attitude and Attitude Change* (New York: Wiley, 1971).

6. Fritz Heider, "Attitudes and Cognitive Organization," *Journal of Psychology* 21 (1946): 107-112. Essentially the same approach has been taken by Theodore M. Newcomb, "An Approach to the Study of Communicative Acts," *Psychological Review* 60 (1953): 393-404, and by Rosenberg and Abelson: M.J. Rosenberg and R.P. Abelson, "An Analysis of Cognitive Balancing," in Rosenberg *et al., Attitude Organization and Change* (New Haven, Conn.: Yale University Press, 1960), pp. 65-111; Abelson and Rosenberg, "Symbolic Psycho-Logic: A Model of Attitudinal Cognition," *Behavioral Science* 3 (1958): 1-13.

7. Cartwright and Harary have tried to remedy this problem, but their approach is too complicated to describe here. See: D. Cartwright and F. Harary, "Structural Balance: A Generalization of Heider's Theory," *Psychological Review* 63 (1956): 277-293.

8. Charles Osgood and Percy Tannenbaum, "The Principle of Congruity in the Prediction of Attitude Change," *Psychological Review* 62 (1955): 42-55.

9. Leon Festinger, *A Theory of Cognitive Dissonance* (Stanford, Calif.: Stanford University Press, 1957).

10. J.W. Brehm and A.R. Cohen, *Explorations in Cognitive Dissonance* (New York: Wiley, 1962).

11. William J. McGuire, "A Syllogistic Analysis of Cognitive Relationships," in Rosenberg *et al., op. cit.,* pp. 65-111.

12. Martin Fishbein, "A Consideration of Beliefs, Attitudes, and Their Relationship," in *Current Studies in Social Psychology,* eds. Ivan D. Steiner and Martin Fishbein (New York: Holt, Rinehart and Winston, 1965), pp. 107-120.

13. Martin Fishbein, "The Prediction of Behaviors from Attitudinal Variables," in *Advances in Communication Research,* eds. C. David Mortensen and Kenneth K. Sereno (New York: Harper and Row, 1973), pp. 3-31.

14. Kenneth Boulding, *The Image* (Ann Arbor: University of Michigan Press, 1956), pp. 8-9.

15. See: Kurt Kofka, *The Growth of the Mind,* trans. R.M. Ogden (London: Kegan Paul, Trench, Trubner, 1924); or *Principles of Gestalt Psychology* (New York: Harcourt, Brace and World, 1935).

Social Learning

Learning Theories in General
    Pavlov and Classical Conditioning
    Skinner and Operant Conditioning
    Hull and S-O-R Theory
Learning Opinions and Policies
    Implicit Mediating Responses (Doob)
    Radical Behaviorism (Bem)

Ego-Maintenance

Value-Expression (Katz)
Ego-Defense (Katz)
Ego-Involvement
    Rokeach
    Sherif

Summary

Chapter Seven

Opinions and Policies:
Social Learning
and Ego-Maintenance

In the last chapter I described some ways people use communication to keep their opinions and policies consistent. The consistency theories certainly provide many insights into the reasons people behave as they do. But there is more involved here. People also learn their opinions and policies as a result of social reward and punishment, and they use their opinions and policies so as to maintain their egos.

Social Learning

People learn to use their opinions and policies to increase the social rewards they receive from others and to reduce or avoid social punishment. They learn to express those opinions and pursue those policies which will be socially rewarding.

Any discussion of social learning is bound to involve some references to learning theories.* Briefly, three learning theories seem to stand out in any survey of the field: Pavlov's theory of classical conditioning, Skinner's theory of operant conditioning, and Hull's S-O-R theory. The name Pavlov probably rings a bell, since you may have read about his classic studies of classical conditioning. Meat powder blown into a dog's mouth was what is termed the "unconditioned stimulus." The dog produced an "unconditioned response" by salivating. A bell, tone, or light (the "conditioned stimulus") was paired with the meat powder a number of times and eventually produced salivation by itself, which was identified as the "conditioned response." Early in conditioning, if the dog was being conditioned to salivate in response to a 400-cycle-per-second tone, he might also salivate in response to 300-cycle-per-second and 500-cycle-per-second tones. That is "stimulus generalization."

---

* *I don't propose to survey learning theories comprehensively or in much detail. If you are interested in more extensive coverage, I would recommend the elementary but informative treatment in* Psychology Today: An Introduction *(Del Mar, Calif.: Communications Research Machines, 1972), pp. 19-77; or the more advanced textbook by Ernest R. Hilgard and Gordon H. Bower,* Theories of Learning *(Meredith, New York: Appleton-Century-Crofts, 1966).*

Later he might learn to respond only to tones in the 375-425-cycle-per-second range. That is "stimulus discrimination."

Operant conditioning experiments of the sort used by Skinner are probably equally familiar. Typically an animal—usually a rat or pigeon—has been placed in a cage in which there is a bar or lever so arranged that if it is pressed or pecked a pellet of food or a little grain will be delivered to the animal. The food "reinforces" any bar-pressing or lever-pecking which the animal performs, so that it comes to press the bar or peck the lever more and more frequently. If reinforcement (food) is not given for a long enough period of time, the animal's conditioned behavior will be "extinguished." Certain "schedules of reinforcement" (food delivery on every fifth peck, or random food delivery, for example) determine how quickly the animal learns, how rapidly it pecks, and how long it will continue to peck after reinforcement is stopped. Early in conditioning the bird may try to peck everything in the cage. That is "response generalization." Later in conditioning it will learn to peck only the lever and to do that very efficiently. That is "response discrimination."

I can only express my deepest apologies to Pavlov and Skinner for my simplistic explanations. I only want to remind you of some concepts you may have studied in more detail in a general psychology course.

Hull's S-O-R theory is more complex. Hull attempted to provide a comprehensive explanation for both classical and operant conditioning and either succeeded or came very close, depending on which psychologist one asks. The theory in general is too complex to describe here, and only one theorist, R.F. Weiss, has even outlined how it might be applied in its entirety to the learning of social opinions through communication.[1]

What is most important about Hull's approach is that he rejected Skinner's "black box" interpretation of behaviorism. Skinner refused and still refuses to speculate about what goes on inside an individual's head—what intervenes between the input stimulus and the output response. Hull included in his theory some discussion of how an incoming stimulus interacts with not only environmental conditions but also with an individual's motivational states and previously learned habits to produce a variety of responses. He argued that it is reasonable to talk about "intervening variables"—states of the individual which one can only infer from his actions. He brought internal states back into behaviorism, or at least made it respectable for behaviorists to talk about them again.

Consequently, Doob was able to use Hull's basic approach in describing "attitudes" as "implicit mediating responses" which an individual produces internally. If it were not for that development we might still be trying to explain human communication in the same terms we use to explain why dogs salivate and rats press levers.

That is essentially what radical behaviorists have attempted to do: to explain human behavior entirely in terms of stimulus input and response output. Some human behavior can be explained that way. But to assume that humans can learn only stimulus-response connections as a result of reinforcement is like using a computer only to check your grocery register slip: the computer can do it, but it can also do things vastly more complex. Similarly, human beings can learn simple stimulus-response connections, but they can do much more complicated things than that. Communication and social behavior are especially difficult to explain in stimulus-response terms. Certainly Skinner has tried,[2] but Chomsky[3] and Osgood,[4] among others, certainly seem to have laid his explanations to a well-deserved rest.

Chomsky has argued that the concepts of "stimulus," "response," and "reinforcement," for example, which have fairly clear meaning when applied to a pigeon in a cage under an experimenter's control, are fairly useless when applied to people talking to one another. Take this sentence, for example. What are the stimuli which produced it? What are your observable responses to it? How are your responses being reinforced? Will you respond the same way the next time you read the same sentence, if you ever do? How long would it take you to learn to speak and understand English if you had to be reinforced for every sentence you are capable of producing? Why am I asking you all these questions?

Osgood has advanced a different argument. When someone tells you "Tom is a thief," it seems possible that he has conditioned you to some extent to respond to the *word* "Tom" as if it were the *word* "thief," just as Pavlov's dogs responded to the tone as if it were the meat powder. But why do you make sure your money is safe the next time the *person* Tom is in the room? The *word* "thief" has never been paired with the *person* Tom. What's more, hiding your money is hardly the uncondi-tioned response to the word "thief," so how could it become condi-tioned to the person Tom?

Implicit Mediating Responses

Osgood's answer is that a mediating response—"meaning"—occurs internally and links the word "thief" to the person Tom through the word "Tom." That seems to have been borrowed from Doob, who defined "attitude" as an "implicit mediating response."[5] More com-pletely he defined attitude as "an implicit, drive-producing response considered socially significant in the individual's society." A radical behaviorist, of course, could never be comfortable talking about such an idea, since the "first commandment of radical behaviorism" delivered by Skinner to his disciples is: *Thou shalt have no internal responses, nor shalt thou look upon those of others, nor shalt thou contemplate them in thy most secret heart. Selah.* To the infidels among us, however, they seem to be convenient, useful, and even sinfully pleasant devices for explaining social opinions and policies.

This internal response described by Doob is implicit in the sense that it is not directly observable by anyone other than the person expe-riencing it; it "may be conscious or unconscious, distinctly verbal or vaguely proprioceptive." The most important characteristic of this implicit response is that it acts both as a response and as a stimulus. It is a response because it is produced by a stimulus. However, it is a stim-ulus because a person can perceive it internally—he can "feel" it, in a sense—and it in turn produces an external, observable response.

The implicit response develops in the pattern of classical condition-ing. Remember when you first saw or heard the initials "S.L.A."? They were just a neutral stimulus at that point, a collection of letters, neutral in the same sense that the tone was initially neutral or "meaningless" to Pavlov's dogs.

But they were promptly paired with the words "symbionese," "liber-ation," and "army." "Symbionese" was probably neutral, but "libera-tion" and "army" probably produced implicit responses of their own, especially in combination, since they had probably been paired with violent actions of radical left-wing groups during the late sixties and early seventies. The implicit responses to "liberation army" then transferred to "S.L.A."

Unless you lived in California at the time, you probably first heard of the S.L.A. in connection with the kidnapping of Patty Hearst, so your implicit responses to kidnapping children of wealthy parents also transferred to "S.L.A." Then you probably heard that this was the same group which claimed to have murdered Marcus Foster, the black Oakland school superintendent, so your feelings about that transferred to "S.L.A."

But then you heard that the S.L.A. was demanding free food for the poor in exchange for Patty Hearst's release, and some implicit responses to Robin Hood robbing the rich to give to the needy may have been mixed in. And you heard Field Marshall Cinque on tape, and your implicit responses to his voice and ideas became part of your implicit response to those mysterious, originally meaningless initials.

Then came Ms. Hearst's apparent conversion, a competent, brutal, flamboyant bank robbery, the evident inability of the F.B.I. to locate the hideout, the news that some members of the group were lesbians, and statements by William Randolph Hearst and various radical groups. Next came the apparent incompetence in Los Angeles when one of the members was caught trying to steal a cartridgebelt, and most of the members were located and surrounded by police. Then came the shoot-out—the ultimate example of futile, insane, suicidal bravery. Finally came Ms. Hearst's capture in San Francisco and her subsequent trial. . . . What an image we all learned, what new meanings and attitudes we came to associate with the simple initials "S.L.A." We developed—learned—an implicit mediating response to those initials. We learned that implicit response socially, by means of communication, in a process very similar to classical conditioning.

But we learned something more, because that implicit response also served as a stimulus, and it led to overt responses. When someone mentioned the S.L.A. at school, you "felt" or perceived that implicit response internally, and it acted as a stimulus to produce opinion and policy statements: "I don't think they're all that bad," "They ought to be shot," or "They may be bad, but they aren't dumb."

Now we come to the part of the learning that seems most like *operant* conditioning. You may have expressed a slightly favorable opinion of the S.L.A. at some time and really caught bad flak for it. So you were more careful next time. Instead of "I don't think they're all that bad," you tried "They may be bad, but they aren't dumb." That resulted in social reward, so you kept it as part of your "S.L.A. discussion policy." Until you tried it on your father, who spent the next hour lecturing to you about just how dumb they were and quizzing you about your political beliefs. And that resulted in a new policy—your "S.L.A. discussion policy when the Man is listening."

We all did it. We all do it all the time. We learn by a process very much like operant conditioning to use our opinions and policies to maximize our social reward and minimize our social punishment. But those opinions and policies issue out of feelings, attitudes, meanings— implicit responses—which we have associated with stimuli such as "S.L.A." by a process similar to classical conditioning. The problem is to express one's "true" feelings and still maximize social reward without compromising one's self-respect. That requires careful planning.

Social Reward and Radical Behaviorism

There is another way one learns to use opinions and policies to maximize social reward, and this one is far more subtle. Surprisingly, it comes from one of Skinner's disciples I reviled so mercilessly a few pages back.

Bem has offered a rigorously behavioristic approach based on radical Skinnerian behaviorism, avoiding any reference to hypothetical constructs.[6] He points out that a child is taught fairly easily to label stimuli which he can observe and which those who teach him can also observe. Thus he soon learns to label father and mother correctly because the parents withhold approval until he gets the labels correct. The child's parents have more difficulty teaching him to label things which they cannot observe; they have more difficulty teaching the child to label "hunger" correctly, for example. Ultimately, according to Bem's analysis, he is taught to say he is hungry when external conditions are such that the parents infer he *should* be hungry. Similarly, in the realm of self-reports about opinions, the parents teach the child to report that he "dislikes" when and what they believe he should dislike. Thus the child adopts the parents' opinions not merely to win their favor but also because he learns to base self-reports upon the

same external cues they use to infer what his feelings *should* be. This
process continues for the adult; he continues to learn to base self-
reports of opinions upon the same *external* cues used by the persons
and socializing agencies which are influential.

Bem's analysis is well taken, but his conclusion seems a bit overdrawn:
he concludes that self-perception is based upon the same external cues
available to those who teach one to give self-reports. This is convenient
for the radical behaviorist because it makes it unnecessary to consider
anything other than observable behavior. However, a child's parents
probably infer correctly more often than not that a child is indeed
experiencing a state of physiological hunger, so that the child learns
to combine internal and external cues as the basis for self-reports. It
has been demonstrated that self-reports of hunger occur when internal
hunger cues are produced artificially in the absence of external hunger
cues: specifically when blood-sugar level and temperatures in certain
parts of the hypothalamus are artificially lowered, and when stomach
contractions are artificially induced. Similarly, no one has to tell a little
boy that he dislikes a little girl who has just kicked him in the stomach,
and it is doubtful that he dislikes her merely because he has learned
that one is supposed to dislike people who kick one's stomach.

Bem's analysis is a considerable contribution, however, in that it
adds new sources of error to self-reports of opinions. Such reports
can be wrong because the respondent misperceives or misinterprets his
own internal stimuli or because he is reporting what he wants another
person to believe are "real" opinions, but they can also be wrong because
he has learned to depend upon the wrong external cues or has mis-
perceived or misinterpreted those cues. The analysis is further useful
because it focuses upon a new way in which self-reported opinions
are influenced by others.

Imagine a mother and child walking down the street. Suddenly a
man approaches from the opposite direction. The man has dark skin
and a "natural" haircut. The mother doesn't have to say "Hate black
people." She involuntarily tightens her grip on the child's hand and
draws the child closer to her, possibly because *her* mother or father
did the same when *she* was a child. The child has just learned that one
of the conditions for expressing tension is the presence of someone

with dark skin and that kind of haircut. Remember the lines from the musical *South Pacific:*

> You've got to be taught to be afraid
> Of those whose skin is a different shade
> Of people whose eyes are oddly made.
> You've got to be carefully taught.

Indeed. And that teaching can be very subtle. When I was about four my parents moved into a racially mixed neighborhood in a small town in southern Illinois. The earliest friend I can remember knowing was black. No one ever told me to like blacks. But my mother obviously liked my friend. She says now it was because he never fought; he would always go home when an argument started. I was encouraged to play with him, and nice things happened when I did (usually cookies and milk, as I recall). Besides, there wasn't much fighting when I was with him, and fighting hurt. I learned that blackness in another person meant friendship, safety, and good food. I haven't had much luck getting rid of that impression.

In the classical conditioning, S-R, and S-O-R models of behavior just described, it has been demonstrated that reinforcement has tremendous long-term influence on one's behavior. It is important to become aware of what subtle rewards and punishments you respond to so that you can better control your social interactions and transactions according to real values you hold. Examine your immediate and past social environments and develop a list of those rewards to which you have been responding. They might include social approval, an "A" or a "4 point," money for a stereo or car, victory in an athletic competition, approval from your employer, intellectual or sexual stimulation, peace of mind, prestige, friendship, power, doing good deeds. To what extent do others who provide you with these rewards also exert a subtle control over your behavior including communicative behavior? For example, how great is the dependence on the instructor for a successful grade? Does he or she want class participation, social interaction, and/or quiet respect, and will these communicative behaviors affect your grade?

Ego-Maintenance

The third major function that opinions and policies may serve for an individual is ego development and maintenance. This is closely related to self-actualization, the third function of communication in general. This parallel between the functions of opinions and policies and the functions of communication should not be particularly surprising, since one's social opinions and policies are largely acquired through communication and are reflected in his or her messages to others.

When I refer to the "ego" I am not using the term in the almost mythical, highly speculative sense in which Freud and his followers have used it. Actually, the term "self-concept" or "identity" will serve equally well, and I will use them frequently and interchangeably. In terms of the Image: Belief-Plan-Value model, I am really referring to a person's image of himself and his place in the world. For most people, this self-image seems to be the center of the image in general. When Boulding described his own image, he described it beginning with himself and moving outward. I suspect most other people would do the same.

Thus the image is "egocentric." I don't mean that in a bad sense, even though "egocentric" in popular use usually has negative connotations. *I only mean that a person's perceptions of the world are necessarily from his or her own point of view. After all, that is the only vantage point one has.* Even the person who succeeds in empathizing with another does so by imagining how he would feel if he were in the other person's position. It should not be surprising that maintenance of one's self-image is important, since one has to spend so much time there.

The functional approach I have taken in this chapter is generally derived from an approach described by Katz, who wrote of four functions: adjustment, ego-defense, value-expression, and knowledge.[7] I treated the knowledge function in the last chapter and the adjustment function in the first section of this chapter. In this section I deal with Katz' value-expression and ego-defense functions as subfunctions under the general category of ego-maintenance. To these two subfunctions I will add a third, ego-involvement, which I believe belongs in the same category.

Value-Expression

Katz says opinions and policies serving the value-expressive function are developed for the purpose of "maintaining self-identity, enhancing favorable self-image, self-expression, and self-determination"; they are aroused by cues associated with the individual's values, by "appeals to the individual to reassert the self-image," or when the individual faces "ambiguities which threaten his or her self-concept"; and they are likely to change when the individual changes the self-concept or discovers new attitudes consistent with this existing self-concept.

Thus the individual who perceives himself to be politically liberal subscribes to those magazines, buys those books, and watches those TV programs which tell him what opinions and policies political liberals are supposed to maintain. The man who wants to be a sophisticated, urbane playboy is likely to buy *Playboy* or *Penthouse* if he believes those magazines will tell him what sophisticated, urbane playboys are supposed to believe and how they are supposed to act. The woman who has just become conscious of her potential as a liberated woman may consult *Ms.* or *Cosmopolitan* to find out what this potential self-image is like.

Now you may have noticed that I seem to be writing about two self-images here, and in fact I am. There is the image one perceives actually represents oneself at a given time, and there is the ideal self-image one would like to become. These two self-images are more similar for some people than for others. For some people the perceived self-image may coincide with the ideal self-image, and for others they may be very different. Of course, the person whose self-images coincide may advertise the fact, in which case he is likely to be seen as very smug and egotistical, or he may simply go about his business confidently and unobtrusively. Similarly, a person whose self-images differ drastically may respond by working hard to make them coincide, or may become discouraged and apathetic.

Communication enters the picture because one's perceived self-image can become quite unrealistic if it is never tested against the perceptions of someone else. It is important to know how others perceive us. It would be absurd, of course, to revise one's perceived self-image whenever it fails to conform to one or two others' perceptions. But

if it does not match the consensus of others, and especially of others who might be expected to know one well, there may be cause for concern. It may be that one is misperceiving himself, or it may be that he is communicating a false image. In either case there may be a problem.

Similarly, communication with others can help one maintain a realistic ideal self-image. Without knowing how others perceive one's abilities, it is easy to set one's aspirations too low or too high. "Self-actualization" requires one to adopt an ideal self-image which is attainable but not too easily attainable, and then work toward that self-image. This process of self-actualization depends heavily upon socially meaningful communication.

We have all known people who seem to have no clear anchors for their self-images, who go from day to day trying on new personalities as they might try on new costumes. We all go through phases when we are dissatisfied with ourselves but are not quite sure just what we want to be. That is perfectly natural so long as it doesn't last too long.

At such times it is important to have others capable of understanding us, with whom it is possible to communicate at a fairly intimate level. Such understanding and capacity for intimate communication is not likely to be developed on command at a moment's notice. It has to be developed and practiced before it is needed.

There is always someone around to tell us what we ought to be and how to achieve it at a very superficial level, and this is frequently to their advantage rather than ours. Advertisers, for example, probably use this device more than any other. Remember the advertising campaign used by the makers of Camel cigarettes? There would be a picture of several people in some situation, and the reader was challenged to find the Camel filter smoker in the picture. Strangely, everyone *except* the Camel filter smoker had some sort of unattractive "gimmick," which really amounted to a superficial, unattractive, and obviously fake image he was trying to project. That image invariably involved smoking some sort of weird cigarette. The Camel smoker, of course, was obviously natural, sincere, and self-confident. Guess whose image the Camel manufacturers were trying to get the reader to imitate?

What has been loosely labeled "sex" advertising seems to rely on a similar approach. Of course sex is frequently used in ads simply to get attention. Usually, however, there is more to it than that. At first it may appear that the sexy nude or seminude woman in the ad is offering herself to any man who buys whatever product is being hawked. Now some men are gullible, but I don't know many who are *that* gullible, and most of those I do know are locked up. Instead, what such ads are usually portraying the woman as saying seems to be something like: "The kind of man who can have me is the kind of man who (uses Satyr deodorant, wears Bodyform clothes, drives a Studmobile . . . your product name here). If *you* want to be the kind of man who can make it with women like me (use Satyr deodorant, wear Bodyform clothes, drive a Studmobile . . .)." That is talking directly to the self-image and, I might add, bypassing the brain.

Which helps explain why sexy nude women appear so frequently in *women's* magazines. They are saying, in essence, "If you want to be the kind of woman who can compete with me, you'd better (use Mink perfume, wear Next-to-Nothing swimwear . . .).

CAN YOU SPOT THE DEEP THROAT FILTERS SMOKER?

(1) No, not him. He's Sy Koe, apprentice hoodlum, smokes rolled sunflower seeds. (2) Nope, he's Stanley Koklutzky, loves brass knuckles, torn T-shirts and cigarettes with gummed filters that stick to his bottom lip. (3) Still wrong—he's Marvin Middleclass, thinks slumming in the Bowery is fun. He smoked Tasmanian cigarettes. (4) Yup, he's the one. He's Sydney Bland, smokes Deep Throat Filters. He's a hack writer for soap operas. (5) No, as usual—this is "Chicken" Cacciatore, the last surviving Italian Kamikaze pilot. (6) He's Spiral Askew, seen here on his front porch waiting for cigarette butts to come in.

Self-images have to be carefully tailored, and they cost more than money. Buy one off the rack and you'll find when you get it home that you look ridiculous in it.

Ego-Defense

Opinions and policies serving the function of ego-defense develop so as to protect oneself against internal conflicts and external threats to the ego. Threat and frustration, appeals to "hatred and repressed impulses," and "authoritarian suggestion" lead to arousal of these attitudes. Change occurs when the threat is removed, after successful aggression or "catharsis," or after recognition and acknowledgment of the defense mechanisms.

It is important to remember that ego-defense mechanisms are those of which the individual is not consciously aware, *by definition*. The mechanisms, in fact, serve to eliminate threat and fear from conscious awareness, but general anxiety level remains high without being related to any specific threat the individual can verbalize. Obviously, these threats are not those we encounter every day; they are threats which tend to produce fear so strong that the individual will not or cannot deal with it. While Katz and Sarnoff[8] distinguish between anxiety and guilt, and deal only with anxiety, guilt also can be so strong that the individual banishes it from awareness. Consider some of these ego-defense mechanisms:

Denial: The individual denies (even to himself) that any threat exists. The overt verbal denial may be recognizable in that it may be stronger and more frequent than seems appropriate. ("Methinks the lady doth protest too much.")

Repression: The individual simply fails to recognize the existence of any threat. Thus he may fail to deal with or talk about an obvious threat.

Reaction formation: The individual professes attraction to the threatening agent.

Identification with the aggressor: The individual models his own behavior and/or appearance after the threatening agent.

Projection: The individual attributes to others the fear or motives which he refuses to recognize in himself.

Scapegoating: The individual blames others for conditions which they have not caused and which he himself may have caused. The blame is especially likely to be placed on stereotyped social groups with little power or on persons the individual perceives to be weak.

Paranoid reactions: Paranoia is a complex syndrome of mental disturbance. An individual may exhibit paranoid reactions, however, without suffering from the general syndrome. This involves perceiving other persons and agencies to be conspiring to harm him, thus avoiding blame for his own failures and at the same time providing a "rational" explanation for the generalized anxiety he feels but cannot otherwise explain.

Displacement: The individual exhibits fear in situations in which it is not appropriate or at such intensity that it is not appropriate. It is assumed this allows him to express fear without acknowledging the threatening agent. This is one possible explanation for some instances of phobia. He may also exhibit aggression toward someone who hasn't harmed him, because he has been frustrated by someone too powerful to attack or by someone he can't attack because of the social consequences.

Masochistic reactions: The individual behaves in a way that is bound to result in his being punished (by compulsive gambling or stealing, for example). It is assumed this allows him to receive punishment for inconsequential acts and thus assuage guilt without acknowledging the unacceptable motives which are creating the guilt.

I said at the beginning of this chapter that I am not using the term "ego" the way Freud and the psychoanalysts use it. However, Katz and Sarnoff do use the term that way, and this *is* a psychoanalytic theory. Still, despite my concern about the vague, speculative nature of psychoanalytic concepts in general, I feel this approach can be very useful in analyzing communication. It can lead to identification of some motives underlying communication which might otherwise go unrecognized. It has an obvious drawback in that ego-defense functions are difficult to identify. One can't very well *ask* another if certain opinions and policies are ego-defensive, since the other person doesn't know. If he knew, *by definition,* they would not be ego-defensive. These mechanisms have to be inferred from behavior which is, in fact, designed—although not consciously—to be misleading.

But Freud's notion of the "unconscious" bothers me a great deal. I agree that people deceive themselves with these ego-defensive devices, but to say that they are always completely unaware of what they are doing is pushing the notion a bit far. I would rather assume that one is sometimes totally unaware of deceiving himself, but sometimes, if he thinks about it and if someone has explained ego-defensive motives to him, he can come to recognize that he is using such devices. As a matter of fact, Katz and Sarnoff have reported some success in reducing racial prejudice by explaining ego-defensive motives and mechanisms to those who were prejudiced,[9] which suggests they must be able to achieve some awareness of what they are doing. Further, most of these ego-defensive devices look very much like some techniques people use to fool others when they themselves are fully aware they are deceiving. In short, it appears that people range from being totally unaware to being totally aware of using techniques such as these. To the extent that a person is unaware, it is simply more difficult to deal with his ego-defense, and it is more likely that he should seek professional help.

I mentioned that Katz and Sarnoff had reduced racial prejudice by instructing prejudiced people about the dynamics of ego-defense. Actually, racial prejudice is very frequently a result of a person feeling insecure and using a particular racial group as a means of reducing his or her insecurity. Thus one may feel threatened by blacks or guilty about their treatment, but may deny it, repress it, profess to like them ("Some of my best friends . . ."), or model his or her own behavior and appearance after them. He or she may feel socially unacceptable motives such as high sexual desire and may project that sexual motive, attributing sexual promiscuity to blacks or other racial, cultural, or social groups. The person who is especially concerned that he or she may be homosexual is the one most likely to refer to others as "fairies," "queers," "gay," "butch," and the like. A person may feel guilty about his or her own affluence when there is so much poverty and so may accuse those on welfare of being lazy; or may feel threatened by high taxes and inflation and again blame "lazy niggers," "lazy hippies," unwed mothers on Aid to Dependent Children, or any other available scapegoat.

A person may feel highly anxious, incapable of coping with the world, and guilty about his failures, so that one convenient escape is to blame it all on a conspiracy of communism, the devil, "rednecks," Catholics, or the "establishment." He may feel frustrated by his boss, success of a competitor, or by a rival for his or her girlfriend or boyfriend, but may not be willing to take the consequences of aggression against that boss, competitor, or rival, so "takes it out on" someone similar to the frustrating person—a person or group safer to attack. He may feel so guilty about something he has done that he feels the need to be punished, but the thing he has done may be so unacceptable to the person or to others that he is unwilling to admit it and accept the punishment. Instead, he acts in self-destructive ways which are at least socially acceptable but will bring him the punishment he feels he deserves.

Such analyses explain a great deal of behavior, both in oneself and in others, which otherwise seems unexplainable. A friend reading this section reacted by saying, "Sometimes I wonder just how much of me I really am." I can't top that.

But there is a danger to rampant amateur psychoanalysis, especially of others. For one thing, it is difficult to determine if another person is using one of the ego-defense mechanisms. There is a "Catch 22" element about it. If a person says he isn't homosexual, the amateur might conclude that he is using the device of denial; if he says nothing about it, he's repressing; if he likes homosexuals or dresses and acts like one, he's using reaction formation or identification and is really threatened by them; if he accuses others of being homosexual, it's because he secretly would like to be. . . . The possibilities are endless, and the other person just can't win. In reality, such inferences should only be made, if they need to be made at all, from *obsessive* denial of one's own homosexuality or *obsessive* identification of others as homosexual or from absolute *refusal* to talk about homosexuality, and then only when coupled with other indications, and then only by a trained psychologist or psychiatrist.

Further, if someone is really using ego-defense mechanisms to cope with deep and pervasive anxiety, it is not the place of an untrained amateur to rob that person of his defenses. There is too much danger of rupturing the stitches on a deep psychological wound which the amateur will then be incapable of healing. Therapy of this sort sometimes takes months or years; it is not something to play with casually at a party or in the classroom. Honesty is a good thing, but insistence on total honesty and confession of one's most private thoughts can be very damaging to someone who is being dishonest because he is deeply sick or hurt.

I am not issuing a blanket condemnation of "encounter groups," but I am suggesting such groups are best conducted under the direction of someone who has excellent professional credentials.

Certainly I am not condemning honest, open, and even intimate communication encounters among individuals either. I would encourage such encounters. But all participants should be aware of the dangers involved, should have the sensitivity to know when the session is getting too heavy for someone else to handle, and should have the good sense and compassion to back off at such times.

Knowledge of ego-defense mechanisms *is* very useful to an individual who wants to analyze his own communication motives, to determine how he may be using his opinions and policies irrationally to defend his own ego, and to guard against communicators who might take advantage of ego-defenses.

Ego-Involvement

To say one is "ego-involved" in an opinion or policy generally suggests that the opinion or policy is closely related to one's own self-image and necessary to the maintenance of a satisfactory self-image. Defined that broadly, "value-expression" and "ego-defense" could be considered subfunctions of ego-involvement. I want to use the term more narrowly to apply to opinions and policies which are used not merely to *express* one's self-image or to *defend* it, but rather are so closely related to the self-image as to actually *define* it. These are opinions and policies so closely related to one's self-image that without them one would be essentially a different person.

In an earlier chapter I described Rokeach's theory of the dogmatic personality. More recently Rokeach has expanded what began as a personality theory into a comprehensive theory of opinions and policies.[10] You should be aware before I begin to describe this theory that Rokeach uses the terms "belief" and "value" differently from the way

I have used them. He uses the term "belief" sometimes to apply to *evaluation,* whereas I do not. For Rokeach, one can "believe" that a concept is good or bad, whereas in my Image: Belief-Plan-Value model that is not a belief but rather a value. Rokeach's term "belief" is closer to what I have labeled an "opinion" which can be a statement about either beliefs or values or both. Further, a "value" for Rokeach is a very central kind of "belief."

A "belief" is the most basic unit of Rokeach's system. It is defined as "any simple proposition, conscious or unconscious, capable of being preceded by the phrase 'I believe that . . .'." Further: "The content of a belief may describe the object of a belief as true or false, correct or incorrect; evaluate it as good or bad; or advocate a certain course of action or a certain state of existence as desirable or undesirable."

An "attitude," on the other hand, is an organized collection of beliefs: "An attitude is a relatively enduring organization of beliefs around an object or situation predisposing one to respond in some preferential manner."

Rokeach also defines a "value" differently. A "value" in his system is a special type of "belief" which is "centrally located within one's total belief system, about how one ought or ought not to behave, or about some end-state of existence worth or not worth attaining." At another point, a "value" is "a single belief that transcendentally guides actions and judgments across specific objects and situations, and beyond immediate goals to more ultimate end-states of existence."

Since beliefs are the building blocks of Rokeach's system, we will consider them more carefully. Rokeach assumes that all beliefs are not equally important to the individual; rather, more central beliefs are more resistant to change and, if changed, produce more reorganization of the rest of the system.

Beliefs are more "central" to the extent that they are functionally connected with other beliefs. Rokeach proposes four dimensions which may serve as criteria for connectedness. To the extent that beliefs are *existential,* they deal with one's physical and social existence and identity, and have many functional connections. To the extent that they are *shared,* they have social connections and are affirmed by social consensus. To the extent that they are *derived* from other beliefs, they have functional connections with other beliefs. Finally, to the extent that they are matters of *taste* they have few and relatively unimportant functional connections.

Now when Rokeach uses these criteria to arrange beliefs on a dimension of centrality-peripherality, he distinguishes among five general classes of beliefs which, of course, are not clearly and discretely distinguishable: (1) primitive beliefs which are learned by direct experience with the object and reinforced by unanimous social consensus; (2) primitive beliefs learned through direct experience but not socially reinforced; (3) authority beliefs which are supported by negative or positive authority; (4) derived beliefs which result from identification with authority; and (5) inconsequential beliefs.

The conclusion of this analysis seems to be that the only important type of change which is at all likely to occur is change among *values,* and this is especially true of change introduced by *communication.* One's primitive beliefs are seldom changed by communication, either because social consensus is unanimous or irrelevant (because the experience is private), and inconsequential beliefs are just that—inconsequential. Thus it appears that beliefs regarding the nature of authority and beliefs derived from authority are most likely to be changed by communication, although this is never made explicit. That particular class of consequential beliefs which Rokeach labels "values" seem to be of this type.

These values, then, are very important in ego-maintenance, since they essentially *define* the ego or self-image. They are those beliefs a person holds most strongly about what is ultimately good or bad, right or wrong, worth attaining or not worth attaining. The individual makes decisions about how he is going to act—what he will and will not do— on the basis of these general principles. When one talks about choice situations, he is usually talking about situations in which two or more of these central values are brought into conflict, so the individual must decide which of the conflicting values are more essential to his own self-image. That is no mere *expression* of perceived or ideal self-image, nor is it a *defense* of that self-image against some sort of threat. Rather, it is a decision as to what the individual considers to be his *essential* self-image, without which he would not be the same person.

Rokeach does not apply the term "ego-involvement" to his own theory; that is my doing. Another theorist, Muzafer Sherif, uses the term "ego-involvement" to describe his theory.[11]

The key term in Sherif's theory is "ego-involvement," but that term as used by Sherif does not mean exactly what it means in common usage, nor is it used in quite the same sense as intended by other theorists. Taking note of his own research and that of others, Sherif concludes that there is a "latitude of acceptance" around an individual's own opinion. This latitude of acceptance is a range of opinion such that any opinions of others falling within the range will be not only accepted but perceived as lying closer to the individual's own opinion than they really are. It is the width of this range of acceptable opinion which Sherif uses to define "ego-involvement": the narrower the range, the greater the involvement.

On either side of the latitude of acceptance lies a "latitude of non-commitment," within which opinions are perceived relatively objectively and are neither consistently accepted nor consistently rejected. Still further out on either side lies a "latitude of rejection," within which opinions are not only rejected but also perceived as being more divergent from the individual's own opinion than they really are.

Beyond the identification of these latitudes, Sherif's most important contribution seems to be the conclusion that the latitude of acceptance is smaller and the latitude of rejection is greater when the individual's own opinion is near the extreme on either end of the scale. These relationships are diagrammed in Figure 1. Thus, while ego-involvement is defined as the narrowness of the latitude of acceptance, it is also presumed, with considerable research support, that ego-involvement is greater if an individual's own opinion is extreme.

I see this conclusion as an indication that people are very discriminating about opinions which are ego-involving. They make fine distinctions among opinions close to their own, but they are very intolerant of opinions which are very different from their own. I am discussing this theory in relation to Rokeach's because I suspect that opinions which are extreme, which have narrow latitudes of acceptance and wide latitudes of rejection, are either the central values Rokeach refers to or they are closely related to those central values. That is only a suspicion; I don't have any conclusive research evidence for it.

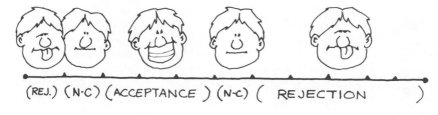

FIGURE 1
Latitudes of acceptance, rejection, and noncommitment per Sherif's theory of ego-involvement.

Note: The individual will perceive opinions falling within the latitude of acceptance as being closer to his own opinion than they really are, and opinions falling in the latitude of rejection as being further from his own opinion than they really are. If an individual's own opinion is extreme, the latitude of acceptance becomes smaller, and he is said to be more ego-involved.

(REJ.) (N-C) (ACCEPTANCE) (N-C) (REJECTION   )

But if it is true, it certainly has some implications for communication, especially for critical listening. Notice that the things Sherif says people do with opinions in which they are highly ego-involved are very similar to the things Rokeach says closed-minded people do most of the time. In other words, everyone is closed-minded or dogmatic about opinions in which he is ego-involved.

We can see that happening constantly. Extreme left-wing groups make fine distinctions among left-wing opinions. An S.L.A. member can distinguish carefully and sometimes emotionally among the Weathermen, the nonviolent S.D.S., the Black Panthers, and his or her own position, but anyone to the right of Mao is a capitalist insect or fascist pig. The John Birch Society member can make fine distinctions among right-wing groups such as the American Nazi party, the Ku Klux Klan, the Minutemen, and the White Citizen's Council, but anyone to the left of Barry Goldwater or Ronald Reagan is either a Communist or a dupe of the Communist party.

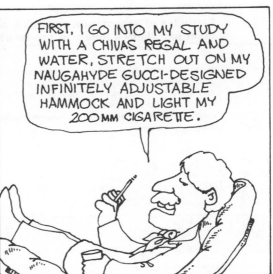

Are you exempt from that sort of thinking? I'm sure I'm not, on opinions which are really ego-involving, which serve to define the essences of my self-image. Yet that kind of thinking would be hard to defend as rational. And the disturbing point about this analysis is that it suggests *we are least rational about those opinions and policies which are most important to us.* Save us from important opinions.

I have tried in these last two chapters to illustrate how we use our opinions and policies to serve the major functions of consistency, social reward, and ego-maintenance. The survey has not been very heartening, since I have discussed a vast number of ways in which one can be misled as he or she tries to make rational decisions in response to communication. But once again this awareness, uncomfortable as it may be, is absolutely essential to communication in a society in which the consumer and the electorate are free to decide what they will buy and who will govern them. Without such awareness, advertisers and politicians could indeed become evil "insects preying on the people," and freedom "just another word for nothin' left to lose."

Summary

People learn to express those *opinions* and adopt those *communication policies* which will maximize social reward and minimize social punishment. Such opinions and policies are probably learned in a two-stage process. First, *internal mediating responses* become conditioned to external stimuli by means of *classical conditioning* or something very similar to it. Then these internal mediating responses, which also serve as stimuli because the individual perceives them occurring internally, come to produce external responses by means of something like operant conditioning. This explanation accounts for a wider range of human behavior than Bem's strictly behavioral theory although Bem's theory does provide additional insights.

People also *use* their opinions and policies for *ego-maintenance*. For example, they use their opinions and policies to express their self-concepts, as ego-defense mechanisms to reduce fear and guilt, and as buffers to defend their most central and ego-involving beliefs and values from attack.

None of these uses of opinions and policies are to be condemned outright so long as one is aware of them. However, some communications are designed to get others to adopt opinions and policies without being aware of their reasons. The best defense against such communication is to be aware of how one's opinions and policies are formed and changed.

Suggestions for Developing Awareness

1. From a recent issue of *Playboy,* choose an example of the ad "What kind of man reads *Playboy*?" Analyze the type of person that advertisers in *Playboy* are trying to appeal to. Describe the intended audience's life-style, jobs, taste in furnishing and clothing, political preferences, etc.

2. This exercise is similar to the preceding one in that it asks you to analyze the type of person advertisers are trying to appeal to. Choose a product advertised on TV that you are familiar with, e.g., coffee commercials. After you have analyzed the kind of audience the commercials are aimed at, note how those appeals have changed over time as audiences have changed. For example, at one time a coffee commercial portrayed a housewife whose marriage was suffering because of her bad coffee. What changes in the audience might have influenced changes in the commercial? Have those changes in the audience influenced most commercials on TV now?

3. Discuss kinds of communication problems that are associated with defense arousal. For example, analyze a specific encounter you participated in where either you or someone else was put on the defensive. What factors contributed to the defensive behavior? What kinds of behavior you observed or felt led you to believe that you or the other person had been threatened? What was the outcome of the encounter? Could it have been handled better?

4. We often hear of the negative aspects of egotism and egotistical people. However, it is vital to good communication and general well-being to develop a strong and healthy ego. Where is the dividing line between a strong and healthy ego and egotism?

References

1. R.F. Weiss, "A Delay of Argument Gradient in the Instrumental Conditioning of Attitudes," *Psychonomic Science* 8 (1967): 457-458.

2. B.F. Skinner, *Verbal Behavior* (New York: Appleton-Century-Crofts, 1957).

3. Noam Chomsky, "Review of *Verbal Behavior* by B.F. Skinner," *Language* 35 (1959): 26-58; reprinted in Leon Jakobovitz and Murray S. Miron, eds., *Readings in the Psychology of Language* (Englewood Cliffs, N.J.: Prentice-Hall, 1967).

4. Charles Osgood, "On Understanding and Creating Sentences" (Presidential Address to the American Psychological Association); printed in Jakobovitz and Miron, *Readings in the Psychology of Language*.

5. Leonard Doob, "The Behavior of Attitudes," *Psychological Review* 54 (1947): 135-156; excerpted in Martin Fishbein, ed., *Readings in Attitude Theory and Measurement* (New York: Wiley, 1967), pp. 42-50.

6. Daryl J. Bem, "Self-Perception: An Alternative Interpretation of Cognitive Dissonance Phenomena," *Psychological Review* 74 (1967): 183-200.

7. Daniel Katz, "The Functional Approach to the Study of Attitudes," *Public Opinion Quarterly* 24 (1960): 163-204.

8. Irving Sarnoff, "Psychoanalytic Theory and Social Attitudes," *Public Opinion Quarterly* 24 (1960): 251-279.

9. Daniel Katz, Charles McClintock, and Irving Sarnoff, "The Measurement of Ego-Defense as Related to Attitude Change," *Journal of Personality* 25 (1957): 465-474.

10. Milton Rokeach, *Beliefs, Attitudes, and Values* (San Francisco: Jossey-Bass, 1968), and *The Nature of Human Values* (New York: Collier-Macmillan, Free Press, 1973).

11. Muzafer Sherif, Carolyn Sherif, and Roger Nebergall, *Attitude and Attitude Change* (Philadelphia: W.B. Saunders, 1965).

Chapter Eight

Reference Persons and Groups: Commitment, Cohesiveness, and Credibility

As explained in the preceding chapters, one's response to communication depends to some extent upon his personality and personal characteristics, and to some extent upon his opinions and policies before the
communication. In this chapter I will discuss the extent to which one's
response to communication depends upon his *commitment* to prior
opinions and the support he receives from the opinions of others,
which depends upon the phenomena of *cohesiveness* and *credibility.*

Commitment

Apparently changing one's mind is not something to be done in public.
It is difficult enough to do in private. Further, opinion change seems
to be retarded even more when one has chosen to perform numerous
irrevocable acts which are consistent with that opinion. In essence,
commitment by means such as these imposes psychological limitations
on opinion change, making the individual more rigid, less adaptable,
less free, and thus less capable of objectively evaluating new information and opinions.

   Understanding the general role of commitment in the communication process is important to anyone involved in that process. The
speaker trying to influence another wants to prevent that other person
from becoming committed to any position other than the speaker's,
or he wants to reduce the effect of any commitment that has occurred.
After the speaker has successfully changed the opinion of the other,
he generally tries to get commitment to the new position so that the
opinion change will endure. The listener trying to make rational decisions, however, wants to avoid commitments which might limit freedom to change opinions if he should encounter new information.
Thus a communicator, regardless of the role he is playing in a particular communication event, can only benefit from knowing the commitments which all the participants have made which might effect
the outcome of that communication event.

   At this point, it would be useful to define more specifically what
I mean by the word "commitment," so it doesn't become another
waste-basket term into which one can throw any concept that doesn't

fit elsewhere. The definition given by Brehm and Cohen seems to be a good one:

> We assume that a person is committed when he has decided to do or not do a certain thing, when he has chosen one (or more) alternatives and thereby rejected one (or more) alternatives, when he actively engages in a given behavior or has engaged in a given behavior. Any one or a combination of these behaviors can be considered a commitment.[1]

This definition does have some problems revolving around the meanings of the words "decide" and "chosen," but it will serve the purposes of our present discussion. An alternative definiton, one which is not so specific but one which is still useful, is that of Kiesler and Sakumura: "the pledging or binding of the individual to behavioral acts."[2]

McGuire defines "commitment" simply in terms of irrevocability,[3] and Gerard follows with a similar definition which I view as being the most useful of those we have encountered:

> Commitment exists to the extent an individual is unable to reverse a decision or to the extent that doing so increases psychological cost and decreases reward.[4]

McGuire follows his definition with a list of four types of commitment in order from that most easily revoked to what he considers most difficult to revoke. He lists private decision, public decision, active participation, and external commitment. McGuire theorizes, on the basis of fairly sound experimental evidence, that decisions which are more *public* are more difficult to change, as are decisions which involve greater *effort* and investment. Thus a decision made in private is committing, but not so committing as a decision announced publicly to people one considers important. Then if one goes further and invests time, money, and effort in the decision (and again, especially if he does so publicly), he becomes even more committed.

Festinger, Rieken, and Schachter have provided a good example of the operation of these variables in their analysis of the actions of members of a religious group whose leader predicted the end of the world at a specific time and predicted that only those in a specific place would be saved. The faithful committed themselves by making their beliefs public and then selling their homes and other possessions so they would be saved from the holocaust.[5] That is commitment in the extreme, and the effect when the world did not end must have been akin to the way Noah would have felt if God had sent a drought instead of a flood. God, of course, would not have done such a thing, first because He is God and, second, because He was publicly committed. Another Old Testament prophet did not fare so well, you may recall; he became quite irritated when God relented and failed to destroy the city the prophet had predicted would be destroyed.

Note McGuire's fourth category: "external commitment." This is the type of commitment which occurs when someone else announces publicly that you hold a certain opinion. There is good evidence that such commitment is effective: if the announced position is the one the individual actually accepts, he will be less likely to change; if the announced position is one the individual has not accepted, he will tend to change in that direction. There does not seem to be adequate experimental justification, however, for regarding this as the most effective type of commitment, as McGuire does.

Thus far I have dealt with the situation in which one's public statements and actions are consistent with his or her private opinion. That is not always the case. In fact, it is only occasionally that one's public statement or action is consistent with *all* his or her private opinions; usually the statement or action is only that compromise which seems to be most satisfactory at that moment. A person may, for example, drive a car to a rally protesting pollution, even though he knows that he is spewing exhaust gases into the atmosphere all the way across town. His action probably is not *totally* consistent with *any* belief he holds, but it represents what he considers to be the "line of best fit" among beliefs which have been brought into conflict in this specific situation.

Then if we can assume for the moment that most commitments are somewhat inconsistent with some of an individual's opinions, consider what such a commitment does to the opinions with which it is inconsistent. Kiesler and Sakumura, whose definition I cited previously, suggest some tentative rules.

The first of these is that individuals attempt to resolve inconsistencies between their opinions and overt behavior. Sometimes this can be accomplished by rationalizing, but very often it will lead to opinion change. If the contradiction inherent in driving to an ecology rally were pointed out, the individual might reasonably be expected to come to view the rally as more important and automobile exhaust as less of a pollutant.

The second tentative rule is that commitment makes behavior less changeable. To the extent that an act is committing or "irrevocable" it is likely to recur, since opinions will be brought into line with the act, making it easier to perform next time.

A third rule seems self-explanatory: The greater the degree of commitment, the greater its effect in perpetuating consistent attitudes and changing inconsistent ones.

Finally, Kiesler and Sakumura list those things which seem to increase the degree of commitment. They say that degree of commitment is increased by a greater *number* of committing acts. It is greater to the extent that the acts are *important, explicit, public, irrevocable,* and perceived to be the result of *deliberate choice.* The matter of choice was discussed in a preceding chapter when I dealt with Festinger's theory of cognitive dissonance. The important point here is that if an individual believes he was coerced into a statement or action by being offered a high reward or by being strongly threatened, he will not feel so committed by the statement or act and will not feel obligated to make his opinions consistent with it. One can more easily recant and blame the act on the reward or threat.

I said before that a speaker trying to change opinions will use knowledge of commitment in two ways: to reduce listeners' commitment to previous opinions and to gain their commitment to the proposition. Often, of course, speakers want to strengthen existing opinions, in which case they will emphasize commitment which has already occurred. The listener will want to be aware of the ways in which his past acts have conspired to "freeze" his opinions and limit future behavior, making future "decisions" empty, meaningless, irrational reflexes rather than the carefully reasoned objective judgments he would like them to be. Finally, the speaker should be aware that, in adapting to the listeners, moving his stated opinions closer to theirs to avoid alienating them, he is in fact becoming committed to an opinion other than his own, and the result may well be that the speaker changes opinions more than the listeners change theirs. The finding in this area that is clearer than any other is this: More opinion change is caused by *making* a statement discrepant from one's own opinion than is caused by *hearing* such a statement.

Cohesiveness

If it were possible to treat communication as the never-ending process it is, there would be no "others" in the present sense; anyone whose opinions mattered would be treated as a participant in the continuing process. In point of fact, however, we generally think of communication events or segments, and we try to analyze them as if they could be drawn out of the total process for analysis. This is another instance of the general rule that language necessarily freezes process, stopping action as does a still photograph. There is no way to avoid segmenting a process if one is to analyze it, but it certainly contributes to one's sanity to remain aware that such segmenting is occurring.

The "others" to whose opinions we refer in this section are those with whom the participants in a given communication event have previously communicated. Two students who meet to discuss doing a cooperative term paper on a controversial topic are haunted by the ghosts of opinions they have encountered in the past and expect to encounter again, just as they are constrained by their previous commitments. The opinions they express to each other will be determined in part by people they have met in the past, whose opinions have become influential for one reason or another. Sometimes these "others" will have been respected and their opinions adopted. Sometimes the "others" will have been highly disliked or distrusted, so that their opinions have been rejected.

In either case, we will refer to such others as "reference persons." They are persons not directly involved in the present communication event who nevertheless, for one reason or another, influence the opinions we bring to that event. They may be close friends or they may be respected authorities we have never met; they may be enemies or public figures we distrust so intensely that we will believe the opposite of whatever they say. The major premise I have maintained in this book has been that all the participants in a communication event should be aware of the means by which their opinions are being influenced. In line with that premise, I will consider the ways in which the opinions of reference persons operate to influence one's own opinions.

A reference person is, in fact, a past source. Thus the credibility of a reference person consists of the same factors as does the credibility of a present source, which I will discuss in the next section: such factors as likeability, expertness, trustworthiness, dynamism, and similarity to oneself. The reference person, however, has one characteristic beyond that of a present source: we know his or her opinions have remained influential and salient over a period of time. What we are really dealing with, then, is this question: What are the characteristics that perpetuate the influence of a source, transforming that source from a presently influential communicator into a reference person having lasting influence?

The answer to that question seems to lie in the concept of "groupness" or "cohesiveness." Previous writers have referred almost exclusively to "reference groups." I agree with that approach as long as it is allowed that such "groups" may contain only two people.

The first step in dealing with the question seems to be to distinguish between "reference groups" and "membership groups." I have already defined a "reference person," and a reference group is simply a group which influences one's opinions and policies. A membership group is, probably not surprisingly, a group to which one perceives he belongs. The two are not necessarily the same. A group can serve as a reference even though it is not a membership group. However, membership groups are especially likely to become positive reference groups; people tend to be unusually persuaded by those within their membership groups and tend to reject "out-group" influence attempts. There are negative reference groups, too; these are groups which *negatively* influence one's opinions, so that one tends to react *against* them rather than toward them.

What is it about the perception of "groupness"—a relationship *vis-a-vis* one other or a number of others—that causes the other or others to maintain influence over a period of time?

For one thing, groups provide social support, especially when judgments to be made are ambiguous. The individual comes to depend

upon the perceptions of others he considers similar to himself or herself in various ways to provide social reinforcement for opinions. To
some extent this may be due to liking or trusting the members of such
a group, but not entirely. Being liked by the group seems to be a very
important incentive in this case.

Groups may also serve to define social reality. An individual imposes
his or her perceptions on social reality probably to a greater extent
than upon physical reality, because social reality is more ambiguous.
Thus one builds expectations regarding various groups and is threatened if those expectations are not fulfilled. The left-leaning radical
who finds his own opinion on a specific issue supported by the Young
Americans for Freedom and opposed by Americans for Democratic
Action may begin to feel he is losing his grip on social reality.

If an individual values membership in the group or values some
relationship to a group, he may use his opinions so as to maintain that
membership or relationship. Some groups demand greater opinion
conformity than do others as the price of continued membership,
and some groups demand opinion conformity in only certain areas.
The group may not demand anything of the individual; he may not
be a member of the group and it may be that no one in the group has
ever heard of the person, yet he may arrange his opinions so as to maintain a self-satisfying relationship to that group. This effect is especially
pronounced when an individual occupies a low power position within
or relative to the group and when he expects to continue to be associated with the group in the future.

It would be easy to become lost in a discussion of the reasons *why*
reference groups are influential and never arrive at the more important question of the effects of such influence. A great deal has been
written about the desirability of maintaining feelings of closeness and
cohesiveness in groups, and about the means to achieve such cohesiveness. Reading the avalanche of writing in the areas of small group
communication, sensitivity training, and general communication
theory, one might conclude that the only purpose of communication
is "mutual stroking behavior."

Social contact and reassurance are extremely important aspects of
communication. When groups are formed for such purposes, social
reassurance is the order of the day. However, when groups are formed

for the purpose of reaching rational decisions, too much cohesiveness and consensus-seeking can turn members into sweet lemmings congratulating one another as they pour over the cliff into the sea.

Janis has labeled this phenomenon "groupthink," which he defines as "the mode of thinking that persons engage in when *concurrence-seeking* becomes so dominant in the cohesive in-group that it tends to override realistic appraisal of alternative courses of action."[6] Janis lists the following symptoms of groups infected with "groupthink":

(1) Most or all of the members of the in-group share an *illusion* of invulnerability that provides for them some degree of reassurance about obvious dangers and leads them to become over-optimistic and willing to take extraordinary risks. It also causes them to fail to respond to clear warnings of danger.

(2) They also collectively construct rationalizations in order to discount warnings. . . .

(3) Victims of groupthink believe unquestioningly in the inherent morality of their in-group. . . .

(4) Victims of groupthink hold stereotyped views of the leaders of enemy groups: They [the enemy leaders] are so evil that genuine attempts at negotiating differences with them are unwarranted, or they are too weak or too stupid to deal effectively. . . .

(5) Victims of groupthink apply direct pressure to any individual who momentarily expresses doubts about any of the group's shared illusions. . . .

(6) Victims of groupthink avoid deviating from what appears to be group consensus. . . .

(7) Victims of groupthink share an *illusion* of unanimity with the group. . . .

(8) Victims of groupthink sometimes appoint themselves as mind-guards to protect the leader and fellow members from adverse information that might break the complacency. . . .

The major advantage of a *group* decision over an individual decision is ordinarily that it is the product of a number of independent judgments based on shared information. When groupthink infects the group process, the judgments are no longer independent. In fact, the group decision may well become less reliable than the decision of any individual, since the tendency is to suppress reasonable doubts which

the individual might entertain if he were not part of such a cohesive group. Janis points out the results of groupthink:

(1) The group limits its discussion to a few alternative courses of action. . . .

(2) The group fails to reexamine the course of action initially preferred by the majority after they learn of risks and drawbacks they had not considered originally.

(3) The members spend little or no time discussing whether there are nonobvious gains they may have overlooked or ways of reducing the seemingly prohibitive costs that made rejected alternatives appear undesirable to them.

(4) Members make little or no attempt to obtain information from experts. . . .

(5) Members show positive interest in facts and opinions that support their preferred policy; they tend to ignore facts and opinions that do not.

(6) Members spend little time deliberating about how the chosen policy might be hindered. . . . Consequently, they fail to work out contingency plans to cope with foreseeable setbacks. . . .

Remedies recommended by Janis include encouraging objections, adopting initial impartiality, setting up independent outside groups to plan and evaluate, asking each member to check group conclusions with outsiders and subordinates, relying on outside experts, assigning the role of "devil's advocate" to at least one member at every meeting, working to get a realistic appraisal of opponent groups, dividing into temporary subgroups, and holding a final "second-chance" meeting at which every member expresses as vividly as he can all his residual doubts.

Cohesiveness, or the perception of "groupness," can be a benefit or a hindrance to effective decisions. A certain amount of cohesiveness is necessary in order that the individuals in a group can share information and test each other's opinions without becoming mutually destructive; it can operate as a lubricant for the group machinery. However, when it begins to become an end in itself, to supplant the proper function of a decision-making group, cohesiveness can lead to disaster.

> *Groups that hang together are sometimes more easily hanged.*

Social Interdependence

Thus one's own opinion and those of others, expressed in social contexts, tend to have an effect upon one's decisions in response to communication. We might subsume both commitment and cohesiveness (in both its negative and positive forms) under the general label of "social interdependence."

The phenomenon of social interdependence is difficult to deal with from the viewpoint of a communication participant, because it is difficult to separate rational from irrational interdependence. Commitment to a position, for example, should not cause one to close his mind and retain that position forever. On the other hand, there are times when one must commit himself to others in such a way that they can have some expectation of continuity. Similarly, the opinions of others are not necessarily any better than one's own, but they may provide important information not otherwise available.

The speaker who wants to deal fairly and responsibly with his listeners is in a similar bind, for he must decide to what extent he can take advantage of his listeners' commitments and dependence on the opinions of others and still retain his self-respect.

I have no intention of making generalizations and pronouncements at this point regarding what is "rational" and what is "ethical" in the area of social interdependence, beyond the premise to which I have adhered throughout the book: All the participants in a decision should be aware of the bases on which that decision is being made. The reader of this chapter should now be more aware of the roles that commitment and cohesiveness play in such decisions.

Credibility

"Credibility" is the word which has been variously used to refer to the "image," "charisma," or "ethos" of a communicator. It is concerned with the extent to which a communicator is perceived as "believable" by another. Credibility can be part of a person's past reputation, and it can also be built during a communication encounter. Although some sources are credible when speaking on a wide variety of topics, most are credible on specific topics under certain circumstances.

Credibility can help or hinder each of the functions of communication. Regarding information-gathering, if one can identify a source who can and will provide reliable information, that can be quite helpful in making critical decisions. Sometimes we have to trust others who have access to information unavailable to us, or who have expertise in technical areas we don't fully understand. However, credibility can also be detrimental to critical listening if the credibility is so high that the listener fails to consider that a generally well-respected source may not have accurate information or ability in some specific area, or that a source who is usually fair and trustworthy may have biases which make him or her untrustworthy in some situations.

Credibility can facilitate cooperation in that it frequently requires a strong, trusted communication leader to pull a variety of factions together. But a selfish or biased source with high credibility can also disrupt cooperation, or can persuade people to cooperate to his or her own advantage or to the advantage of a small unrepresentative group.

A highly credible person can also be very useful in self-actualization A person you trust who knows you well can help you understand and define yourself to your own advantage. But such a person can also be dangerous if you become too dependent. The other person may quite unintentionally impose his or her feelings, thoughts, and perceptions on you, or may understand you at a superficial level and may thus influence you to adopt that superficial self-concept, or may by his or her own apparently superior psychological adjustment provide such a contrast with your own confusion as to cause you to despair. And all those problems can occur if the other person is in fact trustworthy. If not, he can cause additional problems with your understanding of yourself.

The Factor Approach to Credibility

Most of the research in credibility has been designed to identify the "factors" or "dimensions" on which people judge sources. Usually such research has used as the testing instrument semantic differential scales which apply to people, such as those that follow:

Edward Kennedy

competent ___ : ___ : ___ : ___ : ___ : ___ : ___ incompetent

untrustworthy ___ : ___ : ___ : ___ : ___ : ___ : ___ trustworthy

active ___ : ___ : ___ : ___ : ___ : ___ : ___ passive

Gerald Miller, in 1968, wrote of such research:

> Acquaintance with the research suggests only two generalizations about credibility which one can make with much confidence: First, if a communicator has a lot of it, he is somewhat better off than if he has a little of it; second, given the operational procedures typically used in factor analytic research, credibility appears to be a multidimensional construct. (The "operational procedures" hedge stems from the fact that there is little convincing evidence that these dimensions will hold up in a communication situation. . . .) In spite of all the hustle and bustle of research activity, these generalizations reflect little knowledge about credibility.[7]

It does not seem that much more has been learned about credibility since that was written. We know that a source who is credible can cause people to change their opinions and policies better than a source who is not credible. But most communication theorists would *define* a credible source as one who can cause people to change their opinions and policies, so that information is not particularly startling. The research has not told us much about what characteristics of a source make that person credible, although communication theorists since Aristotle have been making some fairly educated guesses. I will discuss some of those guesses in the next section when I describe a functional approach to credibility.

What the factor approach to credibility has indicated is that credibility seems to be multidimensional, as Miller pointed out. People don't simply judge a source to be "credible" or "not credible." They may judge the source to be "trustworthy" or not, "competent" or not, and "dynamic" or not, if one reads a report by Berlo, Lemert, and Mertz.[8] They judge a source to be "valuable" or not and "dynamic" or not if one reads Andersen.[9] They view a source to have "character" or not and to have "authoritativeness" or not if one accepts the report of McCroskey.[10] Norman found that people perceive other people in terms of factors he labeled "agreeableness," "extroversion," "emotional stability," "conscientiousness," and "culture."[11] Whitehead found credibility factors of "trustworthiness," "dynamism," "professionalism (competence)," and "objectivity."[12] All in all, this research is not a great improvement over Aristotle who, in the fourth century b.c., observed that what seemed then to be important about a speaker was his "character," "wisdom," and "good will."[13] If he had only used a computer to discover that, he could still run with the 1976 models.

More discouraging are studies which indicate that different kinds of people perceive different kinds of sources speaking on different topics in different situations on very different sets of factors or dimensions.[14] Different factors also seem to appear depending on what semantic differential scales one includes in the test and what kind of factor analysis one uses. That is why I prefer to talk about the *functions* a specific source serves for a specific listener on a specific topic in a specific situation.

List some people *you* would label as "credible." Let's suppose you listed the following people as credible: your physics professor, your attorney, your doctor, Henry Kissinger, and Walter Cronkite. Are these people "credible" in general or are they "credible" on specific topics in specific situations? For example, would you want your family doctor to prepare your income tax returns? If your doctor is a general practitioner, would you feel secure about him performing brain surgery on you? Would you want your physics professor to defend you against a first-degree murder charge? What information would you believe from each of those "credible" sources you listed? What information would you be skeptical about?

The Functional Approach to Credibility

Suppose we return to the Image: Belief-Plan-Value model and consider how a speaker communicating a message is cognitively processed by a listener.

First, the speaker is a physical stimulus. He is a particular size and shape, has certain voice characteristics, uses certain types of language, including grammatical or nongrammatical usages, and is to some extent fluent or nonfluent. These are sensations organized into perceptual patterns which create an image of that speaker.

Second, the listener elaborates that image by inferring the speaker's educational level, occupation, intelligence, intent, past speaking experience, nervousness, sincerity, knowledge, reasoning ability, and ability to organize, among others.

Third, the listener may further condense his inferences to form opinions as to the speaker's competence, trustworthiness, dynamism, similarity to the listener, and any of a host of others. The listener may also formulate policies with respect to that speaker. That is, he may think, "I would believe this person with respect to nuclear physics, but not with respect to my own psychological adjustment nor with respect to. . . ." This is the level at which the factor approach to credibility has concentrated.

The problem is that listeners form their opinions and policies with respect to the *functions* a speaker is performing for them in a particular topic-situation. When they are asked what "dimensions" or "factors" they use to judge a potential source, they report those dimensions which they view as relevant to the functions they think such a source *might* perform.

Even a specific source performs many different functions at different times. Take the newscaster Walter Cronkite,* for example. Sometimes he provides information, sometimes he teaches, sometimes he verifies or reflects one's own perceptions, sometimes he contributes stability to chaotic crisis situations, sometimes he consoles. . . . In each of those roles different dimensions of his image are relevant. If that

---

* *No, we are not, so far as I know.*

is true of a single individual whose functions are rather restricted by the fact that he is trapped in a television tube, think what a variety of functions *different* sources perform and what a variety of dimensions of credibility are relevant to each of those sources at different times. It is hardly surprising, then, that researchers have failed so miserably in attempting to identify a few dimensions of credibility which are relevant to all sources for all listeners in all topic-situations.

That is why it is important to be able to decide what makes a source credible or not credible in a *specific* topic-situation. To do that one needs to have some idea of the kinds of functions which sources can perform with respect to their listeners.

I described sets of functions in communication in two previous chapters. In Chapter Two I discussed three functions of communication itself: information-gathering, facilitating cooperation, and self-actualization. In Chapters Six and Seven I described three related functions of opinions and policies: maintaining consistency, maximizing social reward, and ego-maintenance. Sources seem to function in three similar roles. Another person can be a source of information or consistency-maintenance, a source of social reward or punishment designed to facilitate cooperation, or a source of social transaction by which one develops, maintains, or regulates his or her own ego or identity.

Insofar as another person functions as a source of information, there are certain criteria which seem relevant to his or her credibility. Such a source can be expected to be most reliable if:

(1) The source is or was *in a position* to observe the facts;
(2) The source is *capable* of observing, in the sense of:
    (a) being physically capable,
    (b) being intellectually capable,
    (c) being psychologically or emotionally capable,
    (d) being sensitive to the facts in question, and
    (e) having had experience in making such observations;
(3) The source is *motivated* to perceive and report accurately, in that he:
    (a) has nothing to gain by deceiving the listener, and
    (b) has goals similar to or compatible with those of the listener;

(4) The source has reported accurately in the past on this and other topics; and

(5) The source is *responsible* in the sense of being in a position to be held accountable for what he says.

Thus, while you may respect your professor in this course, and while he may be in a position to know about communication, he may or may not know more about political events than does anyone else. People frequently assume, consciously or unconsciously, that because another person knows a great deal in one area he is an authority about everything.

Similarly, a person who is capable of making one kind of observation is not necessarily capable of making another, sometimes due to being emotionally disturbed by the second situation, sometimes due to being sensitive to one type of observation but not to another, and sometimes due to lack of experience in making the second type of observation. For example, I find I can fake fairly respectable cocktail party conversation about the races at Laguna Seca, but I don't even pretend to know what to look for at a diving match.

Even when a source is both capable and has had full opportunity to observe the facts, the source may not report accurately if he has some stake in the outcome of the decision. Not that such a person will necessarily lie; it is just very difficult to be objective in a case one really cares about. One of the most obvious studies ever reported in the field of social psychology is by Hasdorf and Cantril titled "They Saw a Game."[15] Students from rival schools saw a film of a game between the two schools. Their task was fairly simple: they were to count the rule violations on the part of both teams. Guess which team committed more fouls according to the students from University A? Guess which team committed more fouls according to the students from University B? Right. Talk about empirical confirmation of the obvious. Let's just hope the researchers didn't get a grant from the President's Commission on Physical Fitness or the National Institute for Mental Health.

Even using a functional approach, the rules only *suggest* some *general* criteria for credibility. The actual decision as to who is to be believed still has to come from the specific case.

A source functioning to induce or facilitate cooperation can be judged by the same criteria, but there is special emphasis on the third. The crucial question in such situations is: Which party will benefit by the cooperation? If the source is going to benefit a great deal, the listener should be mighty suspicious. On the other hand, if the source doesn't appear to have anything to gain but is still trying very hard to persuade, the listener is advised to be even more suspicious. The object of this game is to determine who will gain what by cooperation, so a decision can be made in full view of the motives, goals, and benefits of everyone concerned. *Refusing to cooperate when it is in the best interests of everyone can be just as irrational as being too gullible.*

Most cooperative situations involve some variation of what has been called the "non-zero-sum" game.[16] The "Prisoner's Dilemma" is one such game. A fictionalized version of that game might be something like this:

> Andy and Bart are prisoners in a state penitentiary. Both are serving ten-year terms. Bart approaches Andy and suggests they dig a tunnel under the wall in order to escape. Bart works in the tool room, so he has access to picks, shovels, and wheelbarrows, but Andy is frequently in charge of a work detail which would allow him to dispose of the dirt. The cooperation-competition combinations look like this: (1) If there is no cooperation, both Andy and Bart will serve their full ten years. (2) If Andy cooperates but Bart reports him to the guards, Bart will get off early for good behavior, but Andy will get an extra five years for trying to escape. (3) If both cooperate, both will be free but will still be hunted by the police.

If you were Andy, what would you do? Suppose you really want to escape, but you don't know Bart very well. How would you decide whether you could trust him? Would it make any difference if Bart were serving a life term? if you were serving a life term but Bart was not? Would you want to know how Bart came to work in the tool room? What else would you want to know about Bart's past record of cooperation-competition?

This is typical of cooperative situations. Usually all parties stand to gain from mutual cooperation, or they wouldn't even consider making a deal. However, each party usually stands to lose something if one of the others doesn't uphold his part of the bargain. Further, one party usually stands to gain even more by pretending to cooperate and then backing out. Everyone must decide whether he is going to *trust* the others involved to do what they say they will do. *Mutual trust* becomes the name of the game and the name for "credibility" in a mutual dependency relationship such as this. Obviously, this trust rests more upon the specific situation and upon the specific characteristics, motives, and past records of the people involved than it does upon any general "dimensions" or "factors" of credibility.

Finally, consider the situation in which a source functions to develop or maintain one's ego or self-identity. Generally, the criteria which apply to sources serving other functions apply here as well. One would hardly choose to form a close interpersonal relationship with an ignorant, incompetent, untrustworthy, inexperienced, irresponsible liar if a better alternative were available.

But the criteria we have discussed apply a little differently here. A source can best serve a self-actualizing function for you if he or she is or has been in a position to observe you; is physically, intellectually, psychologically, emotionally, sensitively, and experientially capable of observing you accurately; is motivated to observe and report observations about you accurately, and has done so in the past; and is responsible in the sense of having a continuing relationship with you. There must be some basis for mutual trust—usually a mutually reflective relationship in which you define one another's identities.

Beyond these criteria, however, the other person serving an ego-maintenance or self-identity function will have to be capable of empathic understanding to a degree not required of other types of sources. That kind of understanding may be achieved by another person who is very similar to yourself, who can understand you because he or she is similar to you. That similarity may make the other person very likeable and comfortable to be with. But it can also pose a problem. Recall the discussion of "groupthink." People too similar and too devoted to cohesiveness don't necessarily produce good decisions. If you choose someone too similar to yourself to check your own thoughts and feelings you may as well talk to yourself. Uncomfortable as it may be, it is probably better to choose another person very unlike yourself but capable of empathic understanding. That is a difficult combination to find.

What emerges most clearly from this discussion is the clear impression that "credibility" is no general characteristic. It isn't even a collection of general characteristics. A source is "credible" to the extent that he or she *fits the function* which the listener expects that source to perform in a specific situation. The same is true of reference persons and reference groups in general. Commitment, cohesiveness, and credibility function in a variety of ways in different communication situations, sometimes improving and sometimes decreasing the quality of the communication, but always affecting it.

Summary

People are less capable of responding critically to new information once they have *committed* themselves publicly to opinions and policies. Too much desire for consensus in a highly *cohesive* reference group can also prevent critical evaluation of decisions, although cohesiveness itself facilitates group functioning and task performance. It is important to think critically about why a reference person should be considered credible when he or she expresses an opinion on a specific topic in a specific situation. The criteria which determine *credibility* depend primarily upon the specific function the reference person is performing at a given time rather than upon general factors of credibility across all topics and situations.

Suggestions for Developing Awareness

1. On what basis do you decide to believe or not believe another person? Familiarity? Status? Authority? Have these criteria ever tricked you into believing when you shouldn't have, or not believing when you should have? If so, which ones? Did you change those criteria?

2. What do you do when your family, friends, or instructors have beliefs different from yours? Get depressed? Change your beliefs to match theirs? Ridicule their beliefs? Try to change their beliefs?

3. Cooperation through communication can be constructive or destructive.

Using a group you are familiar with, analyze whether cooperation in the sense of "cohesiveness" and "groupness" (see pp. 180-185 of this chapter) led to constructive or destructive ends. For example, I was a member of a textbook committee. Our purpose was to review introductory textbooks in communication, select those we felt would best suit the nature and scope of our basic communication course and, as a group, decide on which text we would adopt for the following year. Sounds easy. However, the group members had varied approaches to the study and teaching of communication. As we were fully aware of those differences and as we all taught together in the basic course, one would assume that we would argue and be unable to reach a decision. But this was not the case. We worked so hard at cooperating and facilitating one another's viewpoints that we (1) spent hours making the decision about which text to use and (2) ended up with a text that didn't really satisfy anyone.

Have you had an experience similar to this one? What was the purpose of the group? How did the cohesiveness and groupness affect the decision process and outcome?

4. There are many different kinds of reference groups: intellectual, social, religious, business, psychological, and so forth. In this book, an example of an intellectual reference group would be when the author refers to Rokeach, Festinger, Boulding, Sherif, and others. These people provide support to the ideas being presented here and help to define what the author believes is real. What is the difference between invoking the names or ideas of those you respect and name-dropping? On the other hand, what are the dangers inherent in identifying too strongly with a particular group?

References

1. J.W. Brehm and Arthur R. Cohen, *Explorations in Cognitive Dissonance* (New York: Wiley, 1962), p. 7.
2. Charles Kiesler and J. Sakumura, "A Test of a Model for Commitment," *Journal of Personality and Social Psychology* 3 (1966): 349-353.
3. William J. McGuire, "Inducing Resistance to Persuasion," in *Advances in Experimental Social Psychology*, vol. I, ed. L. Berkowitz (New York: Academic Press, 1964).

4. H. Gerard, "Basic Features of Commitment," in *Theories of Cognitive Consistency: A Sourcebook,* eds. R. Abelson *et al.* (Chicago: Rand-McNally, 1968).

5. Leon Festinger, Henry W. Rieken, and Stanley Schachter, "When Prophecy Fails," in *Readings in Social Psychology,* 3rd ed., eds. Eleanor Maccoby, Theodore M. Newcomb, and Eugene L. Hartley (New York: Henry Holt, 1958), pp. 156-163.

6. Irving L. Janis, "Groupthink," *Psychology Today* 5 (1971): 43-44, 46, 74-76.

7. Gerald R. Miller, "Human Information Processing: Some Research Guidelines," in *Conceptual Frontiers in Speech-Communication,* eds. Robert J. Kibler and Larry L. Barker (New York: Speech Association of America, 1969).

8. David K. Berlo, James B. Lemert, and Robert J. Mertz, "Dimensions for Evaluating the Acceptability of Message Sources," *Public Opinion Quarterly* 33 (1969-70): 563-576.

9. Kenneth Andersen, "An Experimental Study of the Interaction of Artistic and Nonartistic Ethos in Persuasion" (Doctoral dissertation, University of Wisconsin, 1961); cited in Kenneth Andersen and Theodore Clevenger, Jr., "A Summary of Experimental Research in Ethos," *Speech Monographs* 30 (1963): 59-78.

10. James C. McCroskey, "Scales for the Measurement of Ethos," *Speech Monographs* 33 (1966): 65-72.

11. Warren T. Norman, "Toward an Adequate Taxonomy of Personality Attributes: Replicated Factor Structures in Peer Nomination Personality Ratings," *Journal of Abnormal and Social Psychology* 66 (1963): 574-583.

12. Jack Whitehead, Jr., "Factors of Source Credibility," *Quarterly Journal of Speech* 54 (1968): 59-63.

13. Aristotle, *Rhetoric,* trans. John Henry Freese (Cambridge, Mass.: Harvard University Press, 1926).

14. A series of studies by McCroskey and others have demonstrated that different types of people rate different kinds of sources on different dimensions: James C. McCroskey, Thomas Jensen, and Cynthia Todd, "The Generalizability of Source Credibility Scales for Public Figures" (Paper delivered at the Speech Communication Association Convention in Chicago, 1972); with Jensen, Todd, and J. Kevin Toomb, "Measurement of the Credibility of Organization Sources" (Paper delivered at the Western Speech Communication Association Convention in Honolulu, 1972); with Jensen and Cynthia Valencia, "Measurement of

the Credibility of Peers and Spouses" (Paper delivered at the International Communication Association Convention in Montreal, 1973); with Jensen and Valencia, "Measurement of the Credibility of Mass Media Sources" (Paper delivered at the Western Speech Communication Association Convention in Albuquerque, 1973). Some data reported by Cronkhite and Liska show that different types of people use different perceptual dimensions to judge different other persons such as "mother," "father," "Liz Taylor," and "Lyndon Johnson": Gary Cronkhite and Jo Liska, "A Critique of Factor-Analytic Approaches to the Study of Credibility," *Speech Monographs,* in press. Liska has demonstrated that the criteria people use to judge credibility depend upon both topic and situation: Jo Liska, "A Field-Dependent Approach to Credibility" (Doctoral dissertation, Department of Communication, University of Colorado, 1976).

15.   A. Hasdorf and H. Cantril, "They Saw a Game: A Case Study," *Journal of Abnormal and Social Psychology* 49 (1954): 129-134.

16.   For descriptions and discussions of these and other types of interpersonal bargaining games, see: Anatol Rapaport, *Fights, Games, and Debates* (Ann Arbor: University of Michigan Press, 1960); Rapaport, *Strategy and Conscience* (New York: Harper, 1964); Paul Swingle, ed., *The Structure of Conflict* (New York: Academic Press, 1970); Martin Shubik, *Game Theory and Related Approaches to Social Behavior* (New York: Wiley, 1964); Thomas C. Schelling, *The Strategy of Conflict* (Cambridge, Mass.: Harvard University Press, 1960). Studies of conflict resolution, interpersonal bargaining, and cooperative-competitive behavior in communication appear regularly in *Journal of Conflict Resolution, Journal of Personality and Social Psychology,* and *Simulation and Games.* One entire issue of *Speech Monographs* was recently devoted to such studies: John Bowers, guest editor, *Speech Monographs* 41 (March, 1974).

3

Becoming Aware of

MESSAGES

The reason no man or woman is an island is
because each one is linked to others by bridges of
communication. Now that we have explored the
geography of these would-be islands, it is time to focus
on the structure of the message-bridges which join
their solitudes. We will consider how messages appeal
to motives by means of reasoning expressed
verbally and extraverbally.

The Image Model and the Paradigm of Persuasion

Plans and Motives or Values
Data, Warrants, and Claims (Toulmin)
Types of Claims

Types of Motives

Physical Motives
    Biological Needs
    Fear Appeals
    Activation Level
Consistency
Social Motives
Ego-Maintenance

Summary

Chapter Nine

Appeals to Motives

Much of the discussion thus far has been in preparation for this chapter. Here I want to consider how people construct messages to appeal to others and how those messages can be evaluated to see if they provide sound reasons for making decisions.

Sometimes this contest appears extremely one-sided. Politicians who need our votes and businessmen who need our money are able to hire some of the most expensive propaganda talent in the world to try to persuade us to give them those votes and money. Then they use television, newspapers, magazines, and the mail to relay those messages to us. Of course, we are always free to refuse to vote, but if we do we are going to be governed by people we didn't choose. We can to some extent refuse to buy, too, but there aren't many people today who can make everything they need to stay alive and comfortable. It seems much more reasonable to learn to choose among messages, to decide which messages are urging us to do things which are in our own best interests. To do that we need to be aware of the motives to which those messages appeal, so we can decide whether those are the motives on which we wish to act. Then we need to decide whether the proposals will actually satisfy those motives.

There are other decisions, too—decisions of a more personal nature— which require critical evaluation of messages. A friend asks you to loan him money, or work on his car, or go on a trip, or transfer to another school, and your decisions may have important consequences. You have to decide what kinds of social and sexual relationships you are going to have, and with whom; whom, when, and if you are going to marry; what your major is going to be and what sort of work you are going to do . . . all of which require that you make decisions on the basis of communication. And always *there are two parts to such decisions:* (1) *what motives are relevant here,* and (2) *will this proposal actually satisfy those motives?*

You may have heard the expression "waving the bloody shirt" applied to a highly emotional appeal. Suppose we take a look at that metaphor. Imagine a mob gathered outside a jail in an old western town. One of the townspeople is holding a shirt drenched with blood and is arguing that Jake, a local tramp, should be lynched for the murder of Dr. Farley, a popular and well-respected citizen of the town. The shirt is a horrible sight, and it is strongly motivating to some sort of action. But what sort of action? Does that shirt actually belong to Dr. Farley? Is that his blood? Does the blood on the shirt mean Farley has actually been murdered? Did Jake do it? If so, should Jake be lynched or turned over to the sheriff?

We are right back to the Image: Belief-Plan-Value model: Strong values require one to choose a plan based on one's beliefs about which plan will produce the most valued outcomes.

Image and the Paradigm of Persuasion

In another book I have described a way to analyze such messages.[1] *A persuasive message is usually an attempt to get a listener to associate a plan with a motive or value.* The plan is one which the speaker wants the listener to adopt. It may be a plan for immediate, overt action (lynching Jake, for example) or a plan for future action (voting for a new sheriff who will give the citizens better protection). It may be a plan for reorganizing one's image (tramps are no good for this town), which has only secondary implications for overt, physical actions.

The *motive* is one which the speaker believes to be a strong value for the listener. It may be a strong positive value such as "safety in our homes and streets," or it may be a strong negative value such as "cold-blooded murder." The speaker's purpose is to get the listener to believe that this strong value is related to the proposed plan. He may argue that the plan (lynching Jake) is positively related to a positive value (safety in our homes and streets): "If we don't hang this murdering tramp, no one of us will be safe from any other no-good drifter who wants our money, our horses, or our women." Or he may argue that the plan is negatively related to a negative value: "Is there anyone here who is going to stand up and say that *murder* should go unpunished?" Of course, since every positive value has an equal and opposite negative value, any argument can be thought of either way.

Notice that the speaker is doing two things in deciding how to argue: (1) the speaker chooses those values which he thinks are most important to the listeners, and (2) the speaker tries to make the listeners believe that those values are related to the proposed plan. The listener, in deciding how to respond, has two parallel questions to answer: (1)

are these the values on which I want to make this decision? and (2) are these the values that are actually most related to this plan?

These two questions imply some others. There may be other values the speaker doesn't mention which may be quite relevant. Since lynching is illegal, this particular plan is related to the value "abiding by law," which the speaker is not likely to mention. Also, there may be alternative plans, such as turning Jake over to the sheriff, which have most of the advantages of lynching and few of its disadvantages.

Sometimes an abstract value such as "safety" requires more complete elaboration before it is strong enough to be really motivating. A speaker frequently elaborates an abstract value by associating it with more concrete values toward which the listener has even stronger feelings: "If we ain't safe from murder, we ain't safe from anything. What about the money from the cattle sale that ya have in the strongbox? Ya think it's safe fer one day if word gets 'round that we set a murderer free in this town? What are ya gonna do without it? How ya gonna pay the mortgage? Yer cattle ain't gonna be safe on the range. Ya'll be *wiped out!* Yer children are gonna be beggin' for food on the streets; yer wife and daughters are gonna be sellin' themselves to the miners in Central City and Cripple Creek to keep body and soul together! All because ya were too spineless to stand up and protect them against outlaws here in Rock Ridge!"

Some of the relationships among these beliefs, plans, and values are diagrammed in Figure 1.

So far all of these statements have been unsupported claims. Suppose we turn now to a description of how claims can be supported. Toulmin[2] has provided a model which can be plugged into the one diagrammed in Figure 1. I will only use three parts of the Toulmin model: data, warrant, and claim. The "claim" is the speaker's statement that the plan is related to a value (that lynching Jake is necessary to safety, in our example). The "datum" is some statement supporting the claim, say, "Second Mesa has had three murders since they let that gunslinger go last spring." The "warrant" is a statement connecting the datum to the claim: "Rock Ridge ain't no different from Second Mesa."

Any argument consists of an assertion of fact (or something assumed to be a fact) and an assertion that the "fact" is related to the claim. Either one may be omitted if the speaker assumes the listeners will supply it themselves.

FIGURE 1
Relationships among beliefs, plans, and values expressed by speaker urging Jake's lynching.

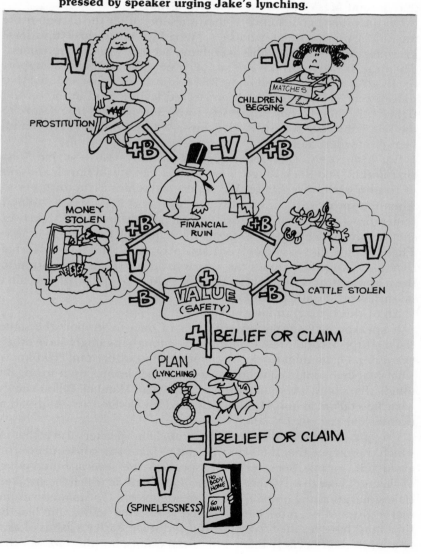

"Look what happened in Second Mesa" might be enough to make the whole argument if the listeners knew what had happened and believed that Second Mesa was enough like Rock Ridge.

On the other hand, someone may question either the datum or the warrant. Up steps Luke, who says, "Whaddya mean three murders? I recollec' some fair gunfights over there, but they warn't no murders." Then the speaker will have to supply a new item of data to support the first: "Now Luke, we all know Fast Eddie drawed first and shot that sixteen-year-old kid 'fore he even cleared leather, and in the second fight. . . ." Then he has to provide a warrant to relate that datum to the first one: "When Fast Eddie drops a kid with no gun in his hand, I call it murder, and. . . ."

But Josh isn't so sure about the first warrant: "Now Second Mesa ain't nothin' like Rock Ridge. They always had a wild bunch and lots of roustin' about over there. We always had a nice clean town here." Then the speaker has to supply data to support the warrant: "Why I remember—and you do too, Josh—when nobody in Second Mesa ever shot nothin' but coyotes. It was ever' bit as quiet as Rock Ridge is now. Then they got that easy-goin' constable over there, and now look what they got." And then comes the new warrant to relate that datum to the first warrant: "I say that can happen right here in Rock Ridge, ain't no different, it's just a matter of time."

All of this is diagrammed in Figure 2.

A speaker may supply several items of data to support the same claim. If the Second Mesa example isn't enough, he might have other examples. Or he might resort to another kind of datum: "You know what Marshall Dillon said how you go about cleanin' up a town. Be tough, that's how." And then the warrant: "And Marshall Dillon knows what he's talkin' about. He shore cleaned up Dodge City. And had a twenty-year run on TV, too."

I've talked so far as if the only kind of claim speakers use is that in which they argue that the plan will lead to favorable consequences or avoid unfavorable ones. Actually, speakers use several other types of claims. Those discussed so far are *causal* claims, in which the speaker claims that adopting his plan will cause safe streets. One may also claim that a given effect must have resulted from some cause: the bloody shirt must have resulted from the murder of Dr. Farley. Claims of *sign* relationships are closely related to causal claims, but they are not the

FIGURE 2

Relationships among data, warrants, and claims expressed by speaker urging Jake's lynching.

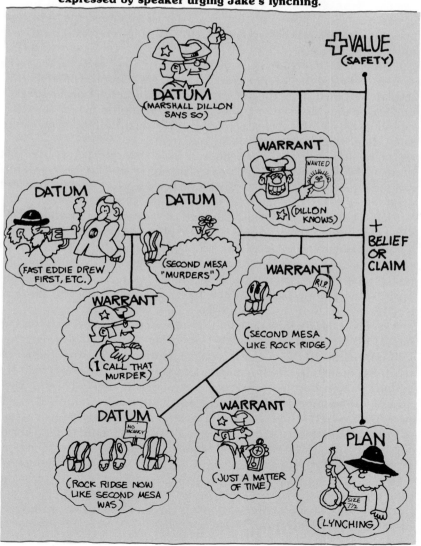

same. All four "murders" in Second Mesa could be a *sign* of an unruly town, but not necessarily caused by it, or by a lazy sheriff. Perhaps Second Mesa is close to a convenient outlaw hideout so that outlaw gangs naturally choose it, "causing" the disruptions, the murders, and the conveniently easy-going sheriff who might be dead if he were more conscientious.

Claims of *similarity* are those in which two things are claimed to be similar, so that if the listener likes the one he will like the other, or dissimilar, so if he dislikes the one he will like the other. Thus the speaker may argue that his proposed plan is similar to another which they like. In our example, the speaker might have compared lynching Jake to defending one's home against an Indian attack.

Claims of *categorization* are those in which the speaker argues that his proposed plan is part of a larger plan which the listeners like. Thus lynching Jake may be just part of a larger plan to maintain law and order.

Claims of *approval* are those in which the speaker argues that a well-liked person or agency approves of the plan, so the listeners' feelings about the person will transfer to the plan. This is *not* the way Marshall Dillon was used in the example. There he was used to support the relationship between lynching and safety, and his effectiveness depended on his believability. He might also have an *approval* effect if he were well *liked* since he himself would become a value.

The last type of relationship, that of coincidental association, can hardly be dignified with the label of "claim." Such relationships are seldom openly "claimed" by a speaker, although they are frequently used. Relationships of coincidental association are those in which the proposed plan becomes associated with certain values because they appear in the same context. Thus while there is no very obvious relationship between smoking Salem cigarettes and fresh spring air, years of advertising which has pictured people smoking Salems in pastoral, fresh, green settings has been designed to produce that association. In our example, the negative relationship between the word "spineless" and the plan to lynch Jake was coincidental association, for the most part.

In general, the most concise thing we can say about these other types of claimed relationships is: *if you don't have good evidence that adopting a given plan will* cause *(or at least contribute to) desirable consequences, why adopt it?* The other types of claims are really kinds of verbal conditioning and, while they are certainly capable of changing the value one attaches to a given plan, they certainly don't constitute good reasons for adopting it. As claims in their own right, these forms of association just aren't adequate, but they may be used as forms of reasoning to support claims of cause. We will discuss that in Chapter Ten. For now, remember the only adequate justification for adopting a plan seems to be the belief that the plan will somehow produce results you value.

With this framework in mind, let's consider the various types of motives or values to which speakers frequently appeal, and the types of reasoning they use to effect your beliefs that such values are related to their proposed plans.

Types of Motives

Chapters Four through Eight were largely devoted to discussing people's motives. In Chapters Six and Seven in particular I described how people use their opinions and policies to serve certain functions, and those functions are in fact general categories of motives. At this point I would like to pull the discussion together a bit more. To do this I will examine briefly four categories of motives: physical pleasure and survival, consistency, social reward, and ego-maintenance.

Physical Motives

Early textbooks in communication and persuasion sometimes made extensive lists of the biological drives to which a speaker might appeal. I do not plan to do that because I am sure you know that people generally do their best to stay alive and comfortable, that they are motivated by needs to eat, sleep, breathe, have sexual relations, avoid pain, and the like. I would like to deal instead with some of the more subtle needs people try to satisfy—needs to which communicators are likely to appeal because they *are* subtle. Most of the more subtle needs are psychological, but there are at least two areas of physical need which require some discussion.

Fear Appeals

It seems a little strange that there has been so much research on fear appeals and so little on reward appeals, especially when experiments in the area of learning have generally found reward to be so much more useful than punishment.[3] Probably that is mostly the result of an historical accident. The first "fear appeal" study was done by two well-respected psychologists, Janis and Feshbach, in 1953.[4] They happened to find that their high fear appeal was *less* effective than their moderate fear appeal. That set off a rash of studies that lasted well into the sixties[5] and has not totally disappeared over twenty years later. Their results are still the ones most frequently cited in textbooks, despite the fact that most of the more recent studies have either failed to find any differences or have found their high fear appeals to be *more* effective. If Janis and Feshbach had studied *reward* appeals and had come up with the surprising finding that their high reward appeal was less effective, we might know a lot more today about the effect of messages which promise rewards. As it is, we know almost nothing about reward appeals.

There is little doubt that high fear appeals are *sometimes* surprisingly ineffective, even though they have usually been found to be more effective. So it is worth asking why they sometimes fail. To answer that question we will look more closely at the Janis and Feshbach study.

These researchers used dental hygiene as the topic of their messages. Their subjects were high school students. The high fear appeal consisted of pictures of horrible and rare dental diseases—pictures which showed rotting gums and teeth fallen out. The moderate appeal mentioned tooth decay as the threat.

Janis and Feshbach suggested one possibility: the students may have actively repressed the rather disgusting high fear appeal, so it may have had less effect on their toothbrushing habits for that reason. A second reason may have been peer pressure. You can probably imagine how a group of high school students would react to a presentation like that— by laughing it up, right? That message may have become such an object of derision that the students were embarrassed to admit they had started brushing their teeth more regularly. Remember this was 1953. Any cat caught with a toothbrush in his hand for the next month probably tried to pretend he was using it to brush up his blue suede shoes or slick back his ducktail haircut. No way he would admit he was using it on his teeth. "You scared of 'pie rea', man? Here, let me see if yer teeth are fallin' out. They ain't the only thing about you that's yella. Hey guys, look at this fag with a toothbrush in his black leather jacket."

Other studies have suggested that a high fear appeal is effective only when it is followed immediately by recommendation of a quick, reliable way to reduce the fear. Sometimes high fear appeals seem to have failed because the recommendations may have *increased* anxiety. One of the studies used high-fear-appeal messages arguing that smoking causes lung cancer, and then it recommended an immediate chest x-ray. Not surprisingly, that appeal did not get many volunteers for x-rays especially among heavy smokers, probably because a chest x-ray at that point was a very threatening thought.

But the most perceptive explanation, and the one with the most far-reaching implications for communication, was suggested by Martin Fishbein in a lecture to a graduate class at the University of Illinois a few years ago. He argued that when you tell a person who has never seen nor heard of some rare, exotic gum diseases that they are the result of not brushing one's teeth properly, his natural conclusion is likely to be that he must be brushing his teeth properly.

That analysis can be applied to many if not most fear appeals. Remember the actor who played Hamilton Burger, the inept district attorney in the Perry Mason series? (You get ten extra points if you can remember his name.) Remember the TV spot which ran a few years ago in which he explained he was dying of lung cancer because he had been a chain smoker for thirty years, or something of that sort? (The TV spot was released—escaped, perhaps—after his death; he did in fact die of lung cancer.) The reaction of someone who had been a chain smoker for only five years might well be: "That's a relief; I have twenty years left before I have to quit smoking."

The gory films of traffic accidents shown regularly in driver's education classes may produce much the same effect, with reasoning something like this: "I don't have accidents like that, and none of my friends do. A bent fender now and then, but nothing like that. We must be pretty good drivers."

Or you may remember the old scare ads against the use of marijuana, the "killer weed." The ads soon became popular wall posters among those who smoked. They implied, and sometimes openly stated, that smoking marijuana led to heroin addiction, prostitution, burglary, and a wide variety of crimes against nature, motherhood, and the flag, not to mention the fact that it rotted one's mind. Now most college students have either used marijuana or know those who do, and since neither they nor their friends seem to be turning into werewolves or eggplants, the campaign against drug abuse seems to have lost a great deal of credibility among those to whom it was directed. That is unfortunate because it means that more realistic warnings against the use of heroin and speed may well be ignored. If evidence is eventually produced that grass does in fact cause long-range damage to the genes or to brain cells, who is going to carry the message?

I am definitely not *recommending* that sort of reasoning on the part of listeners, but I am emphatically recommending that a persuader ought not cry "wolf" every time he sees a stray dog or coyote.

Activation Level
Carmichael and Cronkhite found that frustrated listeners did not change their opinions as readily in response to persuasive messages using highly intense language.[6] They theorized that this effect, as well as some of the instances in which high fear appeals have been ineffective, may be explained by "activation theory," a fairly recent approach to motivation. Briefly, the theory suggests that people try to keep their activation or physical arousal at a level appropriate to the time of day and the task at hand.

For example, I will go to great lengths to avoid stimulation (light, noise, excitement) in the morning, but I will deliberately seek out excitement in the late afternoon and evening. Probably you also have a characteristic daily activation cycle, although it may be quite different, even the reverse of this. However, there are also times when we find our physical activation too high or too low for some task we have to perform. Exam week is a good example. If you have an exam at eight o'clock in the morning and are usually at the bottom of your sleep-waking cycle at that time, especially when you have stayed up late studying, you may feed yourself several cups of coffee or caffeine tablets to get "up" for the delightful experience. On the other hand, if you are too nervous before an exam, you will probably try to calm yourself down.

In short, people sometimes deliberately seek out stimulation and sometimes try to avoid it. That is quite different from the older "drive reduction" theory of motivation, which assumed that people act only to *reduce* drive or arousal. I once saw a mechanical model of the drive reduction approach put together by someone who had nothing better to do with his time. It was a black box with a windup key and a switch. When someone wound it up and turned the switch on, the lid would open, a hand would come out and turn off the switch and retreat into the box, and the lid would close. I don't believe people always act like that. Sometimes they "turn on" and sometimes they "turn off."

This statement has some clear implications for communication. Listeners who are trying to "turn on" for one reason or another, frequently because they are bored, are especially susceptible to appeals to strong motives and to very active, even aggressive, plans. Those who are trying to "turn off" because their levels of stimulation are already uncomfortably high will be likely to reject strong motive appeals and active plans. This is especially true of appeals to physical motives because physical threats and promises are especially potent activators.

Consistency

Little needs to be said about the need to maintain consistency, because that topic was covered fairly thoroughly in Chapter Five. It is probably adequate to remind you that speakers frequently appeal to their listeners to be "consistent" in ways which don't seem very rational: to adopt a plan just because someone they like approves of it; to adopt a policy or an opinion just because it seems to justify a past decision, even though the past decision may have been a bad one; to believe something just because they would like it to be true; or to interpret "facts" in a certain way just because the interpretation fits neatly into a "gestalt," a perceptual pattern, or a consistent comprehensive "explanation."

The research in social psychology does provide some illustrations of "consistency" in action. There are the studies of Milgram, for example, who has demonstrated that most people will administer high levels of supposed electrical shock to others who "fail" an experimental task

if they are told to do so in the interests of science by a prestigious experimenter. Many subjects continued to administer what they thought
were high voltage shocks even after the other person had feigned col-
lapse, even after they had been told the other person had a weak heart,
so long as the experimenter continued to order them to do so.[7]

It has also been repeatedly demonstrated that subjects who believe
another person is being painfully shocked for failing to perform an
experimental task will reject and dislike the other person, even though
they are told his failure was not his fault. The dislike and rejection was
even greater when the subjects were told they would see the other
person suffer more later and when they could do nothing to help.[8]
Fate is just and *consistent*, right? And if it isn't we make sure it is.

> *Life in a maze of irrational "consistency" can be a life
> in prism, where input from the outside world is distorted
> beyond objective recognition.*

Social Motives

In Chapter Seven I discussed how social reward and punishment shape
one's opinions and policies, and in Chapter Eight I dealt with the role
of social motives in communication, under the headings of "Commitment," "Cohesiveness," and "Credibility." Further, some of the personality characteristics in Chapter Five are very relevant to social
motives. At this point I want to pull all of that together into an explanation of ways in which speakers sometimes use social motives to change
listeners' opinions and policies.

Remember from the earlier chapters that some people are unusually
likely to conform to the opinions of others in general or to opinions
of others they consider to be authorities, while some are pushovers
for proposed plans to manipulate others. If you have such tendencies,
people who know you well may use those characteristic social motives
to persuade you.

Remember from Chapter Seven that social reward and punishment
can be used to change one's opinions and policies in very subtle ways,
sometimes so subtly that "social reality" is substituted for one's own

sense experiences. Skillful persuaders know that social threats and promises are sometimes even more effective than physical threats and promises, and they are usually easier to make.

Further, remember from Chapter Eight that once you have committed yourself to an opinion or policy before those who are for one reason or another important to you, it is much more difficult to reevaluate your position in the light of new evidence. Speakers may use your previous commitments to get you to accept plans which don't make good sense. You can avoid this by remaining uncommitted until you are fairly certain all the evidence is in. Remember, premature closure is a lot like premature ejaculation—once it has happened, all the fun is over. Of the two, premature closure is probably the more serious shortcoming. Speakers may also use your desire for consensus with others you respect to keep you from critically and independently evaluating new proposals. Finally, they may use their own general credibility or the general credibility of others to persuade you on topics to which that credibility is irrelevant, about which they know no more than you do. The opinions of experts can be very useful—even necessary—in specific areas in which one lacks adequate expertise on his own, but generalized, uncritical credibility can be a sort of mental Spanish Fly to seduce one into accepting opinions and policies which would look foolish in any other light.

Ego-Maintenance

In Chapter Seven I also discussed how people use their opinions and policies to serve the function of ego-maintenance. Persuaders frequently take advantage of this fact, consciously or unconsciously. When you hear a speaker say something like "Now I know a sophisticated college student like you isn't going to . . ." you know where he's coming from and you'd best watch where he's going. Statements such as "We (your group here) have to stick together" are warning flags to alert you to the fact that the persuader is trying to use your self-image in order to use *you*. Follow the Pride Piper and he will lead you on a veritable Gullible's Travels, littering generalities all the way.

Persuaders also know and use the ego-defense mechanisms. A persuader may say something like this: "Now some people have accused

*The neon lights of San Francisco's North Beach appeal to
obvious motives. Most advertising appeals are more subtle.*

us of hating college administrators. I don't think that's true. I've known
many administrators I've really liked. But this administration is to
blame for a lot of our problems around here. Sometimes I think they
are deliberately shafting the students so they'll look good with the
board of regents." The speaker may be advocating something perfectly
reasonable, but up to that point he hasn't offered one iota of proof.

What he has done is to appeal to the ego-defense mechanisms of denial, reaction formation, scapegoating, and paranoid reactions, at least. Nothing he has said up to that point should have any effect upon the opinions of a critical listener, who is going to be waiting for the evidence. Instead, these should be warning signs that the speaker is trying to appeal to motives of which the listener may not be totally aware.

Ego-involvement is another type of psychological motive, in the sense that people want to agree with those who express support for their most central opinions and try to push *all* the opinions of those who disagree with those central opinions as far away from their own as possible. I know an individual whose most central values seem to be "personal" morality, including especially sexual monogamy and strong family ties. I watched as that person excused all the excesses of the Nixon administration, even after Nixon's confession and resignation. The crucial fact in this judgment was that Nixon and his cohorts all seemed to be sexually faithful to their wives and appeared generally to be good clean family men, whereas some of his detractors were not. Now I don't know whether Richard Nixon was more "moral" in these respects than was Edward Kennedy, but it is hard to see what "personal" morality defined this way has to do with the public, political morality that was at issue. But *all* the opinions and policies of both men were judged on the basis of these few highly central values. On the other hand, I have known people with different central values for whom Nixon could do no right and Kennedy could do no wrong. Either position seems mistaken and seems to be a result of contaminating all of one's judgments by relying too heavily on central opinions in which one is too highly ego-involved. When the twin devices of perceptive selection and selective perception are allowed to roam about, murdering offensive facts at will, they can turn one's image of reality into a "wonderland benight."

Summary

Since sources frequently design their messages to appeal to certain motives and values they assume are important to their receivers, it is important to be aware of those motives and values. Such a message can be thought of as an attempt to cause a listener to believe that the source's proposed plan will produce outcomes valued by the receiver. Unfortunately, sources sometimes try to get their receivers to adopt their plans for irrational reasons: because the plans and values are merely *signs* of one another; because the plan is *similar* to something the receiver values; because the plan and the value both fall into some general *category;* or because some person or agency the receiver values *approves* of the plan.

Messages appeal to many types of motives including some of which the receiver may not be aware. *Physical motives* are the most obvious, and they are used in both fear and reward appeals. *Fear appeals* are generally effective, although in some circumstances fear appeals which are too strong do not produce as much compliance as moderate fear appeals. *Physical reward appeals* are frequently used, but there has been less research dealing with them. Messages also frequently appeal to more subtle cognitive and social motives such as *consistency, social reward,* and *ego-maintenance.*

Suggestions for Developing Awareness

1. A past issue of *Psychology Today* featured an article entitled "Little Brother Is Changing You."* The article discusses the results of an experiment in behavior modification carried out by students labeled as "problems" by their teachers and parents. The "problem" students used rewards to change their relationships with parents, teachers, and other students to more positive ones.

   Design your own "reward" experiment. For example, choose a habit someone has that you wish to extinguish, e.g., your roommate's insistence upon interrupting others or leaving dirty dishes strewn about. The trick is to positively reward the person when he or she allows someone to complete a sentence or when he or she picks up the dishes. For example, when your roommate allows you to finish a sentence you

---

* *Farnum Gray with Paul S. Graubard and Harry Rosenberg,* "*Little Brother Is Changing You,*" Psychology Today, *March 1974.*

might say, "I feel like we can understand one another so well when we hear each other out from beginning to end."

This approach seems to have two advantages: (1) you get to finish your sentences, and (2) the positive feelings that result can enhance your relationship and respective self-concepts.

You might want to write up the experiment's results and share them with the rest of the class.

2. Write two essays or speeches on a topic such as whether to live with someone before you are married. One essay or speech should use *fear* appeals to illustrate what could happen, for example, if you don't live together before marriage. Those fear appeals might include: the high rate and cost of divorce, the impact divorce has on children, and the emotional trauma of dividing money, possessions, and family. The other essay should argue *for* living together, using *reward* appeals. Discuss some of the following: living together gives you an opportunity to test how compatible you are with the other person in more situations than the dating game allows; living together gives you an opportunity to develop a mutually dependent relationship without all the legal problems of ending the relationship if it does not work out; and living together gives you the freedom to develop a close relationship without the social and legal expectations impinging upon it. (The two speeches could equally well be written to *oppose* living together.)

Which essay or speech will be more effective? To what kind of an audience?

References

1. Gary Cronkhite, *Persuasion: Speech and Behavioral Change* (Indianapolis: Bobbs-Merrill, 1969), ch. four.

2. Stephen Toulmin, *The Uses of Argument* (Cambridge, England: Cambridge University Press, 1959).

3. B.F. Skinner has focused on this finding most emphatically, as can be seen by consulting any of his books dealing with learning theory, but the finding is so pervasive that it is confirmed by every textbook in learning theory with which I am acquainted. One brief, simple discussion appears in *Psychology Today: An Introduction* (Del Mar, Calif.: Communication Research Machines, 1972), pp. 58-59.

4. Irving L. Janis and Seymour Feshbach, "Effects of Fear-Arousing

Communications," *Journal of Abnormal and Social Psychology* 48 (1953): 78-92.

5. One summary of the first decade of this research appears in Gerald R. Miller, "Studies on the Use of Fear Appeals: A Summary and Analysis," *Central States Speech Journal* 14 (1963): 117-125. A later discussion can be found in Cronkhite, *op. cit.,* pp. 179-185.

6. Carl Carmichael and Gary Cronkhite, "Frustration and Language Intensity," *Speech Monographs* 32 (1965): 107-111; reprinted in Serge Moscovici, ed., *Readings in the Psychosociology of Language* (Chicago: Markham, 1971), pp. 454-462.

7. Stanley Milgram, *Obedience to Authority* (New York: Harper and Row, 1974).

8. K.E. Davis and E.E. Jones, "Changes in Interpersonal Perception as a Means of Reducing Cognitive Dissonance," *Journal of Abnormal and Social Psychology* 61 (1960): 402-410; D.C. Glass, "Changes in Liking as a Means of Reducing Discrepancies Between Self-Esteem and Aggression," *Journal of Personality* 32 (1964): 531-549; Melvin J. Lerner, "The Effect of Responsibility and Choice on a Partner's Attractiveness Following Failure," *Journal of Personality* 33 (1965): 178-187; Lerner, "Evaluation of Performance as a Function of Performer's Reward and Attractiveness," *Journal of Personality and Social Psychology* 1 (1965): 355-360; and Lerner and Carolyn H. Simmons, "Observer's Reaction to the 'Innocent Victim': Compassion or Rejection?" *Journal of Personality and Social Psychology* 4 (1966): 203-210.

Types and Tests of Reasoning

Comparison and Generalization

Single Examples
Extended Examples
Collections of Examples: Generalization
Collections of Examples: Statistics

Contingency

Hypothesis

Testimony

Categorization: Inclusion and Exclusion

Hitchhiking on the Image

Summary

Chapter Ten

Reasoning and Evidence

In Chapter Nine I described how motives and reasoning are related in a message, and discussed some of the types of motives that messages sometimes involve. Now I will be more specific about the types of *reasoning* you may find in messages, and suggest some ways you can decide whether or not the reasoning in a message is valid.

You might learn that in a course in logic, but then you may not take a course in logic. Even if you do, such courses don't often deal with reasoning as it occurs in everyday communication. That is what this chapter is designed to do.

Types and Tests of Reasoning

I have assumed throughout this book that communication causes a listener to *do* something. In fact, "communication" was defined in Chapter Two in such a way that if the listener doesn't do something, it is assumed no communication has taken place. That doesn't mean the listener has to do anything anyone else can observe. What he does may not be immediately observable; at the moment he may only "change his mind." That is, he may adopt new perceptual plans or policies, so that he comes to *perceive* things differently in the future. He may change his plans or policies regarding future behavior so that, while there is no immediate change in his observable behavior, he *does* things differently in the future. And he may change his beliefs and values in ways that will eventually change his plans and policies which will in turn have consequences for his future behavior.

This idea that communication always causes a listener to do something is important to the way I am going to talk about reasoning in messages. It means that *a person who communicates is always implying, even though he may not be aware of it, that someone else ought to adopt a plan.* Further, the listener is always evaluating the message to decide whether he is going to adopt the proposed plan, even though he may not fully realize that a plan is being proposed or that he is evaluating it.

That means *there is one form of reasoning that is always crucial in a message: "reasoning from cause to effect."* The form of the argument is: "If you adopt my plan it will result in certain desirable consequences." The communicator doesn't always say that explicitly, but the implication is always there. A message as subtle as a raised eyebrow, for example, taken in context, may imply "If you explain your position further you may get me to agree; if you don't I'm going to remain skeptical." Thus the communicator is always trying to get the listener to perceive a relationship between the communicator's proposed plan and the listener's motives.

Let's look at that statement more closely. Reasoning in response to communication takes this form: "If I adopt Plan A (the communicator's proposal), then outcomes 1, 2, 3, 4, and 5 will probably occur; if I adopt Plan B (an alternative to the communicator's proposal), then outcomes 3, 5, 7, and 9 will probably occur; if I adopt Plan C, then outcomes 2, 5, 8, 9, and 10 will probably occur. I prefer the combination of outcomes 3, 5, 7, and 9. Therefore I think I'll choose Plan B."

Since this discussion is becoming so abstract, let's think back to the lynching of poor Jake. Here is Amos, listening to the speaker telling him he ought to help hang old Jake from a limb of the big cottonwood down by the river. That is Plan A. One alternative, Plan B, is to try to persuade the others to turn Jake over to the sheriff. Another alternative, Plan C, is to sneak home and forget the whole thing. Amos' brain is racing like a computer, calculating the probabilities of all the possible outcomes, weighing the probability of each outcome by the value of that outcome, and trying to figure the total value of each plan to decide which one he wants to adopt. His brain isn't doing all that in terms of numbers, of course; it has to work too fast to fool around with numbers:

> Let's see, if I help lynch Jake the sheriff may call in the federal marshalls and arrest us all. We might all be thrown in jail, or we might even be hanged ourselves. But it's a long way to Denver, they prob'ly don't have a jail big enough for all of us, and they surely wouldn't hang us all. Prob'ly what they'll do is get the leaders, 'specially the guy who's talkin' so loud, so chances are I'll get off.
>
> But my wife will raise hell with me, I know, and I wonder what the kids will think. I won't be able to go to Sunday meetin' for months, else for sure the preacher will tell me to my face right there in front of ever'body what *he* thought of it.
>
> Besides, it's murder, and I don't like that. I'd have to live with that the rest of my life, thinkin' I'd *killed* a man. What if it turns out Jake didn't kill old Doc Farley? Then I'd have killed an *innocent* man.
>
> But dammit, the fella's right, we got to protect our homes. Can't have outlaws ridin' through Rock Ridge shootin' up the town and

takin' what they want. I'd kill myself if Jody ended up in a saloon in Cripple Creek.

But suppose we turned Jake over to the sheriff? Reckon he'd do anything? Reckon the law would take care of him? The law shore hanged old Mace and his bunch over in Mace's Hole, cleaned up that place 'til it's nice and peaceful, they're callin' it Beulah Valley now.

But these fellers here ain't gonna turn Jake over to no sheriff without somebody stands up and says they should, and that somebody's prob'ly gotta be me. But I don't wanta make no fool of myself. They sure gonna call me a yaller dog, and they might just hang me alongside Jake. They're purty het up 'bout this.

But s'pose I was to just mosey on home, like I had chores to do? Then I ain't gonna kill nobody, and I ain't gonna be called yaller neither. Reckon I'll jest meander that way, kinda casual-like, and hope nobody sees me.

The plan selected, Plan C, isn't ideal, because if Jake were lynched Amos would still have to live with the fact that he hadn't spoken up. But he would probably warp his perceptions enough to conclude that the mob was too "het up" for him to have stopped them anyway, and would very likely conclude that Jake was guilty anyway, and even if he weren't guilty he "shore weren't worth much," and now there aren't going to be any real outlaws riding through town. And Amos would probably change the value he placed on killing, raising it a few notches. But he would almost certainly alter his general plan for dealing with crisis situations in the future: Stay out of mobs!

The point of this example is that decisions in response to communication are made in terms of *outcomes:* physical outcomes, social outcomes, perceptual outcomes, and cognitive outcomes. And outcomes are the *effects* of which plans are the *causes.* So we will now examine types of reasoning which people use as they try to decide what plans will produce what outcomes.

I will not use the usual division of types of reasoning into "induction" and "deduction," since logicians themselves do not always seem to be clear about what the distinction is. If I were to adopt Beardsley's distinction between deductive reasoning, which produces a necessary conclusion, and inductive reasoning, which does not, then only the last type of reasoning, "categorization," would be deductive.

Incidentally, Beardsley's book *Thinking Straight*[1] is an excellent source for the reader interested in learning more about reasoning in general, as is Emmet's *Handbook of Logic*.[2] Kahane's book *Logic and Contemporary Rhetoric* takes an even more practical approach, drawing a host of examples from everyday life.[3]

Comparison and Generalization

Probably the most basic method of reasoning, actually the second most basic operation of the brain, is the ability to learn from one experience so that the first experience affects the way we act in a second, similar situation. Some of the higher animals are capable of learning by observing the experiences of others; humans, in particular, are even capable of learning from experiences which have only been described to them. We learn by example, and speakers try to persuade listeners by offering them examples.

Single Examples

The use of single examples, or a limited number of examples, is good in that it allows one to visualize each specific instance vividly and to decide if it seems representative. The difficulty is that it is usually impossible to enumerate or describe enough examples to constitute an adequate sample.

Usually the question at hand is how similar an example is to the present instance. I went through that question to some extent discussing the similarities and differences between Rock Ridge and Second Mesa a few pages back. Certainly the two instances should be similar in as many respects as possible, and any differences should be irrelevant or unimportant to the conclusion.

Extended Examples

Sometimes speakers describe the similarities between two instances in great detail, as the speaker might have made an extended comparison between Rock Ridge and Second Mesa. Such extended comparisons are sometimes called "analogies." Analogies don't have a very good reputation among logicians, because they don't seem to have the force of evidence some other types of reasoning do. However, if a speaker is going to use an example, it is probably better to carefully enumerate the similarities and differences between the sample and the present case.

Beardsley, for one, rejects analogy as a valid form of induction except as a type of generalization. His argument is that enumerating thirteen characteristics which two situations have in common produces no rational grounds for inferring any additional similarities *unless* one of the observed similarities puts both situations into some general class about which we have additional knowledge.

Suppose, for example, the argument is that coffee drinking, like cigarette smoking, is hazardous to one's health. One could construct an extensive analogy between the two: coffee drinkers drink more the longer they have been drinking; they become irritable when deprived, in fact they show many withdrawal symptoms when they try to break the habit; both caffeine and nicotine are "artificial" drugs, and on and on. None of these constitute rational grounds for concluding that the two are also similar in being hazardous to one's health. But when we note that coffee and cigarette "addicts" both have chronically fast heart rates, we seem to be on to something important. And we are—because we know that chronically fast heart rates are associated with (probably "cause," but are at least symptomatic of) certain types of heart disease. We now have some evidence for the conclusion, but not by force of the *analogy*. Rather, our new evidence comes from the application of a generalization.

One good approach may be to describe and enumerate a number of examples and then use statistical means to summarize data based on a larger sample or even based on the entire population. Imagine a speaker arguing that the federal government should consider a family of four with income less than $5000 to be within the official definition of "poverty." He might first describe the living conditions of a few typical families at about that income level, allowing the listener to visualize the conditions. Then to demonstrate that the conditions he has described are in fact typical, he could cite statistical data from some source such as *Statistical Abstracts of the United States* regarding the average number of bedrooms in the living quarters of such families, percentages who own various types of appliances, indebtedness, savings, insurance, number who attend college, and other matters with which his examples may have dealt. The examples without the statistics would be difficult to evaluate for representativeness; the statistics without the examples would be difficult to visualize. The two together can constitute a reliable and vivid argument.

Collections of Examples: Generalization

Sometimes one uses examples not just to speculate about the present case, but to make a generalization. Reasoning by generalization attributes some *characteristic* to a *class*. To be certain the generalization is sound, one may ask a number of questions:

(1) Is the class clearly defined? If not, it is difficult to evaluate the adequacy of any sample from that class.

(2) Is the characteristic clearly defined? Any conclusion is going to be at least as ambiguous as the definition of the characteristic. If the definitions of the class and/or the characteristic depend upon measurement, the measurement procedures should be clearly understood and evaluated for adequacy. Remember also that measurement procedures can themselves bias a sample even though the sample may have been unbiased initially. Questions used in an opinion survey, for example, can antagonize respondents or suggest "correct" responses consistent with the bias of the investigator.

(3) Is the scope of the generalization clearly specified? That is, does it contain vague terms such as "most" or "many"?

(4) Is the sample *representative*? There are really two questions involved here: (4a) Is the sample *typical* (random, unbiased, or selected on the basis of relevant variables)? (4b) Is the sample *large enough*? The relation between these two questions is interesting. If *one example* is perfectly typical, then it is a large enough sample; on the other hand, if the sample is large enough to include the entire class, then it is necessarily typical. Of course, these are only hypothetical cases since we never know if a single instance is perfectly typical, and if we had a sample that was, in fact, the entire population, we would not be generalizing. Even if we had surveyed the entire class at a given point in time, we are usually interested in generalizing about that class in the future, and since the membership of most classes is constantly changing we

still would not have the entire class to which we want to generalize. Consequently, in practice the adequacy of a generalization is determined by the balance between the *size* of a sample and its *typicality*. Just what this balance is depends on another concept: the *variability* of the members of the class. Thus we must ask the fifth question before the fourth can be answered adequately:

(5) Is the *variability* of the class adequately represented in the sample?

One reason a sample of one case is inadequate is that any conclusion drawn from it would rest on the assumption that there is *no* variability within the class. Further, with only one case we have no basis for deciding how much variability there is within the class. Even a sample drawn at random might not be typical if it were too small to represent the variability of the class.

One way to check on variability is to draw a fairly large sample and then break that into subsamples. If the generalization is confirmed in some subsamples but not in others, and if the variability between subsamples is too great, we may have to conclude that even the total sample is not large enough to represent the variability of the class. Another way to handle variability is to decide what *subclasses* within the larger class are likely to contribute to variability. The various polling agencies which attempt to predict voting percentages in elections on the basis of sampling have decided that it is important to sample at random from within certain subclasses based on educational level, income, and age, for example. To the extent that the important subclasses are identified and randomly sampled, the problem of variability is reduced.

The scope of the generalization and its accuracy also limit the range of acceptable variability. If the generalization is universal (all the members of the class have the characteristic), then *any* variability is unacceptable. If the generalization is less than universal but specifies some acceptable limits (between 50 percent and 60 percent of the class have the characteristic, or there is a .50 to .60 probability that a member of the class has the characteristic), then too much variability in the sample might lead us to conclude that the percentage of the total class having the characteristic might fall outside the acceptable range even though the sample percentage happens to fall within that range.

Obviously, what constitutes acceptable sample size in relation to sample variability is going to be an educated guess based on common sense, unless one is willing to apply the mathematical criteria available in treatments of statistical inference and sampling procedure. I don't generally propose to do that.

Collections of Examples: Statistics

Beyond the problems involved in generalizations, summarizing collections of examples by the use of statistics has its own difficulties. Shortly after the nationwide 55-mile-per-hour speed limit was imposed, an editorial on station KCBS in San Francisco charged that the California Highway Patrol was ticketing passenger cars but largely ignoring trucks and buses. On March 5, 1974, Commissioner Pudinsky of the C.H.P. responded by saying, among other things: (1) the C.H.P. gave more tickets to truckers in 1973 than ever before, and (2) they had issued twice as many tickets to truckers up to that point in 1974 than during the same period in 1973.

Those figures were obviously designed to make a big impression, and at first glance they do. The problem is that we still don't know how many tickets the C.H.P. was giving to trucks or how that compared to the number given to passenger cars. For all we know from what Pudinsky said, the C.H.P. may have reached its previous all-time high by giving ten tickets to truckers in 1968, set the new record by giving twelve in 1973, and doubled that rate by giving four during January and February of 1974.

I also read a newspaper report that 98 percent of all cases of venereal disease are passed among friends, and only two percent of the cases are communicated (there's that word again) by prostitutes. Obviously it's safer to patronize a prostitute? It may be, but the statistics don't prove it, because we don't know what proportion of all sexual activity involves prostitutes. For instance, if prostitutes account for only one percent of all sexual activity, but two percent of all VD, one would be well advised to save his money.

Not too long after the E.P.A. gasoline mileage report was issued, Mazda came out with an ad saying that its gas mileage was among the top 25 percent "of all cars sold in the U.S." But a quick check of that E.P.A. report showed that Mazda mileage was far from being among the top 25 percent of all *makes* of cars sold in the U.S. and was, in fact, the worst of all the foreign "economy" cars.

One of the greatest books for examples of statistical sophistry is an interestingly written paperback by Stephen K. Campbell, *Flaws and Fallacies in Statistical Thinking.*[4] I can't begin to do justice to the book, but a quick review of the major problems mentioned is certainly worth the space. Under "Some Basic Measurement and Definition Problems," Campbell points out that New York City had a population in 1955 of anywhere from 1,910,000 to 13,630,000, depending on how one defined "New York City," while London's population ranged from 5200 to ten million based on the same criteria. Among the "Far-Fetched Estimates" he cites is Mark Twain's projection on the basis of the rate at which the Lower Mississippi was being shortened by silt deposits that by about the year 2640, give or take twenty years, Cairo, Illinois and New Orleans would be the same city.

On the topic of "averages," he emphasizes the differences among mean (arithmetic average), median (point where 50 percent of all values fall below and 50 percent above), and mode (most frequent value). I have an example for that one: What is wrong with a town which has 90 percent of its population on welfare when its "average" annual income is $100,000? Answer: Nothing, if it has a population of ten, one of whom is a millionaire.

Under "Ignoring Dispersion," Campbell quotes Lord Justice Matthews:

> When I was a young man practicing at the bar, I lost a great many cases I should have won. As I got along, I won a great many cases I ought to have lost; so on the whole justice was done.

Read the book. It's worth the price and the time.

The most disturbing point is that statistics don't have to come from *anywhere* or mean *anything* to convince the average person 75 percent of the time. Try it sometime. It's a great party game. Into a discussion of the relative safety of compacts and full-size cars, drop a line such as: "Statistics show that 78.3 percent of all fatal accidents involve small cars." How often do you think someone will ask you where that percentage came from or what a "small" car is? Right. Less than 2.7 percent of the time.

In short, anytime you hear the average speaker say something that begins "The average American citizen . . ." or "Over 73 percent of the time . . ." you can bet there is at least an 87 percent chance you are about to be taken.

What is the difference between stereotyping and generalizing? Do generalizations that are produced in the "scientific laboratory" escape the dangers of stereotyping? Whenever we refer to groups of people with the word "most," i.e., most professors, most parents, most hippies, most 18-year-olds, what disservice do we do to individuals in the group who are not part of the majority? And even to those who are? And even if we have facts supporting our generalizations?

Contingency

By contingency reasoning I mean reasoning based on the observation that two or more events occur in some fairly dependable relationship. Such reasoning includes both "sign" and "cause." Sign reasoning is the easier of the two because the reliable, dependable occurrence of two events in some relationship makes each one a sign of the other *by definition*. One may, however, conclude too quickly that one event is a sign of another, which produces "superstitious" behavior. On the other hand, some contingency relationships are difficult to detect. I have often marveled at the brilliance of the first person, whose name is unrecorded, who realized the relationship between sexual intercourse and pregnancy, considering the length of time that intervenes. At any rate, there are some rules which apply to contingency reasoning.

If a sign relationship is reliable, we assume causality is involved, but we don't know the nature of that causality. That is, we don't know whether A causes B, B causes A, or some third factor C causes both, or a more complex causal chain or loop is operating. Thus night and day are perfectly correlated, but one does not cause the other. Causal generalizations imply something more, and they will be discussed later. For the moment, remember that all the criteria I have mentioned as applicable to generalization are applicable to sign and causal generalization.

There are, however, some additional criteria which apply specifically to sign and causal generalization:

(6) Were there *control conditions* in which the hypothesized sign or cause was absent (or present to a lesser degree)?

(7) Were the conditions *comparable* in all respects except for the presence or absence of the hypothesized sign or cause?

(8) If there are only certain conditions under which the sign or causal relationships are hypothesized to operate, are those conditions adequately represented?

Some additional criteria apply only to *causal* generalizations:

(9) The nature and direction of the causal relationship must be clearly specified. Sometimes the hypothesized effect will occur *if and only if* the hypothesized cause has occurred. Sometimes, in addition, the effect will *always* occur if the hypothesized cause has occurred. This is the most restrictive case. Sometimes the effect will occur as a result of some other cause as well, so it may occur even in the absence of the hypothesized cause. Finally, other conditions or "causes" may be necessary in order for the hypothesized cause-effect relationship to hold, so that the hypothesized cause may sometimes occur without being followed by the hypothesized effect.

Any causal relationship can be described in these terms, even if it is quite complex, involving multiple causal chains and loops. These complexities need not always be specified, but they do provide additional information which may be useful in subsequent effect-to-cause or cause-to-effect reasoning, or they may provide additional ways of evaluating the adequacy of the generalization.

(10) Has the hypothesized cause been *manipulated*? If not, the hypothesized cause-effect relationship may be only a sign-significate relationship.

(11) Does the hypothesized cause *precede* the effect? A "yes" answer to this question doesn't *establish* causality, but a "no" answer certainly eliminates it. In a causal loop, incidentally, the "effect" may both precede and follow the "cause," since they are mutually causal.

(12) Have you eliminated all the possible *third factors* which might be causing both the hypothesized "cause" and "effect"?

Sign reasoning, reasoning from cause to effect, and reasoning from effect to cause are not themselves part of any process of generalization. They are the application of sign and causal generalizations to specific cases. We use such reasoning constantly in everyday life. We hear thunder and conclude that, since thunder is a sign of approaching rain, it is probably going to rain; we note that the cigarette butts in an ashtray are Bull Durham tailor-mades and conclude that Seth must have been here, since he smokes that peculiar brand of cigarette. In both cases we are using *sign* reasoning. We reason that, since civil disobedience leads to disrespect for the law, illegally blocking traffic on Van Ness Avenue in San Francisco to protest policies at the Presidio will lead to disrespect for the law. This involves reasoning from *cause to effect*. We reason that, since the streets are wet, it must have rained, and use reasoning from *effect to cause*.

Such reasoning is limited by the universality and complexities of the generalization with which one begins. Thus civil disobedience may lead to disrespect for the law only under certain conditions, and wet streets may be caused by rain or by a street sprinkler. Such forms of reasoning are especially useful in the pursuit of *hypothesis*, which I will consider next.

Hypothesis

An hypothesis is an *explanation* of data already available. These "explanations" seem to make use of generalization and deduction, applying generalizations and deductions to specific configurations of data. One criterion by which the adequacy of an hypothesis can be judged is the extent to which it accounts adequately for the data at hand. A second criterion is the extent to which it makes specific, testable predictions regarding data not yet available and the extent to which those predictions are confirmed. Often more than one hypothesis is capable of explaining the available data and making successful predictions. One who is interested in evaluating a given hypothesis will make a serious search for these rival hypotheses. Assuming they are equally capable of accounting for the existing data, he will try to identify circumstances in which they will generate contradictory predictions. By testing these predictions he will eliminate all the competing hypotheses except one. The survival of a given hypothesis does not "prove" its "truth"; the process is only analogous to the evolutionary concept of "survival of the fittest." In practice, such hypotheses do seem to evolve in the sense that they make predictions which are disconfirmed, after which they must be revised to account for the new data, from which revisions are generated new predictions which are also tested. Sometimes the only remaining hypothesis will be disconfirmed at such a basic level that it cannot be revised, in which case it is abandoned and new hypotheses must be devised.

If two rival hypotheses seem to account equally well for all the available data and testing them against one another is presently impractical, the tendency is to accept the simpler of the two (that is, the one requiring the fewer inferences, especially the fewer *inductive* inferences).

The general process, then, consists of the following steps:

(1) Collect data.

(2) Provide an hypothesis to explain the data.

(3) Generate specific predictions from the hypothesis.

(4) Test these predictions.

(5) Revise the hypothesis to account for any disconfirmed predictions.

(6) Generate new predictions from the revised hypothesis.

(7) Test these new predictions.

(8) Continue this process until it becomes more practical to adopt a rival hypothesis which is simpler or accounts more adequately for the available data.

Obviously, hypotheses tend to become more complex as they are revised, until at some point it becomes more appropriate to describe them as "theories." Sometimes complex hypotheses or theories which began as attempts to explain different sets of data come to "overlap" in that they generate similar predictions in certain cases. This is an unusual advantage of this sort of reasoning, since the theories then become mutually supportive.

One of the best books for someone interested in the process of hypothesis is *The Psychology Experiment* by Anderson.[5]

Testimony

We use these methods of induction constantly in everyday life, although we don't usually apply such formal, systematic rules to the process. We gather examples and store them as part of our images of the world. We note certain regularities among those examples—people with shifty eyes seem to be untrustworthy, blondes have more fun, newspaper reporters seem to be politically liberal, that particular sound in a car means the water pump is going bad—and conclude that certain characteristics are signs of others. We speculate about the possible causes involved in such sign relationships: maybe there are so many accidents at that intersection because that tree blocks the stop sign; maybe I feel so sleepy when I come back from skiing because of the change in altitude; maybe. . . . From these cause-effect hypotheses we make predictions which we test using alternative plans: Maybe the reason my eyes burn at night is because I'm allergic to something; I think I'll take an allergy pill tonight and see if it makes any difference. From individual hypotheses we build theories: Well, since the allergy pill worked, I must be allergic; maybe that's also why I'm so tired and cough so much.

But in addition to reasoning by comparison-generalization, contingency, and hypothesis, we use a fourth major type of induction: reasoning from testimony. Testimony doesn't have a very good reputation among logicians either, but the fact is that people use it, and if they didn't they would have problems. It is simply impossible for everyone to be an expert on everything, to know everything he or she needs to know to deal with the world. So in many cases we are forced to rely on experts: professional mechanics, income-tax consultants, attorneys, and the like. The trick, of course, is to know who is actually an expert and which experts can be trusted not to take advantage of us.

I discussed those questions in Chapter Eight under the heading of
"Credibility." However, it might be a good idea to review the criteria
by which one can judge whether testimony is reliable. Briefly, I suggested it seems reasonable to accept testimony from someone if:

(1) He is or was in a position to observe the facts;
(2) He is or was capable of observing, in the sense of:
     (a) being physically capable,
     (b) being intellectually capable,
     (c) being psychologically or emotionally capable,
     (d) being sensitive to the facts in question, and
     (e) having had experience in making such observations;
(3) He is motivated to perceive and report accurately, in that he:
     (a) has nothing to gain by deceiving, and
     (b) has goals similar to or compatible with your own;
(4) He has reported accurately in the past on this and other topics;
     and
(5) He is responsible in the sense of being in a position to be held
     accountable for the testimony.

Now, however, since I presented the message model at the beginning
of this chapter, I can point to another important reservation regarding
testimony in light of that model. This reservation is that speakers use
the opinions of others in more than one way: sometimes as *testimony*
and sometimes as mere *approval*. Take the hypothetical example of a
TV commercial showing Roger Fastback, star of the Detroit Rocker
Arms, extolling the virtues of Greaseless Kid Stuff hairspray. Now
what in the name of Nirvana do I care if Roger Fastback likes Greaseless Kid Stuff? He probably doesn't know Greaseless Kid Stuff from
Shinola, and after charging head first into the line that many times he
probably should be putting silicon or Teflon on his head anyway. The
advertiser is not using Fastback to *testify* as an expert to the causal relationship between the plan of using Greaseless Kid Stuff and the valued
outcome of having attractive or durable hair. Rather, the advertiser
is assuming that the famous Fastback is himself a value in his own right,

and he is trying to associate him directly with the plan by means of an *approval* relationship, hoping the listener's liking for Fastback will transfer to the plan of using that particular hairspray.

It is easy to confuse testimony with approval, but they are very different. As I have already said, the only sound reason for adopting a proposed plan is that the plan will produce valued outcomes. Roger Fastback is not a valued outcome, and using Greaseless Kid Stuff will not produce him anyway.

Let's take another example, just to confuse matters a little further. Suppose the membership chairman for the local Rotary Club tells you that you ought to join Rotary because your boss belongs. What kind of argument is that?

It may be a very good one. If your boss is the type of person who is impressed by that kind of thing and if you want to impress your boss, the argument makes perfectly good sense. Your boss is not being used to testify to the values of joining Rotary, nor is he being used in a relationship of mere approval. What the membership chairman is saying is that the proposed plan will produce valued outcomes, and that's what communication decisions are all about. Now that sort of plan may also wreak havoc with your self-image if you don't approve of kissing up to the boss, but that is just another outcome you will have to take into consideration.

Testimony is a strange case. Its most legitimate use is as a substitute for direct experience. We rely on testimony when we do not have the opportunity or ability to make our own observations, and that is its clearly legitimate use. But *observation* and *inference* are so closely related, and statements involving inference sometimes sound so much like statements of fact, that most listeners accept testimony as a substitute for other types of inference. Consequently, testimony is frequently used as a substitute for deductive inference, comparison, contingency, and hypothesis, so that it can be used to establish relationships of categorization, contingency, and similarity. Since it is so effective and versatile and it is so easy to find "experts" to testify to most anything, it is little wonder that persuaders use it so frequently. I consider, however, that testimony, *when substituted for inference,* serves much the same function as a crutch between the ears.

The same sort of confusion may occur between comparison reasoning and similarity relationships. The similarity of a proposed plan to another well-liked plan does not *directly* constitute a reason for adopting it unless, of course, the two are absolutely *identical,* which is unlikely. The fact that strict gun control is applauded in New York does not mean it will be automatically applauded in Montana. Comparison of similarities between two plans is sound when it is being used to establish causal inferences: that strict gun control in Montana will lead to a reduction in violent crimes, for example. But the soundness of the argument depends upon the causal inference, not upon similarity *per se.* After all, there are few places in New York City where one could fire a gun and avoid hitting another person. There aren't too many places in Montana where one could hit another person if he tried. (I don't recommend that as a model for logical argument, incidentally.)

The same is true of sign reasoning. The fact that a plan is a sign of some value is no reason to adopt it. The story is told of the aborigines who noticed that it rained whenever the missionary carried an umbrella. During a long period of drought they insisted that the missionary begin carrying his umbrella again so it would rain again. Laugh, if you will, at the poor benighted savages, but suppose we take an example from a more prestigious source. In fact, let's take one from a *really* prestigious source: Monroe Beardsley's book *Thinking Straight,* which I recommended a few pages earlier.

On page 115 of that book, Beardsley discusses causal reasoning and cites the example of a study done by Dr. Ernest Wynder of the Sloan-Kettering Institute on the relationship between smoking and lung cancer. To quote Beardsley:

> Wynder . . . looked for a group of people similar in every respect to the rest of the population, except for being strict nonsmokers, and he found it in the Seventh-Day Adventist Church—whose 300,000 members included 20,000 living in the polluted air of the Los Angeles area. In all diseases that could not be connected with smoking (or drinking), the rates for this group were exactly as predicted from the rates in the general population. But of the predicted 10 or 11 cases of lung cancer, only one was found—a man who had been a heavy smoker for 25 years before joining the church. In reporting his results, Dr. Wynder noted that those

defending tobacco have proposed that there is a "neuro-hormonal" factor which causes lung cancer and also causes people to want to smoke heavily. Certainly this is logically possible—that there is no direct causal connection between smoking and cancer, but that both are effects of something else. Dr. Wynder claimed that his own study made this conclusion unlikely: "They would now have to propose that this neuro-hormonal factor not only predisposes to lung cancer and causes one to smoke, but that it also prevents one from joining the Seventh-Day Adventist Church— a combination of factors virtually impossible to accept."

To the contrary, that conclusion is *quite* possible to accept. If there were such a "neuro-hormonal" factor predisposing one both to smoke and to contract lung cancer, it would in fact very effectively predispose one to avoid joining the Seventh-Day Adventist Church—because those who smoke are not *allowed* to join. If those who smoke cannot join, then those having such a "neuro-hormonal" factor would not be likely to join, either. And there goes another cause-effect argument down the drain. Now what do you think of those poor aborigines? At least they're in a little better company.

The point is that sign reasoning cannot, by itself, produce any sound reason for adopting a plan. It can, however, be used in various ways to lead to or support cause-effect relationships between plans and outcomes.

Categorization: Inclusion and Exclusion

Eventually one has to apply generalizations to specific cases. I may know that in general police dogs are likely to bite, for instance. For that generalization to be useful, I have to know that the animal in front of me is a police dog and is therefore likely to bite. That is the essence and function of this sort of reasoning—to make general, abstract information practical and useful by determining how it applies to the instance at hand.

This kind of reasoning is based on the inclusion of specific instances within general categories or the exclusion of those instances from general categories. That may sound a little strange, since most people aren't aware that is what they are doing. Usually they do it too quickly

FIGURE 1

to be aware of what they are doing. But let's take a look at the police dog example. First, I draw a circle representing "all dogs that are likely to bite" (FIGURE 1). Then within that circle I draw another representing "police dogs" (FIGURE 2). Finally, I place an "X" to represent this specific dog within the circle representing "police dogs." In doing that I *necessarily* also place the "X" in the circle representing "all dogs that bite" (FIGURE 3).

That is an essential characteristic of this kind of reasoning, which is also frequently termed "deductive": It will (if used properly) produce conclusions which are exactly as true as its premises. Another way of saying it is that the conclusion necessarily follows from the premises. As they say in computer language, "GIGO"—garbage in, garbage out. If the premises are not true, the deduction can be perfectly valid, and the conclusion will be perfectly untrue. Consequently, one cannot

FIGURE 2

prove anything about "reality" by deduction alone because the premises, insofar as they bear any relationship to experience, have to be provided by one of the other forms of reasoning I have already discussed. What I want to prevent, however, is the wasting of good premises by drawing invalid conclusions—the dreaded "SIGO," meaning "steak in, garbage out."

First, let's see how deduction relates to the model for persuasion I have been using. Deduction can be described in terms of a *syllogism*, which contains three elements: a major premise, a minor premise, and a conclusion. To diagram a syllogism in terms of the Toulmin model, one substitutes the minor premise for the datum, the major premise for the warrant, and the conclusion for the claim. Thus one argument might go:

FIGURE 3

Quick punishment for crime will keep our town safe.

Lynching Jake is quick punishment for crime.

Lynching Jake will keep our town safe.

In the model of persuasion I have been using, that argument would be diagrammed as in Figure 4.

This type of syllogism is called "categorical." The "conditional" syllogism uses a different form. For example:

If this mob hangs Jake, they will be arrested.

This mob is going to hang Jake.

This group is going to be arrested.

FIGURE 4
The relationship between a syllogism and the Toulmin model.

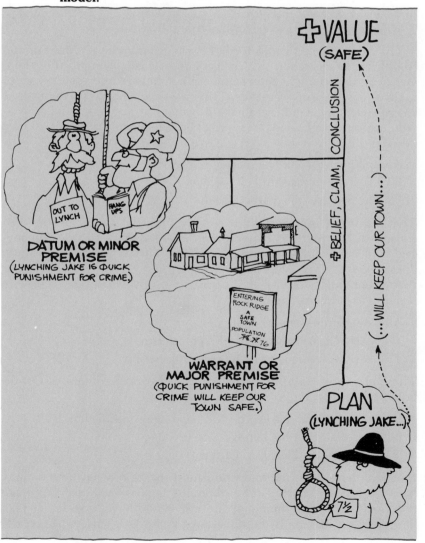

The third, and final, type of syllogism is the "disjunctive":

Either we will hang Jake or we will be overrun by criminals.
We are not going to hang Jake.
We are going to be overrun by criminals.

The rules for the various forms of syllogisms are too numerous and complex to be treated here. Beardsley does an excellent job of explaining them, so you might refer to his book if you are interested. Practice evaluating syllogisms by means of the rules has been shown to produce an improvement in general ability to evaluate arguments, so it is important. Suppose we consider a few invalid syllogisms just to get an idea of what this is:

Any man who'd kill Doc Farley is a worthless skunk.
Jake is a worthless skunk.
Jake must have killed Doc Farley.

That argument is smooth and seductive, but fallacious. For the conclusion to be valid the major premise would have to say that anyone who is a worthless skunk killed Doc Farley, which it obviously doesn't say.

Another fallacy is just as slippery. It involves a subtle change in terms. Take this for example:

All Communists are atheists.
The early Christians practiced communism.
The early Christians must have been atheists.

These are both examples of fallacious categorical syllogisms. Conditional syllogisms can be equally misleading:

If Jake killed Doc Farley, he will have blood on his hands.
Jake has blood on his hands.
Jake must have killed Doc Farley.

Jake may have been the one who found the bloody shirt, or he may have cut himself shaving. The reasoning here is backward. To make the conclusion valid, the major premise would have to read: "If Jake has blood on his hands, he must have killed Doc Farley." Then the

deduction would be valid, but the conclusion still might be *wrong*. The conclusion would probably be wrong because the major premise is probably wrong. It's just another case of "garbage in, garbage out."

I don't know anyone who thinks in syllogisms or anyone who carries rules for reasoning around in his head. But I do believe conscious attention to some of the ways communicators lead and mislead you can increase your awareness of the ways real-life messages are affecting you. Critical response to reasoning is difficult. It requires one to stop and think: What is really being said here? Is the communicator really claiming that adopting his plan will produce favorable consequences? If so, does he have adequate data for his claim? If the data is adequate, does the warrant relate it logically to the claim? And finally, is the warrant acceptable, that is, does it have adequate support?

But enough of that. What I would like you to ponder, the prime question for discussion in your next class meeting, the deep philosophical issue upon which we have focused throughout this entire chapter, is this perplexing puzzle: Who *did* kill Doc Farley?

Hitchhiking on the Image

In conclusion, it appears that most of the means communicators use to short-circuit thinking, to avoid proving that their proposed plans will produce valued outcomes, can be subsumed under a heading such as "Hitchhiking on the Image." What communicators do so frequently is to try to associate their proposed plans—buying their products, voting for them, helping them in some way—with a part of the listener's image.

They try to do this without dealing with the question of just how the listener will benefit by adopting the proposed plan. They do this by encouraging people the listener likes to say they approve of the plan, to associate themselves with it, without arguing its benefits. Communicators do so by trying to make the listener believe that adopting the plan is an absolutely necessary part of his self-image. They do so by trying to get their plans in under the circus tent of some desirable larger plan—making the listener believe, for example, that buying a huge motor home is absolutely indispensable to energy conservation since when he is vacationing in it he won't be using his home air-conditioner. It has been a source of wonder to me how many new ways U.S. industry has developed to save energy since the energy crisis hit—buying bigger cars, for instance, so as to have one more suitable for a car pool. There hasn't been such hitchhiking on the image since the Second World War, when anything you bought somehow contributed to the "war effort."

Communicators hitchhike on the image by trying to make their plans appear similar to others the listener has liked. How the country has been scoured for politicians who look and talk like John F. Kennedy, for example. They do so by taking mere signs of attractive images and using them to spruce up less attractive ones. How many dowdy, under-powered, poor-handling cars have been transformed overnight into ferocious "sporty" cars by adding hood scoops, "spoilers," fake mag wheel covers, racing stripes, bucket seats, automatic transmission selectors mounted on the floor, and rally clocks that look a little like tachometers? Same old pushrod V-8 engines they use in their trucks, same sloppy, soft suspension, same suicide brakes, same slushy two-speed automatic transmission, same fat body—but now a "GT."

Make you angry? You bet. It's a profit-sharing plan: industry uses some of its profits to con you into giving it more of your money. You pay advertising agencies to persuade you that you need something you never thought of before. It's a new way of buying votes: the politician buys an ad agency and TV time, and then he stays out of sight as much as possible while others build an image for him and try to attach it to yours without ever explaining why it is to your advantage to vote for him. I preferred the old Chicago method of buying votes directly. At least the voter got to spend the money.

Don't let these people spend yours. *Know* why you are responding to a sales pitch or a political speech. Know what motives they are appealing to and what forms of reasoning they are using. Then decide at your leisure whether those are the reasons you want to use to make a decision.

Summary

Reasoning and evidence are used in messages to cause the receiver to believe the source's proposed plan will produce certain valued outcomes. To accomplish that, sources use *comparison* and *generalization,* including individual examples, extended examples, and collections of examples (statistics); *contingency reasoning,* including sign reasoning, reasoning from cause to effect, and reasoning from effect to cause; *hypothesis and hypothesis-testing; testimony,* based quite reasonably on the special knowledge of an expert, but also, unfortunately, based sometimes merely upon the person's likeability; and *categorization,* involving reasoning which can be reduced to categorical, conditional, or disjunctive syllogisms. Because sources too often try to "hitchhike" on the listener's image of himself or the world without providing valid reasons for adopting their plans, it is important to be aware of the special tests which apply to each of these types of reasoning.

Suggestions for Developing Awareness

1. Watch some television commercials or look through magazines for ads which use statistics or make claims based on generalization. Does the reasoning meet the criteria suggested in this chapter? Which ones do they fail to meet most frequently? Share some of these with the class.

2. While you're watching those commercials and reading those ads, you'll notice that some of them don't seem to make any claims for their products at all. What *are* they trying to do? I mean, they are spending a lot of money on that advertising, so they must think it works, right? So what connection are they trying to make between that bear and that beer, or between that attractive lady and that cigarette? Does it constitute any reason to buy the product?

3. Listen to a political speech, and write down the reasons the speaker is giving you for voting for him. What motives does he try to appeal to? What evidence does he offer to make you believe he can actually satisfy those motives if he is elected? What kinds of reasoning does he use: generalization, comparison, testimony, causal reasoning, sign reasoning? Which is used most frequently? Can you spot fallacies in the reasoning?

4. Find someone in the class or someone you know who has a different opinion from yours on a controversial issue. First, each of you should try to list all the reasons for your particular opinion: your motives and the

way you see those motives as related to your own opinions. Then exchange lists and evaluate one another's reasoning. Finally, allow time to discuss these evaluations. Do not hit each other, and avoid undue shouting! You may want to have a third person serve as judge or referee. In what areas do you come closest to agreeing? Are there any ways of reaching agreement? Are the biggest differences in your motives *or* in your reasoning?

References

1. Monroe C. Beardsley, *Thinking Straight* (Englewood Cliffs, N.J.: Prentice-Hall, 1966), p. 35.
2. E.R. Emmet, *Handbook of Logic* (Totowa, N.J.: Littlefield, Adams, 1967).
3. Howard Kahane, *Logic and Contemporary Rhetoric: The Use of Reason in Everyday Life* (Belmont, Calif.: Wadsworth, 1971).
4. Stephen K. Campbell, *Flaws and Fallacies in Statistical Thinking* (Englewood Cliffs, N.J.: Prentice-Hall, 1974).
5. Barry F. Anderson, *The Psychology Experiment* (Belmont, Calif.: Brooks-Cole, Wadsworth, 1971).

Language Is a Game

The Nature of Linguistic Rules
Levels of Language Rules
Meaning Is Rule-Governed
Some Alternative Theories of Meaning
Rule-Use Theories of Meaning
Pragmatics Is Rule-Governed

But the Players Are Important

Language, Thought, and Perception
Language Effects on the Receiver
   Clarity
   Intensity, Profanity, and Obscenity
Language and Society
   Social Class
   Sex and Sexism
   Race

Summary

Chapter Eleven

Language:
The Game and the Players

(Kandace Penner)

Communication is an unusually human characteristic, and language is the most unusual characteristic of human communication. Other animals may be capable of using language, but they do not do so with the sense of predestination that is so evident in the human child's acquisition of language.

Language is a behavior that is specific to the human species.

Other creatures are capable of swimming and flying, too, but not with the natural inclination of fish and birds. In a very real sense, humans take to language like a duck takes to water.

But there is a catch. Can you imagine how much thought a fish gives to swimming? About the same amount of thought humans give to talking. That is a problem since the avowed purpose of this book is to make you aware of communication. It is especially difficult to make a person aware of his or her use of language.

Let me use an example from Peter Farb's book *Word Play*[1] and modify it a bit. Any native speaker of English will pronounce the word "bringer" with a soft "g" and "longer" with a hard "g." You do it yourself, of course. But can you explain why? Because you were taught to? In a sense, yes. But you may be surprised to learn that you were not taught to make that specific distinction. Instead, you were taught a *rule,* but you were taught that rule so subtly that you probably don't know what it is, even though you use it many times every day.

Let's pursue that. Imagine a man who has been separated from his wife for two months. He *longs* to be with her, so we might call him a *longer.* How do you pronounce "longer" in this case? With a *soft* "g," right? Why?

Because it is derived from a verb. A verb ending in "ng" with an "er" ending added is pronounced with a soft "g" in English. You "know" that rule and you applied it in this case, even though you were probably unaware that you knew it. The English language, as all languages, consists of hundreds of such rules which we learned as children and use at such a low level of awareness that we are simply unable to recognize them until they are called to our attention.

It took linguists a long time to recognize that language is governed by rules that are applied at a very low level of awareness. I am not referring to the "rules" of grammatical usage that you learned in English class—that "ain't" is incorrect and that you should not end a sentence with a preposition. By the time you first heard those rules of "correct" grammar you already knew the rules of adequate language construction.

Language Is a Game

To say language is a game does not imply that it is frivolous or trivial. Sometimes it is deadly serious, as in the utterances "This is a stick-up," "Choose your weapons," or "I now pronounce you husband and wife." Words such as "Godless monolithic communism," "the domino theory," and the collection of words contained in the Tonkin Gulf Resolution kept the United States at war in Indo-China for a full ten years and killed hundreds of thousands of people. Words such as "defoliation," "pacification," and "protective reaction" disguised the horrors of that war.

No, language is a game in that it operates by means of rules understood by its users who employ strategies to achieve certain goals. A member of one language community observing the language game as it is played in another language community will be at least as mystified as a person who plays only poker and finds himself suddenly in the midst of a bridge game. That is true even if the foreign speaker "knows" the language of the other culture.

Robin Lakoff, a linguist at the University of California, Berkeley, has provided a good example.[2] She points out that most foreigners are taught that "may" is generally a more polite form of address than "must." And it frequently is. But suppose a hostess says to a Japanese guest, "You *must* have some of this cake!" Is she being less polite than if she were to say, "You *may* have some of this cake"?

The native speaker of English knows that she is not—that "must" in this case is more polite than "may," that to say "You *may* have some of this cake" would in fact be mildly insulting. But how to explain that to the Japanese guest? One might say that the hostess' utterance really means "The humble baker of this poor cake begs you to try some in the hope that it will please you." But that is really not quite right; it is at least too formal and stilted and even a little silly. Yet Japanese honorifics — terms used by the Japanese to convey respect—sound just as foolish and are equally misrepresented when translated as "Humble speaker begs honorable American to taste some of this abominable tea."

The Nature of Linguistic Rules

However, when I say language is governed by rules I am not referring to the "rules" of "correct" usage which you were taught in elementary school. Those rules are violated almost as frequently as they are followed and usually without any negative consequences—so long as the speaker knows *when* and *where* they may be violated. As a matter of fact, there are many situations in which it is inappropriate to apply the rules of correct usage. For example, try converting the phrases "Put up or shut up" or "That's where it's at" into correct usage, and see how far it gets you in informal conversation. One of the important rules every native speaker of English knows is that precisely correct usage is inappropriate in informal conversation.

No, the rules I am referring to are more complex, and to violate them brands the speaker as deficient in his or her understanding of the language.

Levels of Language Rules

Linguists generally distinguish among four levels of language study: the phonemic, syntactic, semantic, and pragmatic.

Phonemic rules are concerned with the sounds of a language and how those sounds are combined. They are learned very early; the babbling of Chinese infants can be distinguished from that of American infants before they have reached the age of six months, simply because they have begun to use the sounds and sound combinations required in their respective languages long before they learn to speak.

Different sounds are significant in different languages. The best-known example is probably the English distinction between "r" and "l," a distinction which is simply insignificant in Japanese. The Japanese tendency to confuse words such as "rot" and "lot" is not due to an inability to pronounce the words. Rather, it is due to the fact that speakers of Japanese have not been taught to make the distinction. On the other hand, English speakers trying to learn Japanese tend to pronounce the Japanese words for "door" and "ten" identically, ignoring the distinction the Japanese make between two sounds which can only be poorly represented by the English "o" and "oo." I live in the town of Los Gatos, California, which is pronounced *Loss* Gatos by most of its residents, who simply don't distinguish between that and the Spanish pronunciation, which sounds more like Lōze Gatos.

The rules at the phonemic level are very complex. For example, the English word "fish" could equally well be spelled "ghoto," using the "gh" sound as in the word "rough," the "o" sound as in "women," the "t" sound as in "initial," and a silent "o" as in "rough." Actually such spelling *would* violate some English phonemic rules about the ways letters are pronounced depending on where they appear in a word, but those rules are really wild. Aren't you glad you learned them when you were four years old instead of twenty-four?

Syntax, too, is rule-governed, a fact that has been recognized for some time. Take the sentence, "The bartender ejected the drunk." To produce such a sentence, one needs to know the following rules: (1) a sentence may consist of a noun phrase plus a verb phrase; (2) a noun phrase may consist of an article plus a noun; (3) a verb phrase may consist of a verb plus a noun phrase; (4) an article may be the word "the"; (5) nouns may be the words "bartender" and "drunk"; and (6) a verb may be the word "ejected."

These six rules constitute a very limited grammar, of course, since they are capable of producing only two sentences: "The bartender ejected the drunk" and "The drunk ejected the bartender." By adding more verbs and nouns one could quickly expand the number of possible sentences. Next, one might adopt rules for plurals and different verb forms, and add rules for modifiers such as adverbs, adjectives, and prepositional phrases. Eventually one would have to add rules for other sentence forms as well.

You can see from this simple illustration what linguists have been concerned with for the past few decades. They have been trying to explain what it is a person *knows* when he or she is said to "know" a language. They are trying to produce a limited set of rules by which one can form any acceptable sentence in a language and no unacceptable

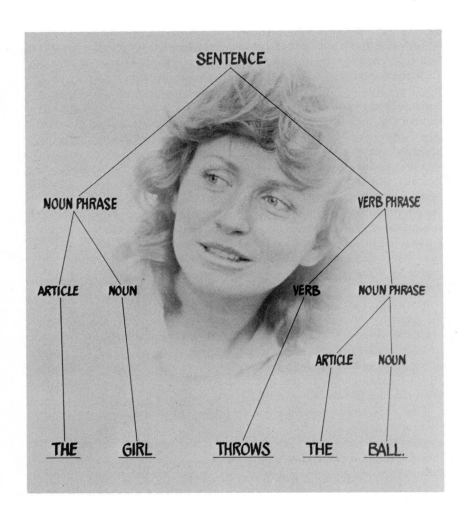

ones. That is a big job, since the number of acceptable sentences in a language is infinitely large.

But it seems obvious that some such rule system must be operating, since we constantly produce and understand sentences we have never encountered before. As a matter of fact, *most* of the sentences we speak and hear every day are "novel" in that sense. Which is why most linguists, and Chomsky in particular,[3] have rejected B.F. Skinner's theory that language is learned by a process of response reinforcement.[4] Among other things, they point out that such a theory cannot explain the human's ability to produce and understand brand new sentences.

But Chomsky points out that a system of "phrase-structure" rules such as I have described has its problems, too.[5] For instance, the following three sentences can all be accounted for by a system of phrase-structure rules:

1. The bartender threw the drunk out.
2. The bartender threw out the drunk.
3. The drunk was thrown out by the bartender.

But these rules provide no indication that the three sentences are similar; in fact, they are equivalent. Similarly, phrase-structure rules provide no indication that the sentence "The attack of the bartender was terrible" may mean that the bartender was *attacked* or that he did the attacking.

Chomsky has argued that this is because phrase-structure rules describe only the "surface structure" of language and ignore the "deep structure" from which surface utterances are derived. Then he proposed that there are "transformation" rules which speakers understand and use to relate surface structures to deep structures. Thus a single deep structure can produce several acceptable surface structures, as in the first example, and they are related by different transformational rules as diagrammed in Figure 1. Or different deep structures can produce the same surface sentence by the application of different transformations, as in the second example, in the way diagrammed in Figure 2.

FIGURE 1

Relationships of several surface sentences to a single deep structure.

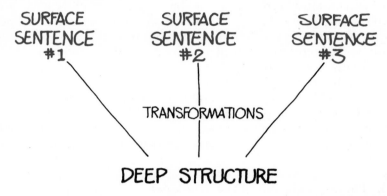

FIGURE 2

Relationship of an ambiguous surface sentence to more than one deep structure.

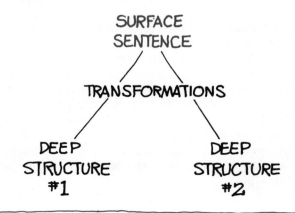

Meaning Is Rule-Governed

At first Chomsky tried to avoid dealing with "semantic" problems involving "meaning." Later, however, he tried to bring the concept of meaning into his system, and other linguists have produced treatments of meaning based on his system.[6] I am not going to try to explain all of those theories, but I would like to explain why it seems reasonable to think of language meaning as the product of a system of rules.

Some Alternative Theories of Meaning

First, however, I will deal with some general types of theories which have tried to explain language meaning in other ways. Those theories are important because many people still accept them and because each one does shed some light on how words and sentences "mean."

I.A. Richards, for instance, is largely responsible for the popularity of "referential" theories, which are based on the notion that a word has meaning because it "stands for" something; that is, it has meaning because it has a "referent."[7] The word "book" has meaning because it *refers to* or *stands for* the object you are presently reading.

That theory has some serious problems. For one thing, some words don't have referents. The word "if," for instance, doesn't seem to "stand for" anything. What is an "if"? Other words, such as "I," have different referents depending on who is using them. Some words or phrases such as "the president of the U.S. in 1976," "Richard Nixon's appointed successor," and "Jerry Ford" seem to have different *meanings* even though they have the same *referent*. Even the referent for a "concrete" noun such as "book" is difficult to point to. Is the referent *this* book you are reading, or *all* the books you and I have known, or all existing books, or some vague notion of "bookness" in general? In short, while it is useful to realize there is some relation between words and things, it isn't adequate or reasonable to argue that words *mean* because they "refer to" things.

Other theorists, following John Locke,[8] have argued that words have meaning because they stand for ideas and images in the minds of those who speak and hear the word. That sort of theory would be difficult to prove or disprove, since it is very difficult to get inside the "minds" of those who use language. All I can say is that I do not have a series of ideas and images flitting through my head as I write this sentence, and I doubt that you have any such series of ideas and images parading through your head as you read it. Of course I have a general idea of what I want to express, but I am not constructing this specific sentence, so far as I know at least, as a reflection of any string of images in my mind. Now some kinds of language—poetry, metaphor, and very vivid language—may produce and be produced by such images. But the theory just doesn't seem adequate to explain *all* language meaning.

So we are back to B.F. Skinner's "behavioral" theory. Skinner probably would never talk about "meaning," but I think it can be said that Skinner uses the term "response" to fill the void left by his refusal to use the term "meaning." Skinner talks about a "response" to a verbal "stimulus." Let's return to an earlier example. Suppose someone sitting at the bar says "Bartender, throw that drunk out." The bartender *may* respond by throwing the drunk out, in which case most native speakers of English would agree that his response matches the meaning of the customer's utterance. But the bartender may say "Flake off, Jack," or he may just continue washing glasses. "Continue washing glasses" is hardly the meaning of "Throw that drunk out." Skinner's theory is important because it emphasizes that there is usually some relationship between a verbal utterance and what a listener does after he hears that utterance, but Skinner's theory doesn't clarify what most people mean when they talk about "meaning."

Some other theories have been *labeled* "behavioral," even though they certainly include a lot more than "behavior" in their explanations. Osgood, for instance, says meaning is an "internal mediating response."[9] You may recall that I described Osgood's theory in Chapter Seven as an explanation of how people learn opinions and policies. Stevenson considers meaning to be a "response disposition."[10] For both of these theorists, meaning is some sort of internal response and is not necessarily reflected in anything the listener actually *does,* at least overtly. Again it is difficult to prove or disprove that sort of theory. "Understanding" and "perception"—even "misunderstanding" and "misperception," for that matter—can all be considered internal responses. "Planning" and "valuing" and "believing," which I discuss throughout this book, are all internal responses. The real problem seems to be that such a theory isn't very specific about *how* people "mean" and "understand" language.

Rule-Use Theories of Meaning

Fortunately, there is another approach that is much more specific. The approach probably originated with a German philosopher by the name of Wittgenstein, who wrote about "language games."[11] It was elaborated by Searle[12] and Austin,[13] whose ideas have recently gained wide acceptance by both linguists and philosophers.

Back to the example. When the customer in the bar says "Bartender, throw that drunk out," he is using language in a way which conforms to certain semantic rules—rules which both he and the bartender understand. If his utterance conforms to those rules, it is meaningful; if it violates some of the rules, it is not. Further, listing the rules to which the utterance conforms (the conditions which must be satisfied in order for it to be meaningful) in fact tells one what the meaning of the utterance is.

Let me be more specific. The utterance "Bartender, throw that drunk out" implies that: (1) there is a person present who meets certain criteria or rules for being addressed as "bartender"; (2) there is another person present who meets certain criteria for being labeled a "drunk"; (3) there is only one drunk present, or the context or some nonverbal act has made clear which drunk the customer is referring to; (4) there is only one bartender present, or it is otherwise clear which bartender is being addressed; (5) there is some sort of enclosure containing the drunk (that is, this is not a catered picnic in an open field, or there would be nothing to throw the drunk out of); (6) the customer believes the bartender is capable of throwing out the drunk; (7) the customer wants the drunk thrown out; and (8) the bartender will not throw out the drunk unless the customer tells him to.

If any of these conditions are not met, the utterance is not meaningful, unless it is *ironic,* in which case a different set of rules applies. For example, rule six might be "violated" for the purpose of humorous irony if the drunk weighs 320 pounds and the bartender weighs 125. Or rule seven (and rule two) might be violated for the sake of humorous irony if the "drunk" is a good friend of the customer. Or rule eight might be violated if the bartender is already carrying the drunk to the door. But even those violations are governed by other rules, and the other customers will probably show their understanding of the rules of irony by laughing. Of course, a good many barroom brawls have started

because a listener is too drunk to detect the irony and instead applies
the straightforward nonironic rules.

Discuss with a friend or with your class the notion that to
understand the meaning of a word is to examine how
that word is used. Does this notion imply an infinite
number of meanings for any word? Or is there a range
or boundary to the possible meanings of any word?

Pragmatics Is Rule-Governed

The customer's choice of the utterance "Bartender, throw that drunk
out" conformed to phonemic, syntactic, and semantic rules.

Still, he had some alternatives he could have chosen. He could have
said instead, "*Please* throw that drunk out," "Throw that *damn* drunk
out," "Why don't you throw that drunk out?" or "My, but this place
is disorderly." All those alternatives are phonemically, syntactically,
and semantically acceptable. In fact, there is a sense in which they all
relate to the same "deep structure." But they are not all equally *pragmatic;* that is, one may be more likely than the others to produce the
desired *effects.*

*Consequently, to fully understand the use of language, we have to know
something about pragmatic rules of language.* Pragmatic rules of language
are extremely subtle. They depend heavily upon the context of the
utterance, and they are embedded in cultural norms and expectations.
A foreigner may have learned the phonemic, syntactic, and semantic
rules of the language, but unless he has spent a great deal of time in
the country where the language is spoken, he is not likely to know these
pragmatic rules.

The customer's choice was governed by rules relating to his status in
relation to that of the bartender, the drunk, and the other customers,
by rules relating to his frequency of attendance at the bar, and by
"house" rules relating to the "atmosphere" of the bar. The utterance
might be perfectly appropriate in a rowdy bar on Chicago's Near North
Side or in the Loop, but quite inappropriate in a bar at the Palmer
House. For other reasons, it might contribute to his early death or
hospitalization if uttered in a South Side bar.

Considering how drastically the pragmatic rules change from one social context to another within the same culture, you can probably imagine how they must change from one *culture* to another. A customer coming into our imaginary neighborhood bar is going to push himself onto a barstool and say "Hey Buddy, make it a Coors, huh?" But Frake, in an article titled "How to Ask for a Drink in Subanun," has described the complex social and linguistic ritual that accompanies drinking among that tribe who inhabit the inland mountains of Mindanao in the Philippines.[14] For the Subanun, the drinking ritual appears to be a test of verbal ability and good judgment, and one must be included in that ritual by specific invitation. In short, Subanun alcoholics have to be the best speakers of the community. Come to think of it, though, Frake's description doesn't sound too much different from some cocktail parties I've attended at communication conventions.

But the Players Are Important

The language game at all levels is closely related to the people who play the game. But it is *impossible* to discuss language at the pragmatic level without dealing with the people who use the language. Obviously, language rules at the pragmatic level are deeply embedded in cultural rules. I have already considered some of those, and many more will be considered in the last chapter of this book, which deals with intercultural communication.

But the discussion thus far has centered on the structure of language and has largely ignored its *effects*. Obviously, one cannot play the language game without being affected by the experience. It is difficult, though, to tell what those effects are, because *the ideal control group does not exist*. Since every human being who is physically, psychologically, and socially "normal" uses language, we have no group of "normal" human nonusers of language with which to compare ourselves. To ask "What would we be like if we didn't use language?" is almost like asking "What would we be like if we weren't human?" Consequently, we have to settle for looking at differences among people who play the game by different rules, and we have to be very cautious when it comes time to decide whether the differences in the language "cause" the differences among the people, the differences among the people "cause" the differences in the language, or both are "caused" by some other factor(s).

Language, Thought, and Perception

There is a point of view, frequently labeled the "Whorfian hypothesis" after Benjamin Lee Whorf, which holds that *the language one speaks affects one's perceptions of the world.*[15] This is also called the theory of "linguistic relativity."

That point of view can be stated very extremely to read "One's language *absolutely determines* one's perceptions of the world," or very weakly, "Language *plays some part* in one's perceptions of the world." Of course, the weaker version is going to be much easier to demonstrate. The extreme version, in fact, would be impossible to "prove" *even if it were true.*

It can be shown that people who speak different languages perceive some things differently, of course, but that doesn't answer the question. Do they perceive things differently because their languages are different, are their languages different because they perceive things differently, or are their languages and their perceptions different because they live in different environments?

I believe the best answer is "all of the above." The best-known example of linguistic and perceptual differences centers around the fact that Eskimos have a large number of words for different types of snow, but no one word equivalent to the English word "snow" which covers the general category.

One can speculate (remembering it is *purely speculation*) that the ancestors of modern Eskimos had a serious need to distinguish among many kinds of snow long before their language made such distinctions —probably, in fact, before they had a language. Small wonder, then, that as their language developed it included a wide variety of words for snow. Historically, environmental conditions probably forced greater perceptual awareness on the part of the Eskimos, and that awareness was reflected quite naturally in their language as it developed.

However, consider a modern Eskimo child born in Fairbanks in a fairly modern home, so that his life does not really depend entirely on making fine discriminations among types of snow. Still, if he is taught the Eskimo language, he will never be able to speak of snow without noticing the *specific type* of snow so he can apply the appropriate word. Whereas an English-speaking child next door can nonchalantly toss off the sentence "Hey, it's snowing again," the Eskimo child must be much more specific in his language and thus in his perception. The Eskimo language (1) calls the child's attention to the differences, (2) forces him to practice making the distinctions, and (3) prevents him from being rewarded by successful communication until he gets the distinctions correct. Thus one's language is an ever-present teacher, a constant reminder of whatever distinctions are embedded within it. Since the distinctions embedded in one's language are probably those which are considered important in one's culture, the language is also a constant reminder of one's culture.

Sometimes the cultural distinctions depend on the physical environment, as they seem to in this case, but sometimes they do not. For example, the Javanese speaker *must* decide, before he begins to speak, which of six possible levels of status he is going to grant the person to whom he is speaking, and he must maintain that level throughout the conversation. But that is certainly no stranger than American English, which forces one to decide whether a woman is married before addressing her as "Miss" or "Mrs.," but forces no such decision when speaking to a man.

So far we have only considered the effects of *vocabulary* on perception. Different language structures may also have different effects on perception. The most common examples come from Whorf's comparison of North American Indian languages, primarily Hopi, with Standard American English. And the most frequently used example is the different treatment of nouns and verbs.

In English the distinction between nouns and verbs seems rather arbitrary. A noun is "the name of a person, place, or thing," right? And a verb is the label for an "action." What, then, is an avalanche? A "thing" or an "act of God"? What about something as stable as a house? Over a hundred-year period (ten years for California "modern") a house appears, grows, deteriorates, and disappears. That is, it is an enduring action. But a "fist" is an action, too, and not any more enduring than "running." Why, then, is "fist" a noun? Why is "phase" a noun and "endure" a verb?

Largely because of the functions they are allowed to serve in English sentences. To use an English word appropriately, one must first find out what part of speech it is. Take the word "grok," a word you may have encountered in Heinlein's *Stranger in a Strange Land.* An adequate definition of that word would begin, "It is a verb, meaning. . . ." You would then know where one could appropriately use it in a sentence.

That is rather arbitrary. Hopi takes a different approach, treating every "thing" as an event, but distinguishing between short-term and long-term events. A wave and a puff of smoke are short-term events. (Remember, there are no long-term waves in Shongopavi, Arizona. As a matter of fact, water is almost a short-term event there.) Anything lasting longer than a "cloud" or a "storm" is a long-term event. Thus a Hopi dwelling is an event, but a long-lasting one.

Now the question is, does a Hopi child learn to view the world as a more changeable, fluctuating, ongoing *happening* than does a child who learns Standard American English? His language forces him to acknowledge the changeability of his most stable surroundings whenever he speaks and to distinguish among the elements of his surroundings on the basis of how long they endure. On the other hand, does the speaker of Standard American English learn to expect greater stability of events which are nouns than those which are verbs? Whorf has compiled impressive evidence to show that the Hopi and Navajo languages, in particular, treat the concept of time in a way which is consistently different from that of Standard American English. That *may* be the result of living in a world in which one does not constantly encounter clocks and calendars and planes which leave at 8:45 P.M., and it *may* result in a different view of the world, but that remains pure speculation. No one really knows why the Hopi language is like that or what effects it has, any more than we know why the Hopi never saw the need to invent clocks and calendars so they could lead their sheep out to graze at *exactly* 8:00 A.M., thus blessing themselves with traffic jams and ulcers and the like.

This leads directly to a somewhat different but related question: How does language affect *thought* patterns? Those who have been primarily concerned with that question have labeled their area of study "general semantics," and they owe their allegiance to Korzybski, who wrote *Science and Sanity.*[16]

General semanticists frequently talk about language as a "map" of reality—the "territory." They point out that *there are many ways in which language not only* does not *but* cannot *accurately reflect reality.* And they argue that our constant attempts and failures to adequately represent reality by means of language produce psychological discomfort, stress, and in some cases mental disturbance.

There is a notation system developed by these theorists to help correct the many failures of language. If used seriously and constantly it would undoubtedly put us all in the booby bin, but it is very useful as a device to remind us of the ways language warps reality.

First, reality is constantly changing, whereas language pictures it as static. Language freezes a constantly changing reality the way a still photograph stops a pole-vaulter in mid-air. The Beatles may have been writing about something like this in their song "Ruby Tuesday." Part of it goes:

> Goodbye Ruby Tuesday.
> Who could hang a name on you
> When you change with every new day?
> Still I'm gonna miss you.

People change, but their names remain the same. The general semanticists' proposal to help remedy this problem would be to write the name:

$$Ruby_{Tuesday}$$

Then there could be $Ruby_{Wednesday}$, since Ruby changes with every new day. Certainly $Ruby_{1976}$ would not be the same as $Ruby_{1978}$. This causes problems when we expect people and situations to stay the same because our names for them don't change. Paradoxically, a friend and I once spent some time arguing over what general semantics is all about. I was basing my interpretation on an article by Irving J. Lee titled "General Semantics$_{1952}$," whereas she was basing hers on a course she took in 1972. Lee was right. General semantics, like everything else, changes even though the name remains the same. My friend and I could have saved a lot of energy had we simply concluded that general semantics$_{1952}$ is not general semantics$_{1972}$.

Second, in reality no two things are identical, but language treats them as if they are. This leads to stereotyping and overgeneralization, which I will go into more deeply in a later chapter on intercultural communication. One of the major difficulties in that area is that Chicano$_1$ is not Chicano$_2$, but they are frequently treated as if they are. What if we had no words for *classes* of people; what if we had only people's *names*? Stereotyping might still survive, but it would be a lot less healthy.

Third, it is impossible to *totally* describe *anything* in reality, but language invites us to try. Suppose you have been dating a man for several weeks, and one night you tell him you love him. He asks what you mean by that, and you try to explain. You are bound to be left with a sense of failure, because you can't explain *exactly* what you mean and how your love for him differs from that you feel for your father, your mother, and your best woman friend. A year later, suppose you are engaged to be married, and you are still using the same word. *Now* try to explain. "How do I love thee? Let me count the ways. . . ." It isn't possible. Just do the best you can, and then add "etc." at the end of the list. The journal of general semantics is titled *ETC*.

Another mismatch between language and reality is that, while there are no abstractions in reality, language is full of them. You and an acquaintance may agree that you believe in "fair play," but as you spend more time together you come to realize he doesn't mean the same thing you do. So you ask him what he means by "fair play." Chances are his definition will be even more abstract; defining *up* the "ladder of abstraction" is a common practice. Thus he may say he means "justice." You now know less than you did before. The better way to define is to "point to"—sometimes quite literally—some concrete examples. So your friend might better say: "Remember when Bob was going with another girl when he was telling Cecily she was the only girl he was dating? That's *not* fair play." A few such examples and it will be much easier to see what his idea of fair play really is.

There are other ways language fails to match reality, but these will have to suffice. *Now the problem is that we are kept in a constant state of uncertainty and psychological stress by the fact that nothing we say or hear ever fits the facts exactly.* I'm not talking about outright lies; those would be easier to deal with. Instead, we are constantly uncomfortable because we "know" at some low level of awareness that what we say and hear is not and cannot be entirely "true," but there is no way to correct it. Most of us just learn to live with this psychological stress, although we may develop strange neurotic tics to compensate for it. Some people, however, are unable to cope with the stress, have mental breakdowns, and are hospitalized. Conversely, one way of diagnosing mental illness is by observing how far a person's language differs from reality. In the face of all this, one ancient Greek philosopher is said to have entirely given up the use of language in his later years. He may have been the father of general semantics or the father of schizophrenia. Possibly both.

Language Effects on the Receiver

Some work has been done to determine what makes language clear and intense, but any comments about what makes language pleasing would have to rest almost entirely on speculation, so I will omit that topic.

Clarity
In the 1940s a man named Rudolph Flesch was busily devising formulas to predict how "readable" language passages were.[17] His formulas produced a "readability index" which supposedly corresponded to the grade level at which the passage could be comprehended. He took into account such things as average sentence length in words, average number of certain parts of speech per 100 words, and number of "unfamiliar" words (those not in the Dale-Chall list of the 500 most common English words). The formulas were widely used by newscasters and newspaper writers, among others, to make certain their copy could be comprehended by their listeners. Unfortunately, the Flesch formulas were never adequately validated in research. Dale and Chall, in fact, reported that the number of unfamiliar words *alone* was a better predictor of reader comprehension than the most complex of Flesch's formulas.[18] Unfortunately, that hasn't put an end to the use of the formulas; they are still fairly popular in some circles.

   We do know one thing from all this: The use of unfamiliar words makes language less easily understood. But that is hardly news. More recent research in psycholinguistics indicates that complex sentences (those requiring more transformations between deep and surface structure) are harder to understand. Thus passive constructions are more difficult than active ones: "The cat was eaten by the woman" is not as easily processed as is "The woman ate the cat." Negative sentences are more difficult than affirmative ones, and *double* negatives are a real puzzle. And embedded sentences sometimes totally exhaust listeners' processing abilities: "The fat cat which my father left with the skinny old lady with the hungry look on her face never came back," for example. Probably one should avoid such constructions if one wants to be understood. Probably one should avoid such little old ladies if one is a fat cat.

Intensity, Profanity, and Obscenity

John Bowers seems to have been responsible for the first study of the effects of language intensity.[19] His somewhat unexpected finding was that highly intense language produced less attitude change among listeners than did language of low intensity. A friend and I speculated that this was because all Bowers' listeners were frustrated, and we conducted an experiment to test our speculation. We found that frustrated listeners did react badly to highly intense language, but language intensity didn't seem to make any difference to listeners who weren't frustrated.[20]

Then (if I recall correctly) John Bowers and Mike Osborne got in an argument at Donnelly's bar one Friday night in Iowa City. Mike allowed as how John just couldn't write intense language and that he was willing to bet *he* could write intense metaphorical conclusions that would be *more* persuasive than literal conclusions of low intensity. So they made the bet and did the study, and Mike was right.[21]

A number of other experiments have explored other effects of language intensity and opinionated language. Rather than deal with those findings, which you can read at your leisure, suppose we move to this question: What *makes* language intense? Bowers has reported that the most reliable predictor is this: Language will be judged as intense if it is part of a sex or death metaphor.[22] What that means can be seen most easily by comparing one of the metaphorical conclusions which

won the bet for Osborne with the corresponding literal conclusion.
First the literal version:

> From what we've learned here today it is obvious that we have
> listened too long to the voices of those who represent special inter-
> est groups. Too long, we ourselves have stood by and permitted
> the ruination of our western economies by those who have pro-
> claimed the doctrine of protective tariff. We have neglected our
> larger interests for the sake of the smaller interests of these spe-
> cial groups, and the result has been—not a vigorous, protected
> economy—but rather economic stagnation.
>
> I say the time has come to listen no longer in our legislatures
> to those short-sighted lobbyists. For only when we shut our ears to
> them, and remove the tariff barriers which stand as so many harm-
> ful restrictions on our general welfare, can we achieve the goal
> of free trade, giving to the entire world new economic hope and
> a new sense of economic well-being.

And now the conclusion based on the sex metaphor:

> From what we've learned here today it is obvious that we have
> listened too long to the seductive whispers of special interest
> groups. Too long, we ourselves have stood by and permitted the
> rape of western economies by those who have proclaimed the doc-
> trine of protective tariff. We have prostituted our own interests to
> satisfy the lust of these special interest groups, and the result of this
> impotent union has been—not a vigorous and healthy economy—
> but economic abortion.
>
> I say the time has come to banish from our legislative chambers
> these economic seducers. For only when we shut our ears to them,
> and remove the barriers which stand like so many ill-advised paren-
> tal restrictions, can liberty and economy lie side by side, stimulating
> each other, giving through free trade a new birth of hope to the
> world and a new manhood of economic well-being.

The sex metaphor appeals to *my* prurient interests, but it must have
some redeeming social value, since it hasn't yet been banned by the
Supreme Court.

Which leads rather directly to the next question: What are the effects of profanity and obscenity in communication? Which leads to an
equally direct answer: I don't know. But I am willing to speculate.

The reason I don't know is that I haven't been able to find any published studies dealing with the question. I can see at least three problems
in conducting such a study: (1) The effect of profanity and obscenity

probably depends overwhelmingly upon the specific speaker, audience, topic, and communication situation, so that a study of the *general* effect of such language probably wouldn't be very useful; (2) Attitudes toward obscenity are changing so rapidly, and indeed what constitutes obscenity is changing so rapidly, that a study done today would be outdated tomorrow; and (3) Obscenity undoubtedly differs in intensity just as nonobscene language does.

But let me return to that first problem and amplify it a bit. If the foreman of the department in the steel mill where I used to work had ever stopped swearing, the workers (1) couldn't have understood a word he said, (2) would have thought it was quitting time, (3) would have filed a grievance with the union steward (they thought it was Muzak piped in to make their working conditions more pleasant), and/or (4) would have sent him to the company hospital on the assumption he was having a seizure.

Obscenity is expected from some speakers by some listeners in some situations. The rule seems to be: You can swear at some of the people all of the time and all of the people some of the time, but you can't swear at all of the people all of the time.

But one of the most striking changes in our society is one which has occurred in this very area of communication, and it is one which has occurred in your lifetime. As recently as the early 1960s, and even later than that in some parts of the country, one could be arrested and convicted of a crime for using certain "taboo" words in public—especially in public speeches and performances, but their use even in conversation in public places could be construed as "disturbing the peace." These same words are now at least tolerated in common conversation as well as more public types of communication.

For example, Lenny Bruce was arrested and convicted for using an "obscene" word in a Chicago night club.* The word at that time was used almost exclusively by men, and a rather small proportion of men at that, and for all practical purposes never in the presence of women.

---

* *If you want to know what word Lenny Bruce used, you will have to see the movie "Lenny" or read one of the books on his life. The Publisher has decided it is not appropriate for this word to appear in this text.*

The same word is used fairly commonly today, both in print and in private conversation, by both men and women.

I remember administering a test to college students in a mass lecture hall in the early 1960s. We were writing on the board the time remaining before we collected the papers, and a colleague of mine had the misfortune of writing "69" there in huge numerals. A nervous titter ran through the audience and spread until it disrupted the whole scene. My friend was really puzzled as to what he had done. He looked around, checked to see if his fly was open . . . I finally explained to him, and he turned red. I don't think that would happen today.

About the same time another friend of mine convulsed us with a story about how someone in a bar in New York had asked him if he was "gay." He too was puzzled, but he allowed as how he was probably as happy as the average person, whereupon the questioner looked at him strangely and found something to do at the other end of the bar. My friend was *not* especially naïve, either; he had been a cab driver in New York City.

Now "four-letter" words (and even Lenny Bruce's eleven-letter word) are used much more openly by men and women alike. Not that *everyone* uses them, but it would be difficult to get through a day without hearing more such language than you would have heard in public places during the entire year of 1960. Even George Carlin's "Seven Dirty Words" on his album *Class Clown* is rapidly losing its punch. I suspect your younger brothers and sisters may not even understand what's funny about it, and I'm sure your children won't.

The revolution which has occurred can probably be traced rather directly to the Berkeley "free speech movement" in 1965. Lenny Bruce was the prophet of the revolution, but Mario Savio actually kicked it off. The student protests of the late 1960s and early 1970s made obscenity a major strategy in provoking the "establishment" into overreacting. Much of the violence of the police riots at the 1968 Democratic convention in Chicago has been attributed to the protesters' use of verbal and nonverbal obscenity. The Chicago police seem to have blown their cool when they heard girls the age of their sisters and daughters using language they had previously heard only from prostitutes and "loose broads." That strategy simply could not succeed now.

Farb has done a good job of analyzing obscene language and "dirty jokes" as a communication strategy. He notes that such language can serve the functions of expressing one's self-concept, of making political or social statements of rebellion against the power structure, of insulting and provoking another, of substituting for physical aggression, of demonstrating verbal ability and wit, of covering and simultaneously relieving sexual anxiety and, in the game of sexual seduction, of testing another person's sexual values and predicting his or her readiness for further advances. If you are interested in the area, I would recommend that you read Farb's treatment.

Whatever its effects and uses, the phenomenon of obscene language is a strange one. A martian would indeed be puzzled to discover that some of the words of earthlings are "obscene," while others which have identical dictionary definitions are socially acceptable. Kitten, a black prostitute in Robert Gover's book, *One Hundred Dollar Misunderstanding,* discusses that strange state of affairs in her characteristic style:

> I ain never gonna fergit that mothahless word long's my blackass alive! Cop You Late! Keeryess! I git me so godam fuss up bout dat dadio, I bout flip.
> I say, Madam, don' it mean somethin' else sides jes plain fug? She say, No.
> I say, Madam, it mean fug, how come it don' jes *say* fug? She say, Fug is bad word. . . . I say, Madam, how come it bad? She say, It like White and Black. She say, Like, Cop You Late is like White, and fug is like Black. She say, Cop You Late is like it got loot, and fug is down an' out broke.[23]

Kitten is understandably confused. The decisions of the Supreme Court over the years, although expressed in more formal language, have been so changeable and contradictory as to suggest that those honorable justices are no less confused as to what constitutes obscenity and why certain words thus arbitrarily labeled evoke such emotional reactions.

What makes some words go bad, while others which seem to refer to the same sins can nevertheless do no wrong? I have found no profound answer to that question. For that matter, I haven't even found a simplistic answer.

Language and Society

Language reflects social structure in many ways. I have already noted that we have different rules for language depending upon the social context and upon the social status of the people we are speaking to or speaking about. But language also reflects and maintains prescribed social roles.

Social Class

Bernstein and other writers and researchers have demonstrated that those of different socioeconomic classes have different *characteristic* language codes.[24] Specifically, he seems to have shown that those of lower socioeconomic class use what he calls a more "restricted" code compared with the "elaborated" code of the middle and upper classes. A restricted code is one which has less variety in vocabulary and less complex syntactic structures. It does not appear that users of restricted code *cannot* use more elaborated language, but rather that they *do* not. In fact, other researchers have questioned Bernstein's whole notion, arguing that high-status interviewers may intimidate lower-class respondents so that they use a more restricted code than they do when talking to people they consider to be their equals.[25] However, while some of Bernstein's results may be explained away, there does seem to be some substance to his observations.

This is important because, as I noted earlier, the language one uses seems to have some effect on the way one perceives the world. If lower-class people in our society do in fact tend to use a more restricted code, that may tend to produce a more simplistic view of the world on their part, that is, less cognitive and perceptual complexity (see the discussion in Chapter Five of cognitive complexity). And one of my students has pointed out rather convincingly, I believe, that Bernstein's description of the restricted code user is *strikingly* similar to Rokeach's description of the dogmatic person (see Chapter Five again).[26] Further, Bernstein's notion is also important because of the idea drawn from general semantics that one's anxieties are greater insofar as one's language fails to match reality. And reality is *not* simplistic or restricted. Finally, when a person from a lower-class background is interviewed for a "white collar" job by an upper-class interviewer, the restricted code of the interviewee may reduce his or her chances of success.

Thus another of those famous "vicious circles" may be operating here, as lower-class background tends to produce restricted-code use and restricted-code use tends to keep those from a lower-class background from getting out of the lower class.

This has some implications for the teaching of language to children, both at home and in the very early grades of school. Bernstein makes it clear that it is the environment in which language is learned which makes the difference, not the family's socioeconomic class *per se*. Restricted codes seem to develop in children who are not encouraged to elaborate their descriptions of the world or give reasons for their behavior and their decisions; who are not given a variety of experience; who are *ordered* to behave in certain ways because "that's the way it's done" or because "I say so"; and whose roles and duties in the home are fixed rather than achieved or earned. Does that suggest anything about child-rearing practices or elementary-school teaching?

Sex and Sexism

Many writers have noted how the English language is rigged to maintain the inferior status of women in our society. One of the more obvious is the fact that it is conventional to use the *male* pronouns "he," "him," and "his" whenever one is referring to a hypothetical person of unknown sex. That is a convention which has plagued me in writing this book, one which I have fought against with only limited success, a fight which has produced some awkward sentences, I'm afraid. How do you say "A communicator has problems when _____ speaks to a dogmatic listener" without using "he" as the pronoun in the blank? You can use "he or she" or you can rewrite the sentence or you can alienate half your readers, that's how. None of those solutions are very satisfactory.

But Robin Lakoff has pointed out some much more subtle ways language discriminates against women.[27] Women's "active vocabularies," for example, are expected to be different from those of men. When was the last time you heard a man describe something as "magenta" or "aquamarine"? Or "lovely" or "divine"? And even though obscenity has been considerably liberated, as I mentioned a few pages ago, women still are not expected to use strong expletives as frequently or at least as publicly as are men. Lakoff's view is that these social restrictions stem from the assumption that women's speech and the things they talk about are trivial, and at the same time these restrictions reinforce that assumption.

She also says that the expected female syntax or sentence construction is different. Women generally use more "tag questions" and

"Wh-imperatives" where men use declarative statements and outright commands. Thus women are more likely to say "Politicians are certainly underhanded, *aren't they?*" and "*Why don't you* help me with this?" Further, she believes that even when women use declarative sentences to state their opinions, they frequently use an intonation pattern which makes them *sound like* questions. All of which makes women appear less self-confident, more deferential, and approval-seeking.

Finally, women are generally expected to use more "polite" constructions. The "Wh-imperative" just mentioned is one such polite construction. Others include tags such as "won't you?" as in the utterance "You'll be home early, won't you?"

Charlotte Hall has reported an analysis she did of tapes of some television shows.[28] While she failed to verify some of Lakoff's observations, she did add some of her own: that the women tended to use more exaggerated patterns of stress and intonation than did the men, except when the men were speaking condescendingly to women or when they were portraying "cute," effeminate, or obnoxious male characters.

The picture seems clear: The vocabularies and sentence construction women are expected to use seem well adapted to maintaining their stereotyped social roles.

Race

Unfortunately, much of what was said about language and social class also applies to language and race. That is because, for reasons which will be detailed in the last chapter of this book, non-Anglo members of our society tend to be pushed into the lower socioeconomic class and thus are more likely to suffer from the problems of restricted-code use as well. That is *not* to say that non-Anglo dialects are restricted codes. They are not; they are capable of being *either* elaborated or restricted. But the problems of restricted-code use *tend* to be inflicted on non-Anglos along with all the more tangible problems of economic discrimination.

The additional injury and insult I want to discuss now is a separate social problem: non-Anglo dialects are likely to be used by Anglos as cues for racial discrimination. Despite the fact that most dialects are not so different as to interfere with communication, Anglos who occupy the upper positions in our socioeconomic hierarchy seem devoted to eradicating them, rather than accepting them as additional enrichment of our cultural heritage. Sometimes this discrimination is practiced at a high level of cultural awareness, and sometimes not. It is difficult to tell, when a personnel manager says "Customers just can't understand that kind of talk," whether he or she really believes it or whether it is just being used as another rationalization for discrimination.

The problem of the black who is forced to be fluent in two different and complex dialects—Anglo English and Black English—is the major example. A major problem is that many Anglos assume a black speaking his native dialect is trying to speak Anglo English with only partial success, when in fact the black is speaking a dialect that is at least as rich in vocabulary and syntax as is Anglo English. It also has a long history which is inextricably interwoven into black history and culture in general.

Farb lists five sources of or influences on Black English: African languages, West African pidgin, Plantation Creole, Anglo English, and urban slang. Three examples from Farb's discussion will have to suffice to illustrate how what appear to the Anglo to be ungrammatical constructions are in fact the result of the correct application of consistent syntactic rules of Black English. "He be workin'" and "He workin'," for instance, have quite different meanings which require longer constructions in Anglo English. "He workin'" means he *is* working *right now.* "He be workin'" means he *has been* working *for some time.*

The various uses of "ain't" constitute another example. "He ain't go," Farb says, does not mean simply that he *didn't* go; it means either that he didn't go *or* is not now going. "He ain't goin'" means that he is not likely to go in the future. "Dey ain't like dat" does not mean they *aren't* like that, it means they *didn't* like that.

And for a final example, again from Farb, "He don't know can she go" is the perfectly logical result of applying if-deletion and verb-inversion transformations to the same underlying deep structure from which is derived the Anglo-English sentence, "He doesn't know if she can go."

Linguists have identified the phrase-structure rules and transformations used by speakers of Black English in the same way they have identified those of Anglo English—by constructing rules which consistently produce utterances which native speakers of the language regard as acceptable.

Yet the black speaker who lapses into black dialect is immediately classified by most Anglos as uneducated and/or not very bright, when in fact he has demonstrated a fluency in what is essentially a second language, an accomplishment most Anglos cannot match. Anglos may adopt specific items of black vocabulary such as "cool" and "rip off," but Black English syntax is fairly safe from such petty thievery, since most Anglos not only will not take the trouble to master it, they don't even know it exists.

Summary

It is useful to think of language as a sort of game which is governed by certain rules which apply at the phonemic, syntactic, semantic, and pragmatic levels. We learn these rules so early and so subtly that we are seldom aware we are using them. *Phonemic* rules are those which specify the sounds and sound combinations used in a given language. *Syntactic* rules specify how sounds can be combined to produce acceptable sentences in a given language. *Semantic* rules specify the meanings of sentences and utterances in various contexts, and the conditions under which such utterances can be said to be meaningful. The *rule-governed approach* to meaning seems more useful than earlier approaches which held that meaning depends on referents, mental images, or behavioral responses. *Pragmatic* rules are those which specify how language can be used to achieve certain effects in different contexts.

But the language game cannot be considered independently of the people who play the game. In particular, the language one uses seems to have some effects on the ways one perceives the world, as well as some effects upon one's thought patterns and mental health. Further, certain types of language are more easily understood—especially those which use familiar words and are syntactically less complex. Finally, language of *high intensity* is sometimes preferred and sometimes rejected by different receivers under different conditions. Obscenity, which is an especially intense type of language, can enhance or disrupt communication depending upon the context in which it occurs and upon the communicator's feelings about it. Social opinions regarding obscenity have changed radically over the past few years in two ways: (1) What is considered obscene has changed, and (2) Obscenity has come to be considered appropriate or at least tolerable in a wider variety of contexts. Obscenity is a puzzling phenomenon in that certain words are considered obscene even though their dictionary definitions are identical to other words which are not considered obscene.

Language is also a potent social force in that it frequently and subtly perpetuates status and role differences between social classes, between the sexes, and between races.

Suggestions for Developing Awareness

1. Writers sometimes construct their own systems of rules. Try to decipher the rule systems used by lyricists such as Leonard Cohen* or Bob Dylan, or the writings of James Taylor during his stay in a mental institution. For example, the song "Fire and Rain" ** written by James Taylor was completed while he was in a mental institution. Can you find a system of rules or is their work lunacy?

2. Young children often talk what we call "gibberish" with their friends or to themselves. Is their talk really "gibberish" or are they using a rule system deliberately constructed so adults will not understand and thus will not listen? Observe some young children and try to decipher their code.

3. Think about the language you regularly use around your friends and in the dorm. Do you use that same language at home with your family? Why not? What are the pragmatic rules that apply in these instances?

4. Construct concrete examples for what you mean by "I love you," "monogamy," "justice," "hate," and "reality." Share those examples with a friend,

---

 * *See the album* Songs of Leonard Cohen *(Columbia, 1968).*
** *See the album* Sweet Baby Jane *(Warner Bros., 1970).*

your parents, and a stranger. What are the results? Is it difficult to think of concrete examples for those words? What happens when you try to define those words with more words? Do you create an "illusion" of understanding?

5. Once upon a time there was a "Doonesbury" cartoon series about a little boy named Michael who wore a note pinned to him that read: "My name is Michael. Please don't hit me. Signed, Mother." Well, to make a long story short, our little Anglo friend Michael landed in a hospital due to a beating he received when he called a black man a "honky." What rule or rules were violated in this instance?

References

1. Peter Farb, *Word Play: What Happens When People Talk* (New York: Knopf, 1974).
2. Robin Lakoff, "Language in Context," *Language* 48 (1971): 907-927.
3. Noam Chomsky, "Review of B.F. Skinner's *Verbal Behavior*," *Language* 35 (1959): 26-58.
4. B.F. Skinner, *Verbal Behavior* (New York: Appleton-Century-Crofts, 1957).
5. Noam Chomsky, *Syntactic Structures* (The Hague: Mouton, 1957); and *Aspects of a Theory of Syntax* (Cambridge: M.I.T. Press, 1965).
6. For descriptions of some applications of the assumption that language is rule-governed at the semantic level, some of which have developed from Chomsky's work, see: John T. Grinder and Suzette Elgin, *A Guide to Transformational Grammar: History, Theory, and Practice* (New York: Holt, Rinehart and Winston, 1973); and Geoffrey Leech, *Semantics* (Baltimore: Penguin, 1974).
7. C.K. Ogden and I.A. Richards, *The Meaning of Meaning* (London: Kegan Paul, Trench, Trubner, 1936).
8. John Locke, *Essay Concerning Human Understanding,* book III, 1690.
9. Charles E. Osgood, "On Understanding and Creating Sentences," *American Psychologist* 18 (1963): 735-751.
10. Charles L. Stevenson, *Ethics and Language* (New Haven, Conn.: Yale University Press, 1944).

11. Ludwig Wittgenstein, *Philosophical Investigations,* trans. G.E.M. Anscombe (Oxford, England: Basil Blackwell, 1958); and *Tractatus Logico-Philosophicus,* trans. D.F. Pears and B.F. McGuinness (London: Routledge and Kegan Paul, 1966). Don't read Wittgenstein first. Even after it's translated it still isn't translated.

12. John R. Searle, *Speech Acts* (Cambridge University Press, 1969).

13. J.L. Austin, *How To Do Things with Words* (New York: Oxford, 1962).

14. Charles O. Frake, "How to Ask for a Drink in Subanun," in John Gumperz and Dell Hymes, eds., *The Ethnography of Communication,* American Anthropological Association Special Publication, vol. 66, pp. 127-132.

15. Benjamin Lee Whorf, *Language, Thought, and Reality,* ed. J.B. Carroll (Cambridge: M.I.T. Press, 1956).

16. A. Korzybski, *Science and Sanity* (Lakeville, Conn.: International Non-Aristotelian Library, 1958).

17. Rudolph Flesch, *The Art of Plain Talk* (New York: Harper, 1946).

18. E. Dale and J.S. Chall, "A Formula for Predictive Readability," *Educational Research Bulletin* 27 (1945): 11-20, 28, 37-54.

19. John Bowers, "Language Intensity, Social Introversion, and Attitude Change," *Speech Monographs* 30 (1963): 345-352.

20. Carl Carmichael and Gary Cronkhite, "Frustration and Language Intensity," *Speech Monographs* 32 (1965): 107-111; reprinted in Serge Moscovici, ed., *Readings in the Psychosociology of Language* (Chicago: Markham, 1971).

21. John Bowers and Michael M. Osborne, "Attitudinal Effects of Selected Types of Concluding Metaphors in Persuasive Speeches," *Speech Monographs* 33 (1966): 147-155.

22. John Bowers, "Some Correlates of Language Intensity," *Quarterly Journal of Speech* 50 (1964): 415-420.

23. Robert Gover, *One Hundred Dollar Misunderstanding* (New York: Ballantine, 1961), pp. 183-184.

24. Basil Bernstein, *Class Codes and Control,* vol. 1 (London: Routledge and Kegan Paul, 1971). This is a collection of Bernstein's papers dating through the previous fifteen years.

25. William Labov, "The Logic of Non-Standard English," in P. Giglioti, ed., *Language and Social Context* (Baltimore: Penguin, 1973).

26. Alice Hardy, "Communication Codes and Dogmatism: A Descriptive Study" (M.A. thesis, San Jose State University, 1975).

27. Robin Lakoff, *Language and Woman's Place* (New York: Harper and Row, Colophon, 1975).

28. Charlotte Hall, "Sexism Is Alive and Well on TV . . . Isn't It?" (Paper prepared for a course titled "Dialectology" taught by M. Campbell in the linguistics program at San Jose State University, 1974. Two of the TV shows analyzed were "The Mary Tyler Moore Show" and "All in the Family.")

Extraverbal Communication

Teachers and students of public speaking have vacillated between almost exclusive fascination with the speaker's delivery and studied ignorance of the topic. The excesses of the elocution movement in the nineteenth century, when every twitch of the finger and squeak of the voice was specifically defined and prescribed, led to a reaction against the teaching of delivery which occupied easily the first half of the twentieth century. Now comes a sudden surge of interest in the study of "nonverbal communication" which bids fair to rival if not surpass the earlier interest in elocution.

Those who study nonverbal communication, however, are not very interested in *prescribing* nuances of voice, gesture, and posture during the speech act. Rather, they are interested in *describing* the various elements of nonverbal communication and the meaning transmitted by each element. The field is so young that few researchers have gone beyond attempts to describe the kinds of behaviors which seem to be communicating *something;* no one is very deep into the description of what it is that is to be communicated. If there is any advice to the speaker to be gleaned from the research to date, it would seem to be this: There are so many nonverbal communication channels, so many of which are not under the conscious control of the speaker, that one is almost bound to appear insincere if he tries to "fake" his delivery. Awkward delivery can be smoothed out, and the speaker may learn to use gesture, vocal variety, and eye contact to maintain the attention of the audience. Such things develop as the beginning public speaker comes to feel more at ease in speaking situations. They are helped along by the suggestions of a friendly observer, or by the speaker's observation of himself by some device such as videotape equipment or a full-length mirror. They are *not* learned by reading books such as this.

It is the communicator in his or her role as *listener* who can profit more by some knowledge of the language of nonverbal communication. It is not that the "naïve" listener *misses* the nonverbal messages; anyone likely to be reading this book must have had at least seventeen or eighteen years practice in decoding nonverbal messages. The problem is that he is probably receiving more nonverbal messages than he realizes, and he may be reacting to some of them without being fully aware of them. Further, just as one learns to attach incorrect meanings to words, one may learn to attach incorrect meanings to nonverbal symbols and to react inappropriately. Some conscious attention to nonverbal communication should allow the listener to be more sensitive in this area.

Discuss the need to improve critical listening—both listening for *feeling* and listening for *information*. Do these two forms of listening differ? If so, how?

Actually, the concern of this chapter is not so broad as the entire field of nonverbal communication. Nonverbal communication may include the study of tactilics (touch), aromatics (odor), objectics (objects and symbols), graphics (configuration of writing and printing), chronemics (timing), kinesics (body movement), and vocalics (nonverbal elements of vocalization), among others. Since this book focuses upon face-to-face or interpersonal communication (although not exclusively), I will direct my attention in this chapter to those nonverbal communication symbols which accompany and most clearly modify face-to-face verbal interaction. We might label this focus the study of extraverbal elements in interpersonal communication. At any rate, I will deal briefly with general appearance, kinesics, proxemics, and paralinguistics (or vocalics).

Most researchers agree that the nonverbal channels carry more social meaning than do the verbal channels.[1] If so, this is very important to the study of interpersonal communication in general. What has prevented it from being studied in any detail is probably the difficulty of isolating and describing its elements. Until quite recently most students of communication despaired of ever describing all the combinations of facial expressions, gestures, and vocal inflections, to consider only three of the numerous nonverbal channels. Further, context seems to play an even more important part in nonverbal than in verbal communication, so that generalizations are even more difficult to make. Finally, the attempt of the elocutionists to teach nonverbal communication to speakers was such an abject failure that few speech experts saw any hope of applying knowledge about nonverbal communication even if it were available. Writers of recent textbooks have generally assumed that nonverbal behavior (or "delivery") is learned at a low level of awareness so that it is "second nature" and very difficult to teach.

The *reception* and *interpretation* of nonverbal cues are probably easier to teach and of at least equal importance. One is constantly called upon to make decisions on the basis of communication—decisions which necessitate constant and usually rather quick evaluations of the trustworthiness of speakers and their information. Speech textbooks have customarily dealt with the tests of reasoning and evidence, so that the interested listener could use the verbal part of the message for such evaluation. Generally, evaluation of nonverbal cues has been ignored. The study of nonverbal communication still has not progressed to the point that it is possible to compile anything resembling a catalog of meanings. What is possible is to encourage the student to be sensitive to the various nonverbal channels, with some suggestions regarding nonverbal cues he may miss and others he may misinterpret.

General Appearance

One study concluded that an "attractive" female student had more persuasive impact upon male students than did an unattractive female student.[2] Another seemed to indicate this was true regardless of the sex of the persuader and persuadee.[3] And one of these suggests that listeners are flattered and responsive when an attractive communicator reveals that she intends to try to persuade them, but they are put off when an unattractive communicator does the same.[4]

The area of "general appearance" probably should be divided between those matters of appearance which are physically fixed and those which the speaker can manipulate. The listener who judges the credibility of speakers on the basis of their inherited physical attractiveness is basing his or her decision on an irrelevant and irrational factor; pretty people can be pretty stupid and pretty dishonest. Matters of dress and grooming are a little more complicated. The speaker has a choice in such matters, so they do communicate something. What the listener must decide is, first, what is communicated and, second, whether it is relevant to the speaker's credibility regarding the matter at hand. The employer who is a pushover for a suit and tie may discover to his or her dismay that even the village idiot can be trained to tie a Windsor knot, and the prisons are full of drug pushers who didn't think a narcotics agent would grow a beard and long hair.

The speaker must decide just how much he can manipulate his appearance for the sake of impression and still maintain self-respect. The listener had best be aware that he can easily be misled by the speaker's attire and grooming; appearance bears no necessary relation to competence or trustworthiness. What the listener can look for are signs that the speaker is using physical appearance in the service of communication. It may be important to decide what image he is trying to project in order to know what he perceives to be his role in the communication event.

Kinesics

The field of kinesics can be most grossly divided into the study of facial and body movements. Ekman has contended that facial movements or expressions generally communicate the *type* of emotion an individual is experiencing, while body movements reveal the *extent* of the emotional intensity or level of arousal.[5] These are two channels to which the listener will become sensitive if he is to receive *all* the messages the speaker is sending. They are especially important precisely because the speaker is often unaware of the messages they are carrying so that the listener, if he knows something about the code, can gain insight into the uncensored feelings of the speaker. As Hall puts it:

> All people communicate on several different levels at the same time but are usually aware of only the verbal dialog and don't realize that they respond to nonverbal messages. But when a person says one thing and really believes something else, the discrepancy between the two can usually be sensed. Nonverbal systems are much less subject to the conscious deception that often occurs in verbal systems. When we find ourselves thinking, "I don't know what it is about him, but he doesn't seem sincere," it's usually this lack of congruity between a person's words and his behavior that makes us anxious and uncomfortable.[6]

Types of Kinesic Behaviors

Not all nonverbal communication occurs at such a low level of awareness. Ekman and Friesen offer a breakdown consisting of five different types of kinesic behaviors, each developing somewhat differently and

each operating at a somewhat different level of awareness.[7] *Emblems* are nonverbal acts which can be given relatively precise verbal definitions. They are learned and culture-bound, actually an extension of the language. The crew of the *Pueblo* temporarily confounded their North Korean captors by raising their middle fingers in the well-known gesture of derision when they were photographed for propaganda purposes. The North Koreans, not familiar with this extension of the English language, publicized the picture widely, inadvertently reassuring Americans that the crew had not lost its spirit. The gesture is an excellent example of an emblem, because of the preciseness of its meaning. Note that emblems are transmitted and received at a high level of awareness. They may contradict an oral message, but if they do, the contradiction is probably intended.

Illustrators accompany and complement the oral message. Their meanings are less precise and more dependent upon oral language, they are probably learned by imitation, and they are used at a high level of awareness. A speaker who holds his hands apart to indicate the length of an object he is describing is using an illustrator.

Affect displays are facial expressions which indicate emotional states. They probably originate in a combination of physiology and learning. That is, the coordination of facial muscles may be largely determined physiologically with little learning, but the relationship between the behaviors and the cues which evoke it are probably learned. Thus we may not learn *how* to smile, but we learn *when*.

The source and observer of affect displays may or may not be aware of them. Obviously there are such things as polite smiles and studied frowns of which everyone is aware. However, some affect displays appear to be unwittingly transmitted and unknowingly received. Ekman has reported what he terms "micromomentary facial expressions," for example, which are expressions so fleeting (1/5 or 2/5 of a second) as to be consciously undetectable, imposed as they are on expressions of longer duration.[8] They serve the purpose of "emotional leakage," according to Ekman, and neither sender nor receiver appears to be aware of their existence. Dilation of the eyes appears to be similar. We are seldom aware of the dilation of our pupils, but there appears to be a close correlation between dilation and attention or interest. We are seldom aware of the dilation of the pupils of others, but there is

evidence that we depend on such dilation as an index of the interest on the part of others.[9]

Regulators are devices by which we encourage or discourage the speaking of others; we nod if we want to encourage or look away if we want to discourage. They seem to be learned. We are generally not very aware of using them, but are usually quite aware when others use them. Of course, if we should define pupil dilation and micromomentary facial expressions into the class of regulators, which they may well be, they certainly do not operate at a high level of awareness.

Adaptors are nonfunctional behaviors, vestigial sublimations of more active behaviors which are not presently socially acceptable. Thus foot shuffling and fidgeting may be vestiges of escape. They are probably learned, but we are not generally aware of them. We may be aware of them as we observe them in others, but are not usually totally aware of their meanings.

Birdwhistell has developed an elaborate classification system for body movement and facial expression.[10] It is beyond the scope of this book, although you may want to explore the subject further. I will be satisfied if you develop an increased sensitivity to cues you already understand in the channels of facial expression and body movement, so you can more readily judge the reliability of verbal messages.

Deception and Control

There appear to be three dimensions of feeling communicated non-verbally, that is, three kinds of information one looks for in nonverbal channels. One expects information about the direction of the other's interest or attention, his or her attitude or affect toward the object of his attention, and the level of his or her anxiety.

Ekman and Friesen distinguish among three general areas of the body from which emanate cues regarding these dimensions of feeling; the face, hands, and legs (including the feet). They hypothesize that the information capacity of a given channel depends upon the length of time required to transmit signals in that channel, the number of distinguishable stimulus patterns available in that channel, and the visibility of the channel.[11]

Thus the face appears to have the greatest capacity for transmitting information since facial expressions change rapidly, there are a great many which are distinguishable, and the face is generally visible. The hands are not so facile nor so visible; they therefore have a more limited capacity than does the face but have a greater capacity than do the legs and feet.

That order is not so clear in terms of capacity for deception or "emotional leakage." It appears that observers tend to watch most closely those channels which have the greatest information capacity. Probably as a result of this, those who are attempting to deceive, send conflicting messages without detection, or "leak" strong but unacceptable feelings tend to use those channels which have the least information capacity and are least likely to be monitored by the observer. Consequently, the inadvertent expression of feelings one wishes to conceal might seem most likely to occur in the legs and feet, then the hands, and least likely to occur through the face.

As a general rule that is true. It is *entirely* true as long as the "facial" channel is restricted to relatively long-lasting facial expressions. *However, there are a number of what might be termed "subliminal" facial channels which are heavily used for the disposal of emotions which yearn for expression but are for one reason or another unacceptable.*

One of these "subliminal" channels is pupil dilation, as I have already mentioned. Another "subliminal" channel is the rate of speed at which one's eyes blink, with faster eye-blink rates indicating greater anxiety. A third is the muscular tension of the face, and a fourth is what Ekman terms "micromomentary" facial expressions, described earlier as an affect display.

A general increase in the level of activity of the hands and legs is indicative of increased overall physiological activation, usually nervousness, anxiety, or stress of some sort. The activity may be more specific, however. Many motions of the hands and legs are of the class labeled "adaptors," which I discussed earlier. These are vestiges of activities which under other circumstances would be useful, but they are for some reason socially unacceptable. Shuffling of the feet and shifting from one foot to another, for example, may be vestiges of walking, perhaps indicative of a desire to leave an uncomfortable situation.

Proxemics, Gaze, and Physical Orientation

Proxemics is the study of the space relationships maintained by persons in social interaction.

People act so as to maintain between themselves and others distances which are physically and psychologically comfortable and appropriate to the limitations of whatever communication channel may be used, to the behavior in which they are engaged and, most importantly for our purposes, to the feelings they have about the others. In doing so, they may communicate a great deal, sometimes intentionally and sometimes quite unintentionally. However, the distance that will be judged comfortable and appropriate depends so heavily upon the gaze and body orientations of the participants that it is impossible to discuss the three separately.

It is customary in discussions of proxemics to distinguish between the phenomena of personal space and territoriality. I will not defy that convention. *Personal space* is a sort of portable territory surrounding oneself—a territory into which others are not expected to trespass. *Territoriality,* on the other hand, is a form of behavior characteristic of humans and animals alike, in which a more or less fixed and permanent territory is marked out and defended from intrusion. I am reminded of the device used by the custodian of the county dump at Fish Camp, a tiny town at the south entrance to Yosemite where I camped one summer while writing this book. Bears outnumber the people in Fish Camp, especially near the dump, so Rain dealt with them by urinating on all the major trees and rocks within a radius of one hundred yards from his trailer. He reported the bears respected his territory so long as it seemed reasonable, but they seemed to feel one hundred yards was about the limit of reasonableness. The concept of personal space seems more important than territoriality in interpersonal communication; we will not concern ourselves with the phenomenon of territoriality at this point.

It is also customary to begin a discussion of personal space with Hall's description of the four categories of informal space: intimate, casual-personal, social-consultative, and public.[12] Intimate space, to which one admits intimate friends, ranges from actual physical contact to about eighteen inches; casual-personal from there to about four feet; social-consultative (impersonal business) on up to about twelve feet; and public space from twelve feet to infinity. These figures were for a particular sample of white professional-class Americans. Wide cultural variation has been observed; most of the examples in the literature indicate that most other cultures not only tolerate but expect closer physical proximity during conversation.

The dimensions of these protective buffer bubbles don't seem to be uniform; closer approach will be tolerated from the back and sides than will be tolerated from the front. This is probably due to the effect of seeing and being seen by the other individual. Research seems to lead to the conclusion that direct eye contact has the effect of reducing interpersonal distance, making both parties less comfortable than they would otherwise be at a given physical distance.[13]

TABLE 1

Seating preferences at rectangular tables.

	X‾X̄ (◻ corner)	X̄ (◻ opposite end)	X̄ X̄ (◻ same side)	X̄◻X̄ (ends)	X̄◻·X̄ (side by side)	X̄◻ / X̄ (diagonal)
Conversation	42%	46%	11%	0%	1%	0%
Cooperation	19%	25%	51%	0%	5%	0%
Coaction	3%	31%	7%	13%	43%	3%
Competition	7%	41%	8%	18%	20%	5%

SOURCE: R. Sommer, "Further Studies of Small Group Ecology." *Sociometry* 28 (1965): 342.
NOTE: These figures are based on a sample of U.S. students. British subjects expressed rather different preferences.

The picture is actually more complex than that; perceived interpersonal distance depends also upon the body orientation to the other participants in the conversation as well as the angle of one's own body with respect to them. Thus perceived interpersonal distance at a given physical distance is least when two people are directly facing one another, and it is greatest when they are back to back.

The intervention of physical objects such as furniture will generally increase perceived interpersonal distance, allowing closer physical proximity. Thus two people may try to sit with a table between them in a small or crowded room when perceived distance would otherwise be uncomfortably close, or the intervening table may allow them to sit closer in order to hear each other in a noisy room. The uses people make of intervening objects under different conditions are illustrated in Tables 1 and 2, according to Sommer.[14]

It seems clear that when another person attempts to decrease interpersonal distance, one generally interprets it as an indication that the other is interested and attentive.[15] If the other person provides additional cues such as smiling and head nodding, one will perceive favorable attention; if he frowns and makes threatening gestures, one may make a sudden decision to leave the area. This appears true also when

TABLE 2

Seating preferences at round tables.

	$\times\bigcirc$ $\times$	$\times$ $\bigcirc$ $\times$	$\times\times$ $\bigcirc$
Conversation	63%	17%	20%
Cooperation	83%	7%	10%
Coaction	13%	36%	51%
Competition	12%	25%	63%

SOURCE: R. Sommer, "Further Studies of Small Group Ecology," *Sociometry* 28 (1965): 345.

NOTE: These figures are based on a sample of U.S. students. British subjects expressed rather different preferences.

perceived interpersonal distance is decreased by another who maintains a more direct gaze[16] or more direct body orientation.[17]

Spatial relationships also reflect status relationships among communicators. High-status persons generally occupy and are encouraged to occupy positions above and in front of others, except when a central position commands more attention and provides greater access to communication channels, as in a group discussion or communication network. High-status persons are also accorded greater personal space and approached less than low-status persons.

Design a field experiment to investigate personal space requirements of different people. Approach people from different angles (front, back, sides). How close will a stranger, friend, or instructor allow you to be? How do eye contact and closeness interact? What have you learned about your own personal space needs?

Practical Proxemics

A knowledge of proxemics can be useful in at least three ways.

First, it can be useful in planning the physical contexts in which communication events are going to occur. Architects, interior decorators,

conference planners, and teachers should be especially sensitive to the constraints imposed upon communication by the arrangement of physical objects. The person who has control of such arrangements can practically dictate the amount and kind of communication which takes place. The teacher who seats students in straight rows facing a platform upon which he or she stands can be fairly assured that the students will be primarily engaged in listening and occasionally asking questions, and that they will perceive him or her as expecting deference. If that is the goal, the teacher will be delighted with the outcome, but if the goal is to facilitate group discussion he or she will be disappointed.

Second, an understanding of proxemics can be useful in deciphering the verbal communication of another. *People communicate a great deal about the way they perceive a situation or the way they wish it to be by the way they use interpersonal space.* One indicates whether he is interested in another, whether he considers the other a friend, and what status he accords the other, among other things.

Finally, such knowledge is useful to the speaker, who can use it to some extent to indicate interest and sincerity, and to focus and, indeed, almost force the attention of the listeners at vital points in the message. When he moves toward the listeners, faces them directly, and maintains maximum eye contact at a certain point in the speech, he can bring audience attention to a peak at that point. Needless to say, that part of his speech had best be worth all the fuss, and the less conscious and deliberate verbal cues had best reinforce the impression of sincerity, or the speaker may become an unwilling impromptu comedian.

Paralanguage

Mehrabian concludes from several of his studies comparing the effects of inconsistent messages transmitted by the verbal, vocal, and facial channels that listeners depend very little upon verbal cues, very heavily upon facial cues, and almost as heavily upon vocal cues.[18] That conclusion with respect to vocal cues must be considerably qualified, however, on the basis of other research. Variations in the physical characteristics of the voice (pitch, rate, volume, etc.) seem to produce reliable differences in listeners' perceptions of speakers and their emotional states, but these perceptions are not necessarily accurate. Further, neither the variations in speakers' vocal characteristics nor the stereotyped perceptions they elicit from listeners seem to have any appreciable effect on listener comprehension or opinion change.

Vocal Stereotypes

The clearest vocal stereotypes are those we term *inflections,* which obviously and usually quite intentionally modify verbal meanings. Actually, a discussion of inflections probably doesn't belong in a chapter on extraverbal communication, because inflections are really part of language, carrying both syntactic and semantic cues. Besides, it would be insulting to your intelligence for me to spend pages of expensive paper and ink explaining how inflection indicates a question, exclamation, emphasis, irony, sarcasm, and the like. So I won't.

Instead, suppose we consider some of the personal and personality characteristics which listeners stereotypically attribute to speakers on the basis of their vocal characteristics.

Perhaps not surprisingly, sex can be identified quite accurately on the basis of vocal characteristics alone, but race cannot. (More specifically, persons having sex can be identified with 90 percent accuracy on the basis of voices alone, while persons having a race cannot be thus identified with better than chance accuracy.)*

The research dealing with the relation between vocal and personality characteristics has been plagued with methodological problems, most stemming from the extreme vagueness of the concepts involved in perceptions of both personality and voice. The general thrust of the studies seems to be toward the conclusion that people *reliably* associate certain personality stereotypes with certain vocal characteristics, but the associations are not very *accurate*.

Probably the most complete study in this area has been done by Addington, whose findings are summarized in Table 3.[19] There are a number of interesting suggestions to be derived from this table. The most obvious are that the speaker can probably improve his or her image by increasing rate and pitch variety and guarding against nasality.

Listeners appear to judge the social status of a speaker not only reliably but accurately on the basis of voice alone, even when speakers are attempting to fake status cues.[20] No one seems to be able to find what voice characteristics listeners are using as status cues, however. The finding also has to be qualified in cases when speakers having regional or national dialects are being judged, because such speakers are generally judged to be of somewhat lower status than those who speak Standard American English.[21]

Studies in which listeners have been asked to judge emotions from voices alone have also suffered from methodological problems. The first of these is that such a test depends as much upon the speaker's ability to express emotion as it does on the listener's ability to identify it. A second is that the experimenter usually supplies the labels which

---

* *Surely no source note was expected for such an obvious fabrication.*

TABLE 3

Simulated vocal cues and personality stereotypes.

Simulated vocal cues	Speakers	Stereotyped perceptions
Breathiness	Males	Younger; more artistic
	Females	More feminine; prettier; more petite; more effervescent; more highly strung and shallower
Thinness	Males	Did not alter listener's image of the speaker; no significant correlations
	Females	Increased social, physical, emotional, and mental immaturity; increased sense of humor and sensitivity
Flatness	Males	More masculine; more sluggish; colder; more withdrawn
	Females	More masculine; more sluggish; colder; more withdrawn
Nasality	Males	A wide array of socially undesirable characteristics
	Females	A wide array of socially undesirable characteristics
Tenseness	Males	Older; more unyielding; cantankerous
	Females	Younger; more emotional, feminine, high strung; less intelligent
Throatiness	Males	Older; more realistic, mature; sophisticated; and well adjusted
	Females	Less intelligent; more masculine; lazier; more boorish, unemotional, ugly, sickly, careless, inartistic, naive, humble, neurotic, quiet, uninteresting, apathetic. In short, "cloddish or oafish" (Addington)
Orotundity	Males	More energetic, healthy, artistic, sophisticated, proud, interesting, enthusiastic. In short, "hardy and aesthetically inclined." (Addington)
	Females	Increased liveliness, gregariousness, aesthetic sensitivity, and "increasingly proud and humorless" (Addington)
Increased rate	Males	More animated and extroverted
	Females	More animated and extroverted
Increased pitch variety	Males	More dynamic, feminine, aesthetically inclined
	Females	More dynamic and extroverted

SOURCE: Mark L. Knapp, *Nonverbal Communication in Human Interaction*, p. 154. © 1972 Holt, Rinehart and Winston, Inc.

the listeners use to identify the emotions, and there is a great deal of room for misunderstanding the meanings of those labels and the shades of meaning by which they are distinguished. Could you, for example, tell the difference between "fear" and "panic"? Still, there is considerable evidence that such judgments can be made with surprising reliability and accuracy.[22] Table 4 represents one summary of the vocal cues which observers judge to be associated with certain emotional states.[23] The table should be interpreted cautiously, because the research findings on which it is based are scanty, sometimes contradictory, and indicate many differences among individuals.

Perceived credibility of a speaker and perceived "persuasiveness" of a message appear to suffer as a result of certain vocal characteristics. (This doesn't mean that voice characteristics actually make a difference in the effect of the message, however. That is discussed in the next section.) A study conducted by Mehrabian and Williams indicated that less pitch variety, lower volume, slower rate, and a greater number of nonfluencies resulted in less perceived "persuasiveness."[24] Studies by Sereno and Hawkins[25] and by Miller and Hewgill[26] concluded that vocal nonfluencies reduced listeners' perceptions of speakers' competence and dynamism, but not their trustworthiness. Studies by Pearce and Conklin[27] and by Pearce[28] concluded that two different styles of delivery produced differences in audience ratings of speaker's dynamism, likeableness, and trustworthiness, but had no effect on their ratings of speaker credibility. Unfortunately, these last two studies confounded quite an array of variables, making it impossible to tell which variables accounted for which effects.

Comprehension and Attitude Change

One would expect that *some* of these vocal stereotypes, especially those related to credibility, would also be related to audience comprehension or attitude change. Generally that is not true.

There is a little evidence that vocal *variety* of various types may increase comprehension,[29] and breathiness or nasality may decrease it.[30] Vocal characteristics in general, though, don't seem to have much effect on comprehension. Even very rapid rates of vocal delivery do not seem to reduce comprehension so long as the rate remains below the supernatural.

TABLE 4

Characteristics of vocal expressions contained in the test of emotional sensitivity.

Feeling	Loudness	Pitch	Timbre	Rate
Affection	Soft	Low	Resonant	Slow
Anger	Loud	High	Blaring	Fast
Boredom	Moderate to low	Moderate to low	Moderately resonant	Moderately slow
Cheerfulness	Moderately high	Moderately high	Moderately blaring	Moderately fast
Impatience	Normal	Normal to moderately high	Moderately blaring	Moderately fast
Joy	Loud	High	Moderately blaring	Fast
Sadness	Soft	Low	Resonant	Slow
Satisfaction	Normal	Normal	Somewhat resonant	Normal

SOURCE: *The Communication of Emotional Meaning,* by J.R. Davitz, p. 63. Copyright 1964 McGraw-Hill, Inc. Used with permission of McGraw-Hill Book Company.

Results of research using opinion change present much the same picture. Sereno and Hawkins, Pearce and Conklin, and Pearce all failed to find any significant differences in opinion change due to the vocal characteristics they studied, which included nonfluencies, pitch, pitch variety, volume, volume variety, and inflection.

It is not too difficult to accept the fact that listeners may dislike certain vocal characteristics of a speaker and still comprehend his or her message. This may be especially true of college students, who have been carefully trained to comprehend under the most adverse conditions, including poor delivery on the part of the speaker. However, the fact that certain vocal characteristics affect perceived speaker *credibility* but have no detectable effect on opinion change seems really difficult to explain; it raises some basic questions about the acceptability of the operational definitions and/or the conceptualizations of credibility and attitude change.

What does all of this do for the advice most speech teachers and textbooks offer in the area of vocal delivery? Knapp lists them:

Inflection	Rhythm	Enunciation
Steady and slight upward	Regular	Slurred
Irregular up and down	Irregular	Clipped
Monotone or gradually falling	—	Somewhat slurred
Up and down; overall upward	Regular	
Slight upward	—	Somewhat clipped
Upward	Regular	
Downward	Irregular pauses	Slurred
Slight upward	Regular	Somewhat slurred

Typical prescriptions for use of the voice in delivering a public speech include: (1) Use variety in volume, rate, pitch, and articulation. The probabilities of desirable outcomes are less when one uses a constant rate, volume, pitch, and articulation. Being consistently overprecise may be as ineffective as being overly sloppy in your articulation. Although it has not been formally studied, it is quite possible that when vocal variety is perceived as rhythmic or patterned, it is no longer variety and this decreases the probabilities of desirable outcomes. (2) Decisions concerning loud-soft, fast-slow, precise-sloppy, or high-low should be based on what is appropriate for a given audience in a given situation. (3) Excessive nonfluencies are to be avoided.[31]

Generally, the findings suggest that the speaker should follow these suggestions if he wants his audience to be comfortable, to like him, and to perceive him to be a high-status, credible person. There is little evidence, however, to lead the speaker to expect all of this to have much noticeable effect on audience comprehension or opinion change.

Summary

Extraverbal communication is especially likely to contain messages of which the communicators are not fully aware, but messages they nevertheless use in making decisions. Some types of extraverbal communication which are especially important are *general appearance, kinesics* (posture, gesture, and facial expression), *proxemics* (interpersonal distance and spatial arrangement), and *paralanguage* (extraverbal elements of voice).

People frequently judge others erroneously on the basis of physical appearance which cannot be changed, or on the basis of dress and grooming which may be irrelevant to the judgment.

While it is difficult for a communicator to prevent his true feelings from being revealed in posture, gesture, or facial expression, the knowledgeable observer can still enhance his chances of detecting deception by learning to watch for those physical mannerisms which most often serve as means of "emotional leakage."

Interpersonal distance frequently affects interpersonal communication in subtle ways, and the ways people manipulate interpersonal distance can serve as cues to their perceptions of themselves, others, and the communication events in which they are involved.

Finally, extraverbal characteristics of speakers' voices are likely to be misleading, in that listeners show high agreement in their judgments of others' voices even though those stereotyped judgments are frequently inaccurate. Variety in vocal volume, pitch, and rate, as well as a moderate amount of fluency and careful articulation, all seem to make a speaker's image more favorable with listeners even though, paradoxically, there is little evidence that such vocal characteristics contribute much to listener comprehension or opinion change.

Suggestions for Developing Awareness

1. Analyze a communication event you participated in or observed in terms of kinesics, proxemics, and/or paralinguistics.

2. Try this exercise in class or at home. Have one person deliver a prepared short speech or poem. The first time you listen to it, wear earplugs and watch the person deliver the speech. The second time you listen to it, wear a blindfold. The third time, listen with both your eyes and your ears. What are the differences in the ways of listening? Which is the most desirable? Why?

3. Speculate as to how your class behavior would differ in environments other than the typical classroom. You might want to use the following examples: a dark, intimate bar, a conference room, someone's living room, or the out-of-doors. Which environment is most conducive to your interest, attention, and ability to concentrate? What are the aspects of each environment that would most influence your behavior?

4. Consider this situation: You have just met a person for the first time. He or she is in a class with you and you end up waiting in line together at the grocery store. You have a short conversation concerning the course you are taking together. As you are leaving, you think about the strange feeling you have about the person. You cannot trace it to anything he or she said, but you feel that this person is very insincere.

    What extraverbal cues might have led you to this conclusion? Have you ever had an experience similar to this one? If so, can you point to the extraverbal cues that contributed to your feelings? If you had an opportunity to pursue the relationship, was your initial feeling wrong?

References

1. See, for example: R. Birdwhistell, *Kinesics and Context* (Philadelphia: University of Pennsylvania, 1970); and A. Mehrabian and S.R. Ferris, "Inference of Attitudes from Nonverbal Communication in Two Channels," *Journal of Consulting Psychology* 31 (1967): 248-252.

2. Judson Mills and Elliot Aronson, "Opinion Change as a Function of the Communicator's Attractiveness and Desire to Influence," *Journal of Personality and Social Psychology* 1 (1965): 73-77.

3.   R.N. Widgery and B. Webster, "The Effects of Physical Attractiveness Upon Perceived Initial Credibility," *Michigan Speech Journal* 4 (1969): 9-15.

4.   Mills and Aronson, *op. cit.*

5.   P. Ekman, "Body Position, Facial Expression, and Verbal Behavior During Interviews," *Journal of Abnormal and Social Psychology* 68 (1964): 295-301; and P. Ekman and W. Friesen, "Head and Body Cues in the Judgment of Emotion: A Reformulation," *Perceptual and Motor Skills* 24 (1967): 711-724.

6.   E.T. Hall, *The Silent Language* (Garden City, N.Y.: Doubleday, 1959).

7.   P. Ekman and W. Friesen, "The Repertoire of Nonverbal Behavior: Categories, Origins, Usage, and Coding," *Semiotica* 1 (1969): 49-98.

8.   P. Ekman and W. Friesen, "Nonverbal Leakage and Clues to Deception," *Psychiatry* 32 (1969): 88-106.

9.   Eckhart H. Hess, "Attitude and Pupil Size," *Scientific American* (1965): 46-65.

10. Birdwhistell, *op. cit.*

11. Ekman and Friesen, "Nonverbal Leakage and Clues to Deception."

12. E.T. Hall, *The Hidden Dimension* (Garden City, N.Y.: Doubleday, 1966).

13. M. Argyle and J. Dean, "Eye Contact, Distance, and Affiliation," *Sociometry* 28 (1965): 289-304.

14. R. Sommer, "Further Studies of Small Group Ecology," *Sociometry* 28 (1965): 338-348.

15. See: A Mehrabian and S.R. Ferris, *op. cit.*; and A. Mehrabian and M. Wiener, "Decoding of Inconsistent Communication," *Journal of Personality and Social Psychology* 6 (1967): 109-114.

16. Argyle and Dean, *op. cit.*; and M. Argyle and A. Kendon, "The Experimental Analysis of Social Performance," in *Advances in Experimental Social Psychology,* ed. L. Berkowitz (New York: Academic Press, 1967), pp. 55-98.

17. A. Mehrabian, "Orientation Behavior and Nonverbal Attitude in Communication," *Journal of Communication* 17 (1967): 324-332; and A. Mehrabian, "Relationship of Attitude to Seated Posture, Orientation, and Distance" *Journal of Personality and Social Psychology* 10 (1968): 26-30.

18. Mehrabian and Wiener, *op. cit.*; and Mehrabian and Ferris, *op. cit.*

19. D.W. Addington, "The Relationship of Selected Vocal Characteristics to Personality Perception," *Speech Monographs* 35 (1967): 492-503.

20. D.S. Ellis, "Speech and Social Status in America," *Social Forces* 45 (1967): 431-451.

21. W. Wilke and J. Snyder, "Attitudes Toward American Dialects," *Journal of Social Psychology* 14 (1941): 349-362.

22. See: J.A. Starkweather, "Vocal Communication of Personality and Human Feelings," *Journal of Communication* 11 (1961): 69; and J.R. Davitz, *The Communication of Emotional Meaning* (New York: McGraw-Hill, 1964), p. 23.

23. Davitz, *op. cit.*, p. 63.

24. A. Mehrabian and M. Williams, "Nonverbal Concomitants of Perceived and Intended Persuasiveness," *Journal of Personality and Social Psychology* 13 (1969): 37-58.

25. Kenneth Sereno and G.J. Hawkins, "The Effect of Variations in Speakers' Nonfluence Upon Audience Ratings of Attitude Toward the Speech Topic and Speakers' Credibility," *Speech Monographs* 34 (1967): 58-64.

26. Gerald R. Miller and M.A. Hewgill, "The Effect of Variations in Non-fluency on Audience Rating of Source Credibility," *Quarterly Journal of Speech* 50 (1964): 36-44.

27. W.B. Pearce and F. Conklin, "Nonverbal Vocalic Communication and Perceptions of a Speaker," *Speech Monographs* 38 (1971): 235-241.

28. W.B. Pearce, "The Effect of Vocal Cues on Credibility and Attitude Change," *Western Speech* 35 (1971): 176-184.

29. Charles Woolbert, "The Effects of Various Modes of Public Reading," *Journal of Applied Psychology* 4 (1920): 162-185; and G.M. Glasgow, "A Semantic Index of Vocal Pitch," *Speech Monographs* 19 (1952): 64-68. One study reports failure to detect a relationship: C.F. Diehl, R.C. White, and P.H. Saltz, "Pitch Change and Comprehension," *Speech Monographs* 28 (1961): 65-68.

30. C.F. Diehl and E.T. McDonald, "Effect of Voice Quality on Communication," *Journal of Speech and Hearing Disorders* 21 (1956): 233-237.

31. Mark L. Knapp, *Nonverbal Communication in Human Interaction* (New York: Holt, Rinehart and Winston, 1972), p. 165.

4

Becoming Aware of

CONTEXTS

It will come as no surprise that communication
occurs in contexts. Most of our communication occurs
in face-to-face interpersonal contexts, so this book
has been primarily oriented in that direction up
to this point. However, there are certain contexts which
impose special considerations: writing and
public speaking introduce problems of organization
and timing; small groups, formal organizations,
and mass society require attention to communication
flow in social structures; and intercultural and interracial
communication are complicated by collisions among
different cultural assumptions. Your awareness of
general communication processes, of people,
and of messages should help now in developing awareness of the constraints imposed
by these specialized contexts.

Chapter Thirteen

Writing and Public Speaking: Organizing Extended Messages with Restricted Feedback

In some communication situations there is one primary communicator who is more or less designated "the source" and is allowed to speak or write at some length with little or no interruption. This differs radically from most communication situations in which messages are usually short, there is a great deal of interruption and feedback, and messages flow back and forth.

But there are sometimes good reasons for adopting the "monologue" format. When a person has an important and relatively complex idea, it may be more efficient to present it in an extended monologue so it can be explained coherently and developed in some rational sequence. Or it may be that information must be shared with a group so large that to allow unrestricted verbal feedback would produce hopeless confusion. Or it may be that the medium in which the message is presented is one which restricts immediate feedback. This is true in the case of a speech on TV, and it is also true in the case of most written messages.

While you are in college, chances are you will frequently have to occupy the position of "source" in such situations. You will probably be assigned to give reports in some of your classes, for example, or you will be assigned to write papers. After graduation the frequency with which you make speeches, give reports, and write papers will depend on your occupation. If you are going to teach, you will probably do so fairly regularly, as you will if you become a politician or professional writer.

But those in other professions, too, are expected to be able to produce coherent public speeches and written reports. The most successful business people, engineers, scientists, medical doctors, architects — those who are successful in most professions, in fact — will be successful to some extent because they are capable of producing organized and interesting public speeches and papers. And the more successful they become, the more frequently they will be called upon to speak and write. Further, while this type of communication may be a very small proportion of your total communication, it will probably make a disproportionately large contribution to your future success, because such occasions are likely to be very *important* ones. One does not usually speak to large audiences on trivial occasions. It is potentially embarrassing and inconsiderate to waste the time of a large audience with a speech which is disorganized, incoherent, and boring.

Further, some knowledge of public speaking and writing will be helpful to you as a listener and reader. It will help you to know what to look for: how to better comprehend informative messages and how to spot organizational techniques in messages designed to persuade you.

The primary difference between an extended monologue and other communication formats is that of organization. In communication *exchanges,* organization develops as the transaction proceeds, but in a *monologue* organization must be *planned.* The speaker or writer must anticipate audience questions and reactions, because they probably will not be verbalized. This is largely a matter of empathy again. The source must try to imagine himself in the position of the receiver—to imagine what the receiver will be thinking and feeling at each point in the message and what the receiver would like to ask or say if he were free to do so.

The first three parts of this book have been designed to provide a basis for such empathy. If you are aware of the general principles of communication, aware of differences among people, and aware of the various aspects of messages, you are well on the way to putting yourself in the place of an audience even when that audience can give you only limited feedback or no feedback at all. And you can usually pretest how successfully you have empathized by asking some people who are similar to your prospective audience to listen to your speech or read your paper before you present it.

But the empathic ability I hope you have developed needs to be applied to this specific situation, and that application can be facilitated, I believe, if we think about some of the problems involved in organizing extended messages.

Actually, the remainder of this chapter is going to deal with two general topics. The first section is concerned with the *internal* organization of messages, and the second with the ways in which public speeches, articles, and papers which a given audience encounters interact with one another to produce an overall effect.

Internal Organization

Good speakers and writers generally arrange their messages quite deliberately and have good reasons for their arrangement, although

they won't always be able to explain those reasons. On the other hand, it is easy to be *overorganized,* to such a degree that audience understanding depends upon following too many complex turns and interdependencies, or to such a degree that more time is spent in introduction, transitions, and conclusions than is spent in explanation or argument. *Good organization is that which follows naturally from the material, aiding understanding, acceptance, and retention without becoming noticeable and distracting.* I will deal first with some of the considerations which suggest the way in which the body of the message can be organized most clearly, and will deal secondly with some means by which the listener can be helped to follow that organization. I will frequently speak of an organizational device or method as "effective." That is, it is likely to produce an effect which is desirable from the source's point of view. As a receiver, one will be more interested in whether the device will help or hinder a rational decision. Knowing the *effect* of the device will help answer that question.

Patterns of Organization

It is much easier to organize a message when the material to be covered is not controversial, because one does not need to deal with all the organizational considerations which persuasion entails. Persuasion requires that the material be organized so it can be understood, of course, but it introduces new problems which often require that the patterns which would be ideal for understanding and recall be modified so as to achieve acceptance.

Organizing for Understanding and Recall

Often the material to be explained will suggest the order in which it ought to be explained. If you are going to explain a process, it seems reasonable to begin at the beginning and proceed *chronologically.* No one would first explain to his roommate how to twist the ends of a joint and then go back to explain how to dry the leaves, unless he had already been smoking. Similarly, the explanation of an object or scene generally suggests the use of some *spatial order:* left to right, top to bottom, near to far, inside to outside, and so forth.

Those are easy. The difficult organizational material is covered in most textbooks under the heading of "The Topical Pattern." I suspect this is really one of those "etcetera" categories, containing all materials which are not obviously chronological or spatial. In these cases in which the material suggests no obvious order, it is much more difficult for the textbook writer to make astute and profound suggestions. I will, however, explain five important considerations, none of which are either astute or profound, but all of which seem to me to make sense.

First, explanation of some parts of the material will depend upon explanation of other parts. Definitions of basic terms are usually necessary at the outset if those terms will be used later in the explanation. Similarly, there may be basic and relatively simple concepts which need to be explained first because their understanding is necessary to the understanding of more complex concepts to come later. For example, it is useful for the receiver to know about the composition of the atmosphere before encountering an explanation of combustion, and useful for the receiver to understand combustion before coming upon an explanation of the production of carbon monoxide. On the other hand, you may want to explain an overriding or very inclusive concept at the outset and then explain its component concepts; you might, for example, define "atmospheric pollution" in general and then explain the various types or causes of atmospheric pollution.

Second, it may be possible to take advantage of knowledge the audience already has. If they already know something about what you are going to explain, you may be able to begin with what they know and lead them gently into the unknown. If they know about something very similar to what you are going to explain, it may help to describe the similarities and then explain the differences.

Third, remember that the most difficult explanation should come when your listeners are best able to cope with it. That will probably be near the beginning of the message, after allowing a brief warm-up. It is probably best, if it can be arranged, to follow the explanation of basic terms and concepts with the part of the explanation you consider to be most difficult.

Fourth, try to decide where the attention of the audience is likely to lag, and put the most interesting parts of the explanation at those points. Certainly you want to begin the message with something interesting. Probably it is a good idea to follow each very complex explanation with something less complex and more interesting, and to conclude the message with something of high interest value.

Finally, the research does seem to indicate fairly clearly that the first and last parts of a message are better remembered than is the material in the middle, all else being equal.[1] There is a strong suggestion that the first part of a message is remembered *longer* than the last part. Consequently, the material might reasonably be arranged so that the most important information comes early, the next most important comes late, and the least important comes in the middle. This admonition is of primary importance when the material is *easy to understand* and the primary purpose is to cause the receivers to *remember* it; the first four considerations may be more important when the explanation is very difficult to understand. Obviously, there are situations in which each of these five considerations would lead one to adopt a different order, so one must use judgment.

> *Communication is almost always more artistic than scientific, and it probably will remain so throughout our lifetimes at least.*

Organizing for Acceptance

The complexity of the decisions a speaker must make increases considerably when the information in the message is not immediately acceptable to the audience, or when one wants to persuade the audience to take some specific action which they would not otherwise take. There are at least six considerations which may cause one to modify the organization he would choose if he had merely to present information without being concerned about its acceptance.

First, if the source tells the audience at the outset that his purpose is to persuade them to accept a position or perform an action which is at that point unacceptable to them, they may prepare themselves to reject his arguments and may refute each one in turn. This is especially true if the source is for one reason or another somewhat unattractive to the audience, or if they are especially opposed to his point of view.[2] If the audience likes the source and if the position advocated is not too different from their own, they may be gratified to learn that he values their opinions enough to want to persuade them. In that case he will probably be more successful if he states the thesis, purpose, and major arguments clearly at the outset of the speech and proceeds to support each argument in turn. However, if one is not so fortunate, he may obtain better results by presenting the arguments as if they were primarily informational, *leading* the audience instead of *pushing* them to accept the conclusions. The audience may move to the source's position without ever being told what they *should* believe.

This is closely allied to the second general rule: that the source may well begin with those propositions which the audience already accepts and lead them as gently as possible to accept those which they initially reject. He may lead them in successive small steps from their initial position to that which he hopes they will accept, or he may use their initial beliefs as premises and demonstrate how they lead logically to the conclusions. In either case the source avoids the unattractive appearance of attempting to impose his own beliefs on others.

A third question is whether the strongest arguments should be placed first or last.[3] Obviously one should not use *weak* arguments, but usually the arguments will differ in effectiveness. I have already suggested that the strongest arguments will be best remembered if they are placed *either* first or last. If the source's credibility is not extremely high, it will probably raise that credibility to begin with a very persuasive argument. Once credibility is established, the audience may not be so hostile to the rest of the message. On the other hand, if credibility is not in question and if the message is short enough that one can depend on having the listeners' attention at the end, it may be advantageous to build to a climax near the end. This arrangement is especially useful if opposing arguments are going to be expressed by another source immediately afterward. The opposing source will have a more difficult job if that strongest argument is fresh in the minds of the audience.

Generally, a persuasive message can be viewed as presenting a *solution to a problem*. The source will usually demonstrate some reason for a change and demonstrate that the proposal is indeed a solution. However, there are two possible approaches: one may demonstrate that problems exist, describe the proposal, and demonstrate that the proposal will solve the problem, or one may describe the proposal and then demonstrate its advantages over the existing system. The major consideration here is whether the audience is likely to be initially hostile to the proposal. If they are, it is probably better to emphasize the severity of the problems at the outset. Otherwise, and especially if there are no glaring problems in the present system, it may be more effective to present the proposal first and then dwell upon its advantages.

The fifth question concerns the point at which one undertakes to refute opposing arguments.* If the source has reason to believe that the receivers are preoccupied with opposing arguments before the message, he had best deal with those arguments immediately. Otherwise they may not pay much attention to attempts at constructive persuasion. What he may want to avoid at this point, however, is introducing opposing arguments which the audience has never encountered, or reminding them of objections which would not be salient if they were not mentioned. The objections refuted at the outset, for best effect, will be only those of which the receivers are already quite aware and which might interfere with their attention to the constructive part of the message. Objections which they might think of later are probably best dealt with after the constructive argument has been presented and, hopefully, after one has secured from them some sort of commitment to the proposal.

Finally, we encounter the question of whether one should cite the source of information before or after the information is presented. The general rule seems to be this: if the credibility of the source of the

---

* *The reader should be aware that the suggestions on this point are somewhat speculative, being based on personal experience and* a priori *analysis. Nevertheless the suggestions seem to follow logically from the research dealing with the listeners' silent refutation of the source's arguments, cited in footnote two, and from experiments dealing with the interaction of messages. Still, the only study which is directly relevant failed to find any significant effect of placement of refutation, at least when the audience was hostile. See Donald L. Thistlethwaite, Joseph Kamenetsky, and Hans Schmidt, "Refutation and Attitude Change,"* Speech Monographs *23 (1956): 14-25.*

information is higher than your own, it will be most effective if the source of the information is cited first; otherwise it will be more effective if the information is given and then attributed to its source. Research seems to indicate that if the audience knows the source before they encounter the information their opinions of the source will influence their acceptance or rejection of the information, but their opinions of the source have little effect if they hear the information first.[4]

Armed with all of these considerations, you may simply disintegrate into a state of hopeless confusion. The organization of a message is by its very nature complex, and it appears more complex as one learns more about it. The beginning source makes the same decisions as the experienced source but does so without knowing why and often without knowing he or she has made them. At best, the experienced source may use information such as this to improve effectiveness. Obviously, one will not always make all the decisions correctly. At the very worst, the experienced source will have a greater variety of explanations for failures.

Methods of Maintaining Order

In the previous section I discussed the *sequencing* of the material within messages, attempting to provide criteria or rationales which will allow the source to arrange the message in such a way as to achieve maximal understanding and acceptance. In this section I am going to proceed on the assumption that if a message is divided into parts, and if the audience knows what these parts are and understands the relations among the parts, they will be better able to remember and respond reasonably to the message.

That psychological principle is well established and easy to demonstrate. To call San Quentin prison from some office phones one would have to dial 914154541460. That number would be rather difficult to remember, even for someone addicted to calling San Quentin every day. However, it is much simpler to remember if one understands that the number consists of "9" to get an outside line, "1" to reach the Direct Distance Dialing equipment, "415" to reach the San Francisco area, "454" to reach the San Quentin exchange, and "1460" to reach the prison. Thus the number is easier to remember when written 9-1-415-

454-1460, especially for someone familiar with the idiosyncrasies of Ma Bell. Since digit span difficulty increases up to a practical maximum of about seven (plus or minus two) digits or items for the general population, the general rule is that the number of major divisions in a message and the number of subdivisions under each major division should be balanced so as to be as few as possible, generally in the range from two to four. I say "balanced" because if there are fewer major divisions there are likely to be more subdivisions, and vice versa.

It is probably clearest for the source to outline the material so as to make certain the divisions are clear, easy to understand, and more or less equal in that each contains roughly the same amount of material and requires about the same amount of time or space to cover as every equivalent division. At least no gross inequalities should exist, or the purpose is defeated. I will not attempt to prescribe an outline form. Here is a typical and relatively acceptable sentence outline of a message. Since the message was never presented, I cannot report on its effectiveness, which is probably just as well.

Speech Outline

THESIS: Approaching the corner correctly, choosing the best line, and steering with the accelerator are necessary to drift a sports car through a simple corner at maximum speed without wiping out.

DEFINITIONS: (As necessary for the audience)

I. Approaching the corner correctly involves braking, shifting, and placing the car correctly on the road.
   A. Brake as late as possible, but complete braking before entering the corner.
   B. Correct shifting involves use of the tachometer and gearbox.
      1. Watch the rpm indicated by the tachometer to avoid lugging and overrevving.
      2. Choose the lowest gear you will use in accelerating out of the corner, so that the engine will be operating above its torque peak but well below its power peak.

    C. Place the car at the outside of the curve, pointed at an angle toward the inside.

II. The best line depends on the location of the apex and the straightaways.
    A. The apex is the point of maximum curvature.
    B. The best line begins and ends at the outside of the curve and approaches the inside at a point near the apex, which depends on the location of the straightaways.
      1. If the straightaway precedes the curve, brake late and cut the corner after the apex so as to maintain speed as long as possible.
      2. If the straightaway follows the curve, brake early and cut the corner before the apex so as to gain speed for the straightaway as early as possible.
      3. If there are no straightaways at either end, or straightaways at both ends, compromise.

III. Steering when the car is in a four-wheel drift or power slide is accomplished primarily by use of the accelerator, using the steering wheel for minor corrections.
    A. A car is drifting when it is sliding sideways at an angle to the road with the front end pointed toward the inside of the curve and the front wheels pointed toward the outside.
    B. In this situation, accelerating will slide the rear wheels further out, increasing the slip angle of the car and forcing it toward the inside of the curve.
    C. Decelerating will decrease the slip angle, forcing the car toward the outside of the curve.
    D. Too much acceleration will force the rear wheels out too far, causing the car to spin.

CONCLUSION: The novice racing driver who knows how to set a car into a corner and steer it through the correct line by delicate use of the accelerator has only one thing further to remember: if all else fails, aim for the hay bales.

Once the source has divided his material and arranged it in a reasonable sequence, the remaining problem is to indicate to the audience what the arrangement is. The basic procedure, subject to modification due to some of the considerations already mentioned, is to indicate the basic pattern of organization at the outset of the speech, use transitions to let the audience know when you are moving from one point to another, and summarize the major points in the conclusion. This procedure maintains the greatest clarity, but it cannot very well be followed in the sort of persuasive message in which the source wants to lead the audience to a conclusion. Introductions, transitions, and conclusions can also become very obtrusive and mechanical if they occupy too much time and if the source lacks artistry and subtlety.

Introductions

Actually, introductions serve a multitude of purposes in addition to that of clarifying organization. You can try to make the audience like you and respect your opinions sometimes by the use of humor, almost always by emphasizing areas of agreement and, when possible, by allowing them to discover the "credentials" which qualify you to discuss the topic, if you can do this without giving the impression of bragging. *The introduction is also the first point at which you can try to capture the attention and interest of the listeners, but you do not "capture" it in the sense that it can be securely caged and then left alone.* Instead, you will have to use devices to gain attention at the outset of the message and devices to maintain it throughout. Arousing audience curiosity and demonstrating the relevance and importance of the topic or proposal are two of those devices most often used in the introduction.

The introduction is also the point at which you can introduce such background material and definitions as the audience will need to understand the remainder of the message. In an explanatory message it is probably best to state the *thesis* in the introduction. The thesis is a one-sentence summary of the entire message. In a persuasive message the thesis is the statement of the position which you would like the listeners to accept. As I pointed out before, it is not so effective to state the thesis of a persuasive message in the introduction if the listeners will be so hostile to it as to interfere with their acceptance or rational evaluation of the arguments which follow. The same is true of the statement of the purpose: its appearance in the introduction will probably clarify an informational message, but it may interfere with acceptance and reasonable evaluation of a persuasive message. Finally, the major divisions of the message may be somehow indicated in the introductions, except in a persuasive message, again, in which a statement of major arguments will often put a hostile audience on the defensive.

Transitions

Transitions are always important, but they are especially important in the case in which a persuader has chosen to forego the statements of thesis, purpose, and major divisions. The intent in such a case is to *lead* the audience to a conclusion, and the transitions serve as the gentle signposts by which they are led. Probably the worst transition is "Now I am going to my second major point," but the next worse is "Let us consider, secondly. . . ." Of course you will find those in profusion throughout this book. Hopefully you will be more imaginative than I have been.

Transitions, or at least the points at which they appear, are also good places for interest and attention material. Of course the entire speech should be interesting, but just in case the entire audience is not electrified and totally enthralled, the points of transition offer themselves as convenient places to pay some extra attention to attention.

Conclusions

The conclusion can serve at least two functions: it can *summarize* and *provide a climax* for the message. *Too often the message dies at the end of the body, and the conclusion becomes merely an obituary.* Instead, the most effective conclusion is one which brings the listeners to a peak of attention and interest at the same time as it summarizes the major points. You should look for ways to prevent the message from giving the appearance of ending; it should, instead, remain open, inviting the audience to become involved with its material. Question and answer sessions are one standard but not very imaginative means of allowing the audience to become actively involved. You should search your material carefully to find others especially appropriate.

The conclusion of a *persuasive* message will almost certainly be more effective if it contains an appeal for a *specific, immediate,* and *committing* action. If the audience will actually do something at the conclusion of the message, they will later feel obliged to justify having done it and will help persuade themselves even after the message is over. It is much more effective if the action taken is one which would be difficult to justify on any grounds other than rational agreement with the source, so that the audience cannot later rationalize away their commitment. Beyond the advantage of helping to commit the receivers, there is some evidence that such an appeal will cause them to have greater respect for the source.[5] Apparently they view a source who makes an appeal for action as a "doer," not merely a "talker," perceiving him or her as more sincere and active than if there were no such appeal.

There is one case in which the appeal for commitment may well come earlier in the message, however. If the source has chosen to put the constructive arguments first and then refute opposing arguments, the appeal for commitment might reasonably come after constructive argument and before refutation. The procedure is to persuade the receiver, get commitment, and then innoculate the receiver against counterarguments which might come later. After commitment he is less likely to catch some of the disease as a result of the innoculation.

Timing of Messages

Sequencing and timing of messages is important whenever an audience encounters a series of messages, whether those messages are all from the same source or from different sources. Messages can affect each other directly; they can affect each other as a result of having common sources; they can serve as mediators which allow sources to affect each other; and, in combination with feedback, they provide the means by which one audience can affect a source, modifying that source's subsequent messages to other audiences.

It appears that audiences can encounter messages on opposite sides of a question and encounter them in fairly close succession, without the first influencing the second to any appreciable extent. That is true if they merely hear or read the messages. However, if the receivers *commit* themselves in some way after the first message, or if they are *forewarned* that counterargument will follow, then they are likely to be less responsive to a second message contradicting the first.

Most of the research dealing with forewarning has been done by William McGuire or by someone testing his theories.[6] Forewarning and refutations seem to become more effective if the receivers have some time between the first and second messages. McGuire theorizes that forewarning acts as a sort of "innoculation," and receivers need some time to construct "belief defenses" against the countermessage. It is interesting that forewarning appears to work just as well if the arguments which the receivers later encounter are not even those which were mentioned and refuted; in fact, it seems to work best if some of the arguments encountered have actually been refuted and some have not. Further, the effect seems to be enhanced if the source can get the receivers to actively participate in constructing refutations for counterarguments. In fact, the whole procedure begins to take on the appearance of a training session in which the receivers are taught to refute counterarguments. The source taking full advantage of our knowledge to this point would say something like this:

> Look, you're going to run into arguments on the other side of this question. I'll tell you what some of them are and what's wrong with some of them, but I wish you'd help me think up refutations for some of the others. Also, since I can't begin to tell you what all the opposing arguments may be, try to keep alert to what's wrong with any new arguments you may hear.

Whereas the effectiveness of most types of persuasion decreases as time passes, the effectiveness of this sort of immunization appears to *increase,* if anything. There are two important qualifications. One is that there is some evidence receivers who are forewarned may begin changing their beliefs in the direction of the counterattack apparently so that the counterattack will not be so disparate from their own opinions.[7] Getting strong commitment from the receivers *before* they are forewarned will reduce that effect. The second caution is that refutation seems to be far more effective if it comes *before* the counterattack rather than afterward.[8]

When the same source produces two or more messages, an audience aware of his preceding messages will respond to the one at hand in a way that depends at least in part upon what they thought of the others. If the earlier messages caused the audience to perceive the source as less credible, their suspicions regarding his credibility will be reflected in a reluctance to accept what he says now. Further, messages the audience has encountered from other sources will affect their responses to the one at hand to the extent that the previous messages are relevant and salient.[9] Their reaction to the message at hand will also affect their responses to the present source and his future messages. Suppose, for example, Charles Fedders, a relatively unknown speaker, comes on campus urging demonstrations and disturbances just after a speaker the students highly respect has urged them to cool it at least until after the elections to see what they can do by political means. The students could be expected to reject Fedders, his message, and any future messages he comes up with. It isn't entirely a matter of getting there first; Fedders' reputation and his subsequent persuasive effectiveness could have suffered even if he had spoken before the more respected speaker. This chaining can continue from message to message and speaker to speaker longer than anyone cares to observe. It is a good illustration of the statement in an earlier chapter that the process of communication doesn't have a beginning or an end. We may cease to be interested in it, but it goes on and on.

Finally, one audience can interact with another when they encounter the same source. The source states opinions before the first audience. They use whatever feedback channels are available to them to indicate that they like some of what the speaker says and dislike the rest. He is likely to drop or underemphasize what they disliked and increase the emphasis on what they liked when speaking to the next audience. The first audience has affected what the second hears and they in turn, partly as a result of what they have heard, will affect subsequent sources and messages. Again, the chain is endless. Audiences are not "passive." They work actively to change the opinions of speakers they hear, to change messages those speakers produce in the future, which change future audiences so they respond differently to subsequent speakers.[10]

I have generally directed my advice in this chapter to the communicator in the role of message source, since it is in the role of source that

one organizes and sequences messages. However, organization concerns one as receiver also. Unclear organization makes it difficult to decide whether or not a message is rational. A receiver is entitled to know what a source is proposing, what his evidence and arguments are, and how they relate to one another. Otherwise, any chance of evaluating the message rationally may evaporate in the confusion.

Generally, then, the advice I have given about how messages can be more clearly organized should benefit a person in the role of receiver. Some techniques of persuasive organization, however, if used by a source intent on manipulating an audience, could really be detrimental to the receivers trying to listen critically so as to gather reliable information. Such a source might try to get the receivers to commit themselves before they have heard any opposing arguments, for instance. That may not be to the receivers' advantage, so they need to be aware of it. Any organizational technique which makes the receiver less aware of how he is making decisions is likely to be to his disadvantage. On the other hand, a receiver has some obligations in this regard, too. For example, if a source tells the thesis of the message in the introduction and the receiver disagrees with that thesis, he or she ought to be aware that this initial disagreement may produce irrational hostility which will prevent critical evaluation of the new information.

Thus message organization and timing are of concern to everyone involved in a communication event.

Summary

When a source presents an extended message with little audience feedback, several considerations seem important. Some of those considerations have to do with *audience comprehension,* and others have to do with *audience acceptance.* Beyond considerations concerned with the *order* in which the material is presented, there are a number of devices which can be used to make that order more comprehensible and acceptable. When messages occur in a sequence, they can affect one another. *Forewarning* of future counterarguments the audience may encounter will reduce the effects of those counterarguments. Previous messages the audience has encountered will have favorable or unfavorable effects upon audience acceptance of the present message and upon their opinions of its source, as will future messages the audience will encounter. Further, audience response to the present source will have an effect upon the messages he produces in the future, which will in turn affect his future audiences and their future reactions to still other sources and messages.

Suggestions for Developing Awareness

1. Imagine that an acquaintance of yours expresses his or her views on the legalization of marijuana. A week later, a person you respect voices a different opinion on the same topic. What happens to your opinion of your acquaintance? the person you respect? Which of them are you likely to believe? Why?

2. Analyze a political speech, using the organizational pattern suggested in this chapter. The following questions may be used as guides:
   (a) Is the introduction used to tell you that the speaker intends to persuade you or to establish the speaker's credibility?
   (b) How are transitions handled?
   (c) Are jokes or entertaining stories used? If so, where in the text do they appear? Are they appropriate?
   (d) How does the organizational pattern of the speech influence you?
   (e) Does the speaker ask you to do something?
   (f) Does the conclusion summarize the arguments? Is there a climax or high point of interest?

   You might want to try this same approach for an informative message (a chapter from this book, a lecture, or a student's paper).

3. Prepare an outline of a public speech or a paper. Indicate what you will do in the introduction and conclusion, and what transitions you will use. Discuss with the class why you organized as you did. You might try actually delivering the speech.

References

1. See, for example: H.F. Adams, "The Effects of Climax and Anti-Climax Order," *Journal of Applied Psychology* 4 (1920): 330-338; A. Jersild, "Primacy, Recency, Frequency, and Vividness," *Journal of Experimental Psychology* 12 (1929): 58-70; Harold Sponberg, "A Study of the Relative Effectiveness of Climax and Anti-Climax Order in an Argumentative Speech," *Speech Monographs* 13 (1946): 35-44; J.W. Doob, "Effects of Initial Serial Position and Attitude Upon Recall Under Conditions of Low Motivation," *Journal of Abnormal and Social Psychology* 44 (1953): 199-205; Percy H. Tannenbaum, "Effect of Serial Position on Recall of Radio News Stories," *Journalism Quarterly* 31 (1954): 319-323.

2. The effects of forewarning in general are well summarized by William J. McGuire in "Inducing Resistance to Persuasion," in *Advances in Experimental Social Psychology*, vol. I, ed. L. Berkowitz (New York: Academic Press, 1964); and in "Attitudes and Opinions," *Annual Review of Psychology* 17 (1966): 475-514. Studies which are especially relevant here are: Jane Allyn and Leon Festinger, "The Effectiveness of Unanticipated Persuasive Communication," *Journal of Abnormal and Social Psychology* 62 (1961): 35-40; Elaine Walster and Leon Festinger, "The Effectiveness of 'Overheard' Persuasive Communications," *Journal of Abnormal and Social Psychology* 65 (1962): 395-402; Timothy C. Brock and Lee Becker, "Ineffectiveness of 'Overheard' Counterpropaganda," *Journal of Personality and Social Psychology* 2 (1965): 654-660; Judson Mills and Elliot Aronson, "Opinion Change as a Function of the Communicator's Attractiveness and Desire to Influence," *Journal of Personality and Social Psychology* 1 (1965): 173-177; Judson Mills, "Opinion Change as a Function of the Communicator's Desire to Influence and Liking for the Audience," *Journal of Experimental Social Psychology* 2 (1966): 152-159.

3. Research findings on this question are mixed, probably because of the various operational definitions of argument strength and because of different audience attitudes toward the topics and the sources, among other considerations. It seems clear that "strong" arguments by any definition are more effective if placed *either* first or last. See: Sponberg, *op. cit.;* Harvey Cromwell, "The Relative Effect on Audience Attitude of the First Versus the Second Argumentative Speech of a Series," *Speech Monographs* 17 (1950): 105-122; Howard Gilkinson, Stanley F. Paulson, and Donald E. Sikkink, "Effects of Order and Authority in an Argumentative Speech," *Quarterly Journal of Speech* 40 (1954): 183-192;

Halford E. Gulley and David K. Berlo, "Effect of Intercellular and Intracellular Speech Structure on Attitude Change and Learning," *Speech Monographs* 23 (1956): 288-297; and Donald E. Sikkink, "An Experimental Study of the Effects on the Listener of Anti-Climax Order and Authority in an Argumentative Speech," *Southern Speech Journal* 22 (1956): 73-78.

4. See: T.R. Husek, "Persuasive Impacts of Early, Late, or No Mention of a Negative Source," *Journal of Personality and Social Psychology* 2 (1965): 125-128; Percy H. Tannenbaum, J. Macauley, and E. Norris, "Principle of Congruity and Reduction of Persuasion," *Journal of Personality and Social Psychology* 3 (1966): 233-238; and Bradley S. Greenberg and Gerald R. Miller, "The Effects of Low-Credible Sources on Message Acceptance," *Speech Monographs* 33 (1966): 127-136.

5. Phillips R. Biddle, "An Experimental Study of Ethos and Appeal for Overt Behavior in Persuasion" (Doctoral dissertation, University of Illinois, 1966).

6. McGuire, *op. cit.*

7. See: William J. McGuire and Susan Millman, "Anticipatory Belief-Lowering Following Forewarning of a Persuasive Attack," *Journal of Personality and Social Psychology* 2 (1965): 471-479; Melvin Manis and Joan P. Blake, "Interpretation of Persuasive Messages as a Function of Prior Immunization," *Journal of Abnormal and Social Psychology* 66 (1963): 225-230; and Melvin Manis, "Immunization, Delay, and the Interpretation of Persuasive Messages," *Journal of Personality and Social Psychology* 1 (1965): 541-550.

8. See: Tannenbaum, Macauley, and Norris, *op. cit.;* and Charles A. Kiesler and Sara B. Kiesler, "Role of Forewarning in Persuasive Communications," *Journal of Abnormal and Social Psychology* 68 (1964): 547-549.

9. See: Percy H. Tannenbaum and R. Gengel, "Generalization of Attitude Change Through Congruity Principle Relationships," *Journal of Personality and Social Psychology* 3 (1966): 299-304; and Percy H. Tannenbaum, "Mediated Generalization of Attitude Change via the Principle of Congruity," *Journal of Personality and Social Psychology* 3 (1966): 493-500.

10. See: Raymond A. Bauer, "The Obstinate Audience: The Influence Process from the Point of View of Social Communication," *American*

Psychologist 19 (1964): 319-328; and the proceedings of a conference attended by Bauer, Herbert Krugmar, Elihu Katz, and Nathan Maccoby, among others, in *The Obstinate Audience,* ed. Donald E. Payne (Ann Arbor, Mich.: Foundation for Research on Human Behavior, 1965).

The Flow of Communication
in Social Structures:
Groups, Organizations,
and Mass Society

Social structures have a strong influence on communication patterns, of course. That is, communication patterns tend to develop differently in small face-to-face groups as compared with large organizations in which there is some formal hierarchy, and differently again as compared with those which develop in society at large.

In this chapter I would like to discuss specifically why communication *flows* differently in different social contexts. I will not try to discuss group communication, organizational communication, and mass communication *in general;* that would be far too ambitious an undertaking. But I believe we can get an idea of how some of the general communication principles discussed in the rest of this book must be and can be adapted and applied in these specific contexts.

Face-to-Face Groups

I am not going to spend much time worrying about what constitutes a "group." It does seem important to distinguish a "group" from an "aggregate," which is merely a collection of people who *happen* to be together at a particular time in a particular place. In my view:

> *An aggregate becomes a group when its members perceive themselves to be in some relatively important relationship to one another, so that they must depend on one another to achieve certain mutually desirable goals.*

Fifteen people waiting for a bus will probably remain an aggregate. However, if the bus fails to arrive they may form a temporary group as they make arrangements to help one another reach their destinations, or at least relieve the boredom by playing card games and the like.

In an earlier chapter I discussed why groups form and why they attract members: because the members value the *activities* of the group (sports car clubs and mate-swapping groups); because the members value their common *goals* (a group organized to pass a local school-bond referendum); because the members value *affiliation* with others

Appearances suggest this is an aggregate *rather than a* group.

in and of itself; and because the members value certain things external to the group which group membership can help them achieve (for example, country club membership helping a salesman increase his sales).

As groups develop, their communication patterns tend to change. Bales and Strodtbeck studied problem-solving groups using Bales' Interaction Process Analysis model, which was described in Chapter Three. They identified three phases in the development of such groups, which they termed "orientation," "evaluation," and "control."[1] In the *orientation* phase, communication seems to be designed to get the group organized, identify the problem, and share whatever information is possessed by individual members. During the *evaluation* phase, communication centers on resolving conflicting opinions and policies of the members, deciding which information seems to be reliable and which of the possible solutions is most likely to work. In the *control* phase, communication is used to coordinate the activities of the members in order to actually implement the chosen solution.

During these phases, however, communication will also reflect a number of other interesting social phenomena. For one thing, a *leader* and a *power hierarchy* will emerge. Predicting who will emerge as a leader has proven to be a difficult task, but there are a number of factors which at least seem to contribute to leadership. One of these seems to be the physical position of the individual: if he is seated in a prominent position and/or one in which he has greater access to communication channels, he is more likely to assume leadership. However, the emergent leader is also likely to be a person with a dominant, assertive communication style, but one who is perceived as dependable and who does not express opinions too much at variance with those of the rest of the group. It will also improve his chances of leadership if he is perceived as having special knowledge or abilities relevant to the task at hand.

Once a leader has emerged and a power hierarchy has formed, communication patterns will reflect it. Communication will begin to flow through the leader. He will come to assert more and more influence over who speaks, he will speak more often himself, and he will be spoken to more often. Communication directed toward the leader and other persons high in the hierarchy will also be of a different *kind:* it will be more deferential and approval-seeking. The leader's own communication, however, will usually reveal greater devotion and commitment to the group.

Once the power relationships are fairly well stabilized and recognized, communication will begin to reflect and facilitate interpersonal bargaining. That is, individuals will begin to band together in coalitions in order to get the group to accept their points of view. Men seem to join such coalitions for different reasons than do women, although that generalization is undoubtedly culture-bound and is probably not long for this world. Still, men generally seem to join those coalitions which have *just enough* power to achieve their goals; they will not compromise any more than they have to in order to win. Women, on the other hand, seem to form those coalitions which will be least disruptive of social relationships, so they sometimes form coalitions which will not win and at other times include more people than necessary to produce a winning coalition.

People who express unpopular opinions or refuse to cooperate with the majority are also dealt with differently at different stages of group development. Early in a discussion such people will receive an unusually large share of the communication, as the others try to persuade them to change. If they continue to deviate from the opinions of the majority, that communication will become negative; that is, they will be "sanctioned" or punished for their obstinacy. Finally, the others in the group will simply stop talking to them. On the other hand, people who start out conforming to popular opinions will later be given much greater freedom to express disagreement.

Design an experiment to test the notion that "people who express unpopular opinions or refuse to cooperate with the majority are also dealt with differently at different stages of group development." If you are going to use a class discussion for this experiment, you might want to warn the instructor of your plans. Also, a "debriefing" session afterwards might help you avoid serious conflicts with other members of the class.

I have already mentioned that seating position plays a part in the selection of a leader, but it also affects who is likely to speak to whom. Obviously, those who occupy positions which are more "central" in the sense that they allow greater access to communication channels are going to communicate more. More specifically, persons who are seated opposite one another are more likely to speak to one another rather than to those seated next to them (although this depends, of course, on the *distances* involved). But the *type* of communication is also likely to differ: people seated opposite one another are generally more likely to disagree than are people seated next to one another.

During all of this, communication networks will be constantly forming and changing. Of course, it is impossible to predict the shape of such networks, since that shape at any stage of the discussion depends on all the factors just surveyed, as well as many factors (interpersonal attraction, for example) which have not been mentioned. But it is possible to discuss the general effects of *centralized* versus decentralized networks. Those were mentioned in Chapter Three, as a matter of fact.

When a group adopts or a leader imposes a very centralized network in which communication is expected to pass through the leader, group members are usually less satisfied with the discussion. However, if the leader is capable and fair, such a centralized network will be more *efficient* in getting the task completed so that, if the group is very task-oriented, this type of network may be more satisfying. The catch is that, if the leader is *not* capable or fair, he can effectively destroy communication in a centralized network, so that the group members will have to find a way to bypass him in order to get anything done. One thing does seem clear: the closer a person is to the center of a centralized network, the more satisfied he or she is likely to be.

All of these generalizations about communication patterns in groups have exceptions. For example, not *all* communication flows through the leader and not all persons with contrary opinions are left out of the group. Think of specific instances to exemplify other exceptions.

Formal Organizations

Much of what has been said about communication flow in developing face-to-face groups can be applied to communication flow in organizations. The primary differences seem to be that (1) there is a formal pattern of communication flow in an organization; (2) there is a formal power hierarchy in an organization; (3) there is a formal decision process in an organization; and (4) these formal elements are fairly stable and less subject to development. *There are also many informal elements in a formal organization: an informal communication flow, an informal status hierarchy, and sometimes an informal decision process as well.* Coordinating all of these formal and informal structures makes organizational management the headache and the challenge it is.

Now in fact, complex as all this may sound, it is oversimplified. For one thing, many organizations do not actually have prescribed patterns of communication, power, and decision; at least they are not prescribed in the sense that they are *written* anywhere, and frequently they are not even *known* or at least agreed upon by those who should know. Further, the whole picture is additionally complicated by such considerations as: the actual physical structure of the organization, including its plant layout and/or the geographical location of its subdivisions as well as the physical communication network (phone lines, etc.); the economic structure, including the question of whether it is a profit or nonprofit organization; the nature of its output, as to whether it deals in products or services; and the pattern of flow of its products or services through the actual physical plant.

If you have decided this may quickly become impossibly complex, it may. Which is why those in management positions and communication consultants are well paid. In the face of all this, one writer has expressed the opinion that:

> . . . the most significant factor accounting for the total behavior of the organization is its communication system, and that the dynamics of the organization can be best understood by understanding its system of communication.[2]

So suppose we imagine ourselves in the place of a team of communication consultants called in to study the flow of communication in an organization. In terms of the six networks just mentioned, what would we need to know?

First, we would want to know how the management *believes* decisions are made within the organization (formal decision process) as compared with the way they *are* made (which includes the informal decision process). The formal decision process may call for certain decisions to be made or at least approved by a certain person within the organization whereas, in fact, that person simply receives and automatically approves recommendations from someone else. Conversely, someone not included in a given part of the decision process may actually hold the veto power. A mass promotional campaign, for instance, may have to be "cleared with Joe in the mailroom." And you'd better believe that if Joe says he can't get the mailings out in time, that promotional campaign is *dead*.

The reason we as communication consultants want to know how different types of decisions travel through an organization is because we must find out *who* needs to know *what*, and *when*. Poor decisions may be the result of someone receiving too little information or receiving it too late. If management is basing its communication priorities on the *formal* decision process, people who *really* make decisions may be ignored, while people who are only theoretically involved may be inundated with information. For example, if "Joe in the mailroom" had known earlier that a massive promotional campaign was in the works, he might have been able to prepare for it.

We also want to know about the formal power hierarchy and the informal status hierarchy in the organization. People with high *designated* power are likely to be *accorded* high status as well, but not necessarily. It might be useful, too, when we are asking the employees about informal status, to actually ask them two questions: (1) Who in the organization do you perceive to have power? and (2) Who in the organization do you like? Then, instead of an informal status hierarchy, we could construct a "perceived power hierarchy" and an "affiliation network."

Now if those who have high designated power are not perceived to have power and/or are not well liked, there are obvious problems which may result. Also, comparing these hierarchies with the formal and informal decision processes may be highly informative. Some person with high power may be using it to channel all decisions through himself, thus overloading himself, retarding the speed with which decisions are made, and producing a poorer quality of decision. Conversely, a person with high designated power may be acting as a figurehead, when he could be using his power to implement crucial policies.

Finally we would reach the payoff level of our analysis: the level of communication flow. One thing we would like to know is who is "supposed" to communicate with whom about what, and we would want to know whether communication in each link is "supposed" to flow one way or both ways. Probably we would find that this "idealized" formal communication network: (1) will bear a great deal of resemblance to the formal power hierarchy and the formal decision process; (2) will show most communication flowing vertically—that is, up and down the formal power hierarchy rather than horizontally among people at the same power level; and (3) will show most, if not all, communication channels open in both directions, so that communication appears to flow as easily up the hierarchy as down.

But this is the theoretical, idealized, communication network, and it is likely to be more fiction than fact. What we would be most interested in knowing is who *in fact* communicates with whom about what. We might try to find out by asking the members of the organization at all levels. If we use that approach we will have to be careful because they may report that they communicate through the expected, approved channels just as they are "supposed" to, and they may fail to mention the informal channels in which we are interested. We might try to actually observe the communication patterns. If so, we will have to do it very unobtrusively, because people standing around with pencils and clipboards can disrupt the normal communication network. To check our observations, we might inject innocuous rumors or jokes into the organization at various points and then see how they travel through the structure.

Once we were fairly certain our information was accurate, we would try to convert it to a visual diagram or, if that proved too complicated, we might use some sort of computer analysis. However we proceeded, we would want to find out to what extent we could "account for" or explain the actual communication network in terms of the formal communication network, the formal power hierarchy, the perceived power hierarchy, the affiliation network, the formal decision process, and the informal decision process. Assuming that we were called in as communication consultants because the organization was experiencing problems, we might expect to find one or more of the following conditions:

(1)   *The actual communication network bears little similarity to the formal communication network or the formal power hierarchy.* This might not be a drawback; the actual network *might* be more efficient than the formal one. So we should probably ask some more specific questions in this case. For example: Is the management expending time and money trying to impose a formal network in preference to facilitating a more natural and efficient network already functioning well? Is the formal communication network based on the formal power hierarchy and the formal decision process, whereas the actual network better reflects the actual decision process and better serves its information needs?

But the actual network may *not* be efficient, and it may need some attention. For instance, there may be too much *downward* communication in the power hierarchy without adequate upward communication, reflecting a tendency on the part of management to impose its decisions on the members without assuring adequate feedback. Further, there may be a great deal of informal communication operating only *horizontally* in the hierarchy, so that there is a great deal of information flowing at each power level, but it never flows up or down. Thus there may be much dissatisfaction compounded by inaccurate rumors at one level, but since that dissatisfaction is communicated only informally and only horizontally, upper management levels never know about it.

(2)   *The actual communication network bears little resemblance to the perceived power hierarchy.* If the formal and perceived power hierarchies are essentially identical, the problems have already been covered under (1). But if the formal and perceived power hierarchies differ from one another and from the communication network, this would mean that the members of the organization are not even communicating with the people they *believe* to be powerful, which is almost certain to indicate membership dissatisfaction.

(3)   *The actual communication network bears little resemblance to the affiliation network.* This would be an unusual condition, since people usually communicate with those they like and like those with whom they communicate. If such a condition were found, however, it would seem to indicate that the structure of the organization was somehow preventing the members from communicating with those they liked.

(4)   *The actual communication network bears little relationship to the formal and/or the actual decision process.* Whether the actual communication network relates to the *formal* decision process is not especially important, but if it does not relate to the *actual* decision process the organization is in real trouble. People in the decision "hotspots" should also be centers of communication; for the well-being of the organization, such people *must* have maximum access to information.

Now suppose our team of communication consultants identifies some serious communication problems in the organization. What steps can we recommend to reshape the communication network into a more efficient system? Practically speaking, there are two types of moves we might recommend: rearranging the personnel or rearranging the physical layout in which the organization operates. A third alternative is conceivable but not feasible: *ordering* people to change their communication patterns has about as much chance of success as praying for a spontaneous abortion.

Suppose we consider the personnel option first. One theory suggests that certain types of people attract communication the way magnets attract iron filings.[3] *Powerful* people who are *likeable* and *well informed* are communication-magnetic. It seems reasonable to try to fill the decision hotspots with such people, so long as they are also competent to handle the decisions required of them.

Management cannot *create* likeable, competent people, of course, but they can be *chosen.* They can then be placed in the decision hotspots. Their perceived power can then be enhanced by what amounts to a promotional campaign, so long as that campaign is subtle enough to avoid creating jealousy among coworkers and thus destroying their likeability. They can also be fed information others will consider important.

If we observe that there is not enough upward communication in the power hierarchy, we can use our observed communication network to identify the people who are obstructing such communication, and either replace or retrain them. If there is too much informal, horizontal communication at a given level, we can identify the people who are especially active communicators at that level and promote them to the next higher level or appoint them to serve as liaisons with adjacent levels.

Now we will consider the option of rearranging the physical environment. There are two major considerations involved: (1) people tend to communicate more with those physically close to them, and (2) areas which people necessarily frequent tend to become communication centers.

Thus if we want to encourage communication among certain people, one solution is simply to *put them together*. If it is impractical to put them together all the time, it may be possible to devise imaginative ways to get them together *some* of the time.

Which leads to the second consideration. Employee cafeterias, snack bars, vending machines, lounges, drinking fountains, and even restrooms are not just necessary evils which have to be put *somewhere* to appease the employees. Such areas, as well as the routes leading to them, are devices which can be used to facilitate communication patterns. If it is necessary to encourage communication between two isolated departments, one thing we can do is to put all their photocopying machines, vending machines, or drinking fountains together, or place the cafeterias, lounges, snack bars, and restrooms in such a way that the personnel of the two departments will be likely to share them. Separate cafeterias and lounges for staff and management can effectively sabotage communication from one power level to the other, since they effectively segregate those power levels.

All our machinations may fail, of course, because there is much about the flow of human communication which is still unpredictable. But we can certainly improve our chances for success by using all the means which are available.

Mass Society

Those who write or teach about mass communication are usually people who are themselves involved in the game or whose students are studying to be. Consequently, such writing and teaching is usually conducted from the point of view of the person who *does* mass communication. Thus the flow of communication in society is customarily traced from its "origin," usually defined as the point at which some reporter discovers it or some advertising agency creates it, to its "destination," at which the consumer accepts it or rejects it, adopts it or spurns it.

(Kandace Penner)

Ma Bell *versus* **Mother Nature.** *This simple scene would have been incomprehensible 100 years ago. Communication technology has made it possible for us to communicate with people thousands of miles away while we avoid communicating with those several inches away. This has caused drastic changes in patterns of communication flow.*

Now that approach would be perfectly reasonable if one were going to work in the mass media or the advertising industry, or run for political office. But most of us are not. Most of us are going to be *consumers* of mass communication. *Thus I am not so interested in how information is disseminated throughout society as I am in how it is funneled to me.*

So, as usual, this analysis is going to proceed backward. We are going to try to swim upstream, against the flow, to ask how consumers of mass communication can gather information and select that which is reliable from the massive barrage which rains down on us every day. But we are still concerned with the *flow* of communication, because the central question is, simply put: *Where is all this stuff coming from?*

Happily, there is a model which pictures this process from the consumer's point of view. The one I am referring to is Becker's model, described and illustrated in Chapter Three, which represents an individual circulating through a cube of data, encountering some, missing some, and determining what he will hit or miss as he chooses his path through the cube.[4] We can think of ourselves as salmon swimming up the Rogue River, if you will. On the banks are fishermen trying to lure us with all manner of delicious-looking bait. But there is also a lot of good food in that river. We have to eat *something,* so we have to learn how to tell which tasty morsels have hooks in them. Sometimes you can tell by the way it wiggles, and sometimes you can see the line. In some previous chapters I have described how hooked bait wiggles. Now I am going to talk about how to spot the line.

In the same article in which Becker presented his model, he also gave an interesting description of how he first learned about the assassination of Martin Luther King and the events surrounding it:

> If we could reconstruct and compare the ways in which each of us got and continues to get the message of Eugene McCarthy, or of the Ted Kennedy-Mary Jo Kopechne accident, or of the student demonstrations at Berkeley or Columbia University, we would begin to get some sense of the variations in the message which each of us has experienced. To illustrate this conception of message that I am proposing, I have tried to reconstruct as accurately and completely as possible the way in which I was exposed to the message of the murder of Martin Luther King during the forty-eight-hour period following the event. I first heard of the assassination from a Chicago cab driver as we were coming into the LaSalle Hotel for the Central States Speech Convention. He wondered (aloud of

course) whether President Johnson was going on television that night. My query about whether something new had occurred regarding the Vietnam peace feelers brought the information about King. In rather quick but scattered succession over the next two days I heard snatches of conversation about these events in the hallways and lobby and meeting rooms of the hotel; I heard an assortment of newscasters and interviews with Negro and white leaders; I saw film footage of the burning and looting; I heard Whitney Young of the Urban League declaring that it was time for us self-styled white liberals to stop talking and start doing; I read stories in the Chicago papers about the events; I saw the store window across from the hotel broken by one of a group of Negro youngsters who marched by; I heard an impassioned speech in a hotel room by a close friend justifying the burning and looting being done by Negroes in many parts of the country; I saw the hotel employees locking all of the entrances to the hotel but one; and I engaged in discussion with my friends and colleagues about whether it was safe to go out of the hotel for dinner. And these were only a small portion of the relevant bits of the message to which I was exposed during that two-day period. Not only was I exposed to bits of the message, I was forced to respond to many — to create my own bits and, in the process, to develop points of view about the events. Many of these communication transactions were redundant. I saw some of the films on television innumerable times; I heard and read some of the same stories; I even heard myself responding to various individuals with the same phrases. In other words, there were two kinds of processes at work: there was an ever-increasing number and variety of pieces and sources of information and, at the same time, there was a certain amount of repetitiveness, of going through the same or similar transactions again and again.

You can probably recall similar experiences. For example, how did you encounter information about such things as the "Watergate" conspiracy, Nixon's resignation, the threat spray cans pose to the ozone layer, genetic damage related to LSD, opposition to the Vietnam war, the energy crisis, inflation, double-knit fabrics, and automobile emission controls?

The two-step flow is not a new dance. Actually it is a rather old dance. The term refers to the fact that most people do not get their information about a given news event or new product *first* and *directly* from the media. Rather, most of us get our first information from other people who get theirs directly from the media.

But that is a bit oversimplified. In fact, it seems more useful to go back to the concept of communication networks fanning out from the media.

Downstream from the Media

Those who get their information directly from the media and are influential in disseminating it have been labeled "gatekeepers" by those writers interested in information flow, "opinion leaders" by those interested in mass opinion change, and "early adopters" by those interested in the diffusion of innovations.

Actually, of course, there are different gatekeepers for different kinds of information. True, there are people who are *generally* well informed on many topics, but gatekeepers tend to specialize. Thus my sources of political information may or may not be the same as my sources for information about new music, books, and movies, and those in turn may or may not be the same as my sources for information about new automobiles and automotive products, new birth control methods, the availability and effects of drugs, etc.

Further, there are *networks* of such gatekeepers who feed information to one another and then downstream to their "clientele." Thus I saw the new four-passenger Lotus in a parking lot and went immediately to a newsstand to look for a road test report in *Road and Track* or *Car and Driver*. But I wasn't satisfied with that; I had to talk to someone who had driven one. So far I have only been able to talk to someone who has talked to someone who has driven one. Eventually I hope to find someone who *owns* one. In turn, I am anxious to tell the people I know who are interested in sports cars, so I can show off my newfound knowledge and enhance my credibility as a sports car aficionado. So I find myself opening conversations with the exciting gambit: "Hey, have you seen the new Lotus?" This puts nine out of ten of my listeners to sleep immediately, but the *tenth* one . . . ah, *that* is worth waiting for.

How to evaluate the credibility of gatekeepers? Most of the criteria are the same as the criteria for evaluating credibility in general, and those were discussed in Chapters Eight and Ten. But this idea of communication flow through networks adds another. It is important to know where the gatekeeper gets his or her information: how many previous gatekeepers it has passed through, where it originated, and whether it has been confirmed by more than one report.

Upstream from the Media

But there is another network of gatekeepers feeding information *to* the media. Behind the front-page story, the feature article, and the newscaster on the screen is another social structure consisting of several layers of gatekeepers who have different motives, serve different functions, and are capable of restricting or altering the information which flows through the media membrane into the society at large.

For one thing, information has to be chopped up, fragmented, and parceled, so it can be squeezed through the format of a particular medium. A news item has to be considered extremely important before it will be given more than sixty-second coverage on a TV newscast or more than a few column inches on the front page of a newspaper. It must be important, that is, unless it is bizarre or contains some "human interest" factor. A major newspaper published near my home will invariably devote banner headlines to any mass ice-pick murder which has occurred anywhere in the country. Not being a devotee of mass ice-pick murders, I don't buy it unless I want to read the want ads.

Further, news must break at the right time and place in order to qualify for coverage in many media. Sometimes this warps the news event itself. The national political conventions try to time the choice of their presidential nominees so their acceptance speeches will catch a prime-time audience. Butterfield's original admission that Nixon had bugged his own office occurred out of sight of TV cameras, but it was essentially reenacted with appropriate theatricals for the benefit of a nationwide audience.

Thus the formats of the media strongly influence our perceptions of and expectations about the world. It comes to us in fragments. We expect to know about it immediately or not at all. We expect it to reach a climax quickly and dramatically, or we become bored, impatient, or frustrated. And we experience some difficulty distinguishing between reality and illusion. I recall riding between Pueblo and Colorado Springs when the driver suddenly exclaimed "I saw a wreck!" He left the freeway and drove back five miles along the access road to find a car which had driven over an embankment and rolled several times. When I asked him why it took so long for him to react to what he had seen, he explained that it had taken him that long to realize he was not watching TV—that such an occurrence in reality was likely to hurt or kill someone. The victim of the accident apparently thought he, too, was on TV, because he crawled out of the car without a scratch. Only the car seemed to know the whole thing was real, and it was dead.

McLuhan has written extensively about how the media influence our perceptions and thought patterns, to the point that the media *formats* influence is more than the media content.[5] His approach seems to me to be essentially an update of the Whorfian hypothesis discussed in my chapter on language. One's perceptions are influenced by the language one learns, and "language" is frequently indistinguishable from format. The television format, for example, is or is very similar to a language, and it tends to mold our perceptions.

Behind the face of the media, a social structure of editors, advertisers, and media corporations operate to select what we see, hear, and read. The editors are almost completely anonymous as far as the general public is concerned, but it is their opinions and policies, modified by economic and political pressures, which largely determine what comes through to us. They occupy a strange place between the reporters, who tend to be politically and economically liberal, and the owners and advertisers, who tend to be conservative.

There is real pressure on the editors to reinforce traditional American values and to avoid putting the American system in a bad light; there is pressure to adopt editorial policies which do not interfere too flagrantly with the interests of owners and advertisers; there is pressure to maintain circulation or audience ratings, so that it sometimes appears they are determined to appeal to the "lowest common denominator" and to select only bad news—which may be redundant, since it sometimes appears it isn't news if it isn't bad. There is pressure on the one hand to avoid controversial issues, since they may offend the audience and have the additional disadvantage of requiring that equal time be given to all viewpoints. On the other hand, however, editors know that controversy *is* news. They might try to predict trends and fads, and know which are which, but their predictions as a group tend to be self-fulfilling, since the media *en masse* make and break trends.

I tend to sympathize with the plight of the editor and his owner-imposed need to keep his enterprise economically solvent by keeping both advertisers and subscribers relatively happy. But it is unfortunate that economic considerations play such an important role in the dissemination of information in our society. Doig and Doig put it well when they said: "The First Amendment to the Constitution did not intend press freedom simply as a license to print money."[6]

Further upstream in this network are the reporters, who are subject to their own pressures. Some of these are matters of logistics, the deployment of personnel and equipment to meet demands of time and distance. On the national scene, no matter when or where a story breaks there will *always* be a problem with deadlines, so that reporters working with "breaking" news of national significance always work under time pressure. If a story breaks just right for the *San Francisco Chronicle,* it will be just wrong for the *New York Times,* a real panic for the *Chicago Tribune,* and a rush for the *Denver Post.* And that is more than just a *reporter's* problem. It is *our* problem, because stories reported under time pressure are likely to be filled with inaccuracies, misquotes, and limited perspectives.

Just moving the troops and their weapons may distort the news, too. To begin with, news tends to be *created* where the reporters and their equipment *are.* But if news does break in a small town, for example, there is a real dilemma. If the reporters don't arrive there with their equipment, we get a telephoned report from a "stringer," coupled with old photographs dug out of the files and, on TV, a "voice-over" narration by a studio newscaster who may not really know any more about the situation than the listener does. If the reporters *do* get there with their equipment, the army may trample the story right into the grass, and the presence of all those people, cameras, and sound trucks is bound to distort it.

Then there are the pressures imposed by the relationship between the reporter and the newsmakers. These problems may be blatant and obvious, as in the case of "junketing": a group of reporters are invited to report on the opening of a new resort in Acapulco in February, and their expenses, of course, are paid. Or an automotive editor is invited to drive a new model for a few months so he can really evaluate it in depth. At no cost to him or his magazine, of course. Or a corporation

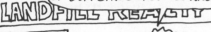

launches an advertising campaign for a new product and throws a bash for the reporters. Or a select group of critics are invited to preview a new movie and have dinner with its stars. And on and on. No one says anything about how the movie ought to be reviewed, of course, but the critics know why their names are on the guest list.

A more subtle problem is that there is frequently one side of a story which is much easier to get. When a federal agency or a large corporation is pitted against a disorganized group of minority renters, for example, propaganda is going to gush from the agency or the corporation through its public relations people.

Which brings us to the problem of the reporter's need to treat his sources with a certain amount of consideration lest they simply dry up. Sometimes this requires maintaining the anonymity of the source, which interferes with our ability to evaluate his reliability. On the other hand, there is a great amount of information which would never become public if the source could not depend on remaining anonymous. But this also raises the possibility of "leaking" false information or sending up "trial balloons" to test public reaction without ever taking responsibility. Many of the "dirty tricks" referred to in the Watergate investigations involved leaking information that was damaging to the reputations of political enemies. John Kennedy "leaked" the story that he was going to appoint Robert Kennedy to the post of attorney general and then weeks later, when he saw there was not going to be any "fire storm" of negative reaction, he actually did so.

Sometimes the need to maintain good relations with his sources puts restraint on the vigor with which the reporter probes his leads. Important news sources can punish reporters by cutting them out of important news breaks or even by giving "scoops" selectively to their competitors.

And of course the reporter is always trying to decide the extent to which he should allow his own values to intrude into his reporting—the extent to which he should practice "advocacy journalism." When a political demagogue makes unsupported charges or when a Nazi makes ethnic slurs against Jews or blacks, is a reporter obligated to report them? Of course not. He is not *obligated* to report any specific item. And therein lies the crux of the problem. He must *choose* what he is going to report, he must *choose* how he is going to word it, and he must *choose* the background information, perspective, or context in which he reports it. Thus Nicholas von Hoffman, columnist for the *Washing-ton Post,* has said:

> What editors and politicians call objective journalism is the present moment, the isolated incident, without any secondary or qualifying information. . . .
> By these standards objectivity consists of limiting oneself to accurate quotation.[7]

And Ron Dorfman, who edits the *Chicago Journalism Review,* maintains that "Every news story you write is advocacy of something, even if it is only neutrality."[8] Still, there is a strong tradition in American journalism which says *editorializing* must be clearly identified as such and strictly segregated from "straight" reporting.

And thus to those gatekeepers furthest upstream in this communication network: the newsmakers themselves. We know too well now that public relations men as prestigious as presidents' press secretaries do in fact evade the truth, tell half-truths, make statements of supposed fact which become "inoperative," and—is it possible?—even *lie.* And the frustrating thing is that the strange system that has evolved in this country makes public lies seem almost necessary. For example, suppose a reporter asks the press secretary if the president is considering imposing price controls. The press secretary knows he is, but if he says "yes" or even "no comment" thousands of corporations will immediately raise their prices while they still can. What *does* he say? What would *you* say?

Does the public have the right to know *everything?* Do we have the right to know whether Ted Kennedy had sexual relations with Mary Jo Kopechne? If so, do we also have the right to know whether the widow Payne is having sexual relations with Jack Frost? Now we may not *care,* but that isn't the question. If for some reason the public *does* care, does the public's right to know supersede the widow Payne's and Jack's right to privacy?

And does the public's right to know supersede the government's right to privacy in cases of "national security"? Always? Ever? Never? And who decides?

Finally, some newsmakers open the gates deliberately and send all manner of nonsense flooding out. They perpetrate hoaxes on the public, they start rumors, and they deliberately stage misleading events

for the media to report. Political demonstrations *for* candidates are frequently staged, and at the zenith of the "dirty tricks" era some candidates allegedly encouraged and sometimes paid "social undesirables" to demonstrate *against* them or for their opposition.

Right-wing political groups have at various times reported straight-facedly that the peace symbol is meant to represent an inverted broken cross and so is anti-Christian, and that the small letter "c" on some canned goods is put there to identify those safe for consumption when the Communists poison our food supplies. But the left wing has its own imaginative propagandists at work. One of their creations, frequently used against Nixon in his law-and-order days, was the following quote attributed to Hitler:

> The streets of our country are in turmoil.
> The universities are filled with students rebelling and rioting.
> Communists are seeking to destroy our country. Russia is threatening us with her might and the republic is in danger. Yes, danger from within and without.
> We need law and order. Yes, without law and order our nation cannot survive. Elect us and we shall restore law and order.

Careful research by scholars specializing in the politics of the Third Reich has thus far failed to unearth any record of such a statement.[9]

With all of these gatekeepers intervening between ourselves and that overwhelmingly large proportion of the world that we cannot experience directly, one is tempted to backpack deep into the wilderness and forget the whole thing. Some of us could do that, but if we all tried it—zap—there goes the wilderness. Perhaps someday there will be TV sound cameras installed everywhere so we can tune in to any part of the world and see for ourselves what is happening there. Or perhaps we will all learn the technique of astral projection so we can send our minds off to observe for themselves while our bodies rest comfortably at home in bed. *But so long as we have to rely on the senses of others, or at best rely on cameras and microphones which others decide where to point, our best bet is to learn all we can about the gatekeepers and how they constrain the flow of communication in mass society.*

Summary

The flow of communication in a *face-to-face group* will depend upon the reasons the members belong to the group, will change as the group goes through various phases of development, will change as a leader and a power hierarchy emerge, will change as interpersonal bargaining progresses and coalitions form and dissolve, will change as members express and then either abandon or retain deviant opinions, and will depend through all of this on the physical setting and seating positions of the members.

Communication flow in *formal organizations* will be affected by many of these same factors, but it will also be affected by the presence of formal and informal communication networks, formal power hierarchies, perceived status hierarchies, affiliation networks, formal and informal decision processes, and interactions among such networks, hierarchies, and processes as well as the characteristics of specific personnel and the physical layout of the organization. Information received by an individual in society can be traced back through a network of "post-media" gatekeepers through the media interface and then back through a network of "pre-media" gatekeepers including editors, media owners, advertisers, reporters, and newsmakers, all of whom are subject to pressures which tend to distort the facts. It is important that the consumer of mass communication be aware of these *gatekeeper networks* and the pressures which bear upon them.

Suggestions for Developing Awareness

1. Interview a college or university department chairperson about the organization of the department that the person chairs. Find out how decisions are made and by whom they are made, who talks to whom, about what, and when. Make your questions as specific as possible and attempt to find out about both the formal and informal communication flow.

2. Some departments allow students to observe department meetings. If you can find a willing department, analyze one of their meetings in terms

of leadership and power. Who appears to be the leader? Is it the designated leader (department chairperson) or does another leader emerge? Does communication flow through the leader? What power does the leader display in controlling the communication flow and the decision process? If a decision was made, was it *really* democratic or was it the leader's choice?

Note: You might want to have one group do exercise 1 and another group do exercise 2. Then compare the results each group obtains. To what extent is the chairperson's perception of his or her department congruent with what you observe actually happening in the department meeting?

3. Listen to, watch, and/or read two different news reports of the same event. Are there differences in the content of the reports? What are those differences? Are they misleading? Which report do you believe? How did you decide?

4. There is an old party game called "rumor transmission." A group of people form a circle and choose a person to start the game. Whoever starts the game might want to choose a picture to compose a story about or an incident they have participated in. This person whispers a story to the next person and so forth around the circle. The last person to hear the story tells the group what he or she has heard.

   Try this game and discuss how the message gets distorted as it moves from person to person. Then consider how this phenomenon can affect your ability to make a good decision. For example, how reliable is information you get from news sources? Consider that a news item travels through several human filters before it reaches you.

5. Euphemisms run rampant in news stories and political speeches. A euphemism is the substitution of a pleasant word for an unpleasant one. The following examples are euphemisms: "pacification of the enemy infrastructure" means "blasting the Viet Cong out of a village"; "aversion therapy" means "beatings in prisons"; "strategic social deprivation" means "solitary confinement."

   Choose a newspaper account of a story and find the euphemisms. Discuss how they bias the story and influence your feelings about the event. Then substitute the "real" meanings in place of the euphemisms. How does this change the impact of the story on the public?

References

1. R.F. Bales and F.L. Strodtbeck, "Phases in Group Problem Solving," *Journal of Abnormal and Social Psychology* 46 (1951): 485-495.
2. Eugene Walton, "A Study of Organizational Communication Systems," *Personnel Administration*, May-June 1963.
3. Walton, *op. cit.*
4. Samuel Becker, "Rhetorical Studies for the Contemporary World," in *The Prospect of Rhetoric*, eds. Lloyd F. Bitzer and Edwin Black (Englewood Cliffs, N.J.: Prentice-Hall, 1971), pp. 21-43.
5. Marshall McLuhan, *Understanding Media: The Extensions of Man* (New York: McGraw-Hill, 1964); and *The Gutenberg Galaxy: The Making of Typographic Man* (Toronto: University of Toronto Press, 1962).
6. Ivan Doig and Carol Doig, *News: A Consumer's Guide* (Englewood Cliffs, N.J.: Prentice-Hall, 1972), p. 47.
7. *Editor and Publisher*, July 4, 1970, p. 44; cited in Doig and Doig, *op. cit.*, p. 110.
8. *Editor and Publisher*, November 14, 1970, p. 18; cited in Doig and Doig, *op. cit.*, p. 111.
9. Jerome Beatty, Jr., "Funny Stories," *Esquire* (November 1970): 44-50.

Communication Among Cultures

Some American Beliefs
Some American Values
Cultural Plans, Policies, and Behavior Patterns
Some General Problems

Interracial Communication

Interracial Beliefs: Stereotyping
Interracial Values: Prejudice
Interracial Plans and Policies: Discrimination
Interracial Communication Plans and Policies
Functions of Stereotyping, Prejudice, and Discrimination
   Social Learning
   Consistency
   Ego-Maintenance

Summary

Chapter Fifteen

Reflections in the Cultural Interface: To See Ourselves as Others See Us

There are many reasons for studying intercultural and interracial communication, not the least of which is to foster understanding among
cultures and peace among nations. But those are long-range goals.
There is a more immediate benefit:

> *By understanding people of other cultures and communi-*
> *cating with them, one can form a better picture of one's*
> *own culture and hence a better understanding of oneself.*

   Americans argue about many things, of course. But the beliefs,
values, and patterns of behavior which are most typical of our culture
are those which are least controversial. They are "truisms" which are
usually assumed and accepted without question. Because they are not
questioned by others within our culture, we often accept them as *facts
about the world* rather than mere culturally-bound opinions. Thus we
are not *aware* that we are operating on the basis of certain assumptions. That brings us back again to the theme of this book—that communication is more reliable insofar as communicators are aware of
what they are doing.
   However, when we study intercultural *communication,* we are not
merely comparing cultures. Rather, we are studying those points at
which cultures meet, merge, and interact—that is, we are studying
cultural *interfaces.* And it is at these interfaces where one can see most
clearly the contrast between cultures. Thus the unstated assumptions
of one's own culture are best reflected in the intercultural interface,
where they are magnified by intercultural communication.

Communication Among Cultures

In Chapter Two I pointed out that individuals have certain beliefs on
which they base their values. They adopt certain plans which they
believe will best achieve those values or will be most consistent with
them. Now obviously I can't talk about *all* cultural beliefs, values, and
plans. Consequently, I will try instead to provide a few examples of

intercultural differences in each area and the ways those differences complicate intercultural communication.[1] First, I will consider some beliefs and values which researchers have concluded seem to dominate American culture, and then I will discuss how these beliefs and values result in specific behavior patterns which clash with those derived from the beliefs and values of other cultures.

Some American Beliefs

One way to divide beliefs into categories is to talk about beliefs regarding *human nature,* the *physical world,* and the *supernatural.*

Regarding human nature, Americans seem to assume that people are basically "rational" and thus, while they may make mistakes, they can generally be trusted to make decisions for themselves. Hence, the democratic ideal, the concept of justice as consisting of a trial by jury of one's peers, and the devotion to free enterprise, which allows the consumer to select for himself the goods he will buy from a selection offered in the open competition of a free marketplace. That, of course, seems to be only a dominant belief. Like much of this discussion, it rests on some guarded stereotyping. Many politicians do not seem to assume much rationality on the part of their constituents. The jury trial system is hedged about with elaborate instructions to the jury and supervised by a judge whose function is to see that the rules of evidence are observed. Ad writers who produce TV commercials and magazine advertisements seem to assume the opposite, relying on unproven associations between their products and audience values. Social psychologists seem to have demonstrated, if anything, that Americans make irrational decisions rather frequently. Consequently, we might have to modify the assertion to say Americans believe human nature is *basically* rational, but frequently corrupted by unscrupulous peddlers of illogic.

To some extent, I suppose, this may be a value rather than a belief: Americans believe they *should* be rational. Here in the late 1970s, however, even that is being contested by those who argue that people spend too much time "intellectualizing" and too little time "feeling." Whether that represents a long-term change in American culture or just a passing fancy remains to be seen.

Americans also seem to believe that humans are some mixture of good and evil: either they are good but corruptible *or* they are evil but capable of rehabilitation. Further, they seem suspicious of too much pleasure and certainly suspicious if not downright antagonistic to *seeking* pleasure for its own sake.

However, fate is just and hard work will be justly rewarded with pleasure and happiness. This means, of course, that the most lowly born can, by virtue of hard work, achieve success in terms of either prestige or money. Similarly, a society can achieve progress by hard work and ingenuity. Unfortunately, the converse is also held valid: when people are *not* successful or societies do *not* progress, the suspicion is strong that someone must have been shirking his duty.

Progress, of course, requires humankind to dominate nature, which Americans generally assume they can do through miracles of science and technology. They assume that science and technology are the most effective means to dominate nature because nature is basically mechanistic and thus susceptible to scientific explanation and technological control. Americans are a little divided at this point with respect to how one is to understand nature. They started out with a very practical, concrete approach, intolerant of abstractions. But "the wonders of modern science" have produced so many practical, concrete results, even though based on abstractions which few people understand, that most Americans have come to accept *scientific* abstractions without question. Nonscientific abstractions, however, are not likely to be tolerated.

One of the more curious aspects of American culture is the peculiar approach to the supernatural. Here we have a culture which places great emphasis on the ability of humans to better themselves and to control nature by their own industry and ingenuity—a culture which accepts a view of nature as basically mechanistic and comprehensible. But despite this general belief system which seems to put humankind at the center of an orderly universe, most Americans believe instead that *a single* all-knowing and all-powerful god occupies that central position. The apparent contradiction seems to be reconciled by two beliefs: (1) God *rewards* a person's industry and ingenuity, just as the owner of a firm might be expected to reward a junior partner, and (2) the orderly, lawful nature of the universe is evidence that it was created by God, since it would not be so orderly had it occurred by chance. Scientific explanations involving such concepts as evolution can be reconciled with the notion of an all-powerful creator by assuming that God *at some point* created the universe and continues to preside over its development.

List examples of behavior which seem to be based on some of the "American beliefs" discussed in this chapter.

Some American Values

Most American values seem to follow rather directly from the beliefs just described. Adapting the organization originated by Kluckholn and modified by Condon and Yousef, both of whom were cited earlier, I will deal with three major value categories: self, family, and society.

As a result of their pervasive belief that a person can better himself by his own ability and hard work, Americans place high value on *individuality;* because this same belief implies a relationship between change and progress, they value youth above age; because this belief implies also that a person's "fate" is in fact his or her own doing, they value equality of opportunity between the sexes and among racial groups; and they place a higher value on *doing* than upon being. The value of sexual and racial equality requires a little explanation, since so much has been said about sexual and racial *in*equality in the United States. First, such equality *does* exist in the United States *to a greater degree than in most cultures.* Second, insofar as it does not exist, it is still proclaimed as a value, resulting in a peculiarly hypocritical posture. The contradiction between the value and the actuality is rationalized by some variation of the "separate but equal" doctrine. Thus men and women are held to be *equal* but *different,* and thus suited to different *but* equal roles in the society. The same rationalization is applied to explain the obvious differences in social roles occupied by the different races, with an additional stinger: races which occupy low socioeconomic positions are held to do so not because they have been denied equal opportunity, but rather because they do not work hard enough to better themselves. These are abhorrent and hypocritical rationalizations, yes, but they are *pervasive* beliefs nevertheless—pervasive because they are necessary to reconcile obvious status inequities with the basic belief that God and/or fate is just.

Regarding the family, Americans prefer an individualistic, democratic, open, mobile orientation. That is, family lineage and identification is not of as great concern among Americans as it is in most cultures; authority is likely to be less centered in one or the other of the parents; rights and obligations of children do not depend rigidly upon birth order and sex; and family members are relatively free to move away to establish homes of their own in other cities or states.

As for social values, Americans are not so quick to assume that one accepts a social obligation whenever one accepts a gift or a favor from another, nor do they hold to rules by which the social classes are obligated to one another. Americans seem to value individuality over group loyalty; they are relatively free to move from group to group. They value directness in social relationships; social relationships and contracts are not frequently "arranged" by third parties. All of this really leads up to one of the most important American social values: informality. Americans tend to be quite impatient with titles, rituals, ceremonies, and the like. But when it comes to *property*, they are generally very acquisitive and jealous. The rule almost seems to be "you are what you own," and property rights sometimes seem to be more important than human rights. Not that Americans necessarily lack generosity, but parting with one's property must be an *individual's voluntary* act.

Think of examples of your *own* behavior that are inconsistent with the "typical" American beliefs and values mentioned in this chapter.

Cultural Plans, Policies, and Behavior Patterns

I *hope* many of you are saying by now: "These aren't beliefs and values of typical Americans. *I'm* a typical American and I don't hold many of these beliefs and values." I hope you are saying that because it is the beginning of *wisdom* in intercultural encounters. "Typical" Americans are hard to find and so are "typical" Japanese, Argentines, and Ukranians.

Nevertheless, these beliefs and values are important to you personally for at least three reasons. First, even if you do not agree with them, they are culturally dominant values with which you have had to deal all your life. Thus even if you rejected some of them, they may have shaped your personal opinions by providing you with dominant opinions against which to react. Second, and more important to intercultural communication, they form the stereotype of "the typical American" held by those of other cultures. If you visit a foreign country, this stereotype may largely determine how you are treated, because the residents of that country *expect* you to be like the stereotype. Third, when you visit another culture you may find yourself almost unconsciously defending this stereotype and even beginning to play the stereotyped American role. The people you meet may accept the stereotype so universally and completely as *American* that it seems almost unpatriotic—even traitorous—to say *"I'm* not like that; *I* think those are foolish and dangerous opinions." At the worst you *may* come to adopt the stereotype; at the very best you will be confused by the way people react to you.

Now suppose we turn this around so as to empathize with the plight of an Arab visiting *this* country. Surely he or she has the same problems. *Thus rather than being visited by "typical" Arabs (and Japanese, and Germans, and Swedes), it may be that we create them by our stereotypical expectations.*

That is one problem which occurs at the intercultural interface. Beyond that, there are certain behavior patterns which are *derived* from pervasive cultural beliefs and values. Since an individual learns the behavior patterns separately from the beliefs and values, he frequently maintains the behavior patterns even after he has rejected the beliefs and values on which they are based. In fact, he may not even realize there is any relation between them. The behavior patterns are simply "the way things are done"; they are not derived from cultural assumptions.

For example, a friend of mine reports that a student in one of her classes in intercultural communication recently said "I don't have any cultural assumptions, and I don't have *time* to *spend* learning about them."[2] The metaphor of "spending time" is based on some very typically American cultural assumptions which the student obviously didn't recognize. The first is the acute value Americans place on property. The second is the notion that time is so valuable a property that it is to be "spent" like money, conserved and doled out among competing interests. Now the student may or may not have accepted those values, but the idiom he used would be quite meaningless if translated literally into the language of a culture which did not share those values.

Now I simply don't have space to "spend" on a detailed survey of specific intercultural differences in verbal and nonverbal behavior. Many have already been mentioned in the chapters on language and extraverbal communication. But a few illustrations might be useful.

As I have mentioned, some other cultures assume that a compliment or a gift imposes an obligation upon the receiver. Consequently, an American visitor, making no such assumption, might out of politeness compliment his foreign host on a particularly valuable and valued possession and then be embarrassed when the host insists on presenting it to him. Similarly, I recall inviting a foreign graduate student to a cocktail party at my home. When he arrived he presented me with not only a bottle of wine, but a set of wine glasses as well. I am to this day unsure whether my profuse thanks was adequate to discharge any obligation this gift may have imposed. That depends, of course, on whether we were operating on his cultural assumptions or mine.

Another student, of Mexican descent who was raised in Arizona, told in class of his embarrassment after he moved to California when he visited a girl to whom he had been introduced at a dance. When her brother answered the door he asked for "Dolores," but her brother would only answer "Who do you want to see?" Fortunately, she heard him at the door and came to help. Later she explained that her brother considered "Dolores" too familiar a form of address when he was calling on her for the first time; he should have asked for "Senorita _____ ."

Because of the American preoccupation with equality, directness, and informality, American audiences do not hesitate to provide public speakers with feedback, whether negative or positive. Japanese audiences, however, are not so quick to indicate that they are displeased with a speaker, and are likely to indicate their displeasure by very subtle nonverbal means. Thus an American speaker before a Japanese audience may have real difficulty knowing whether his listeners are accepting or rejecting what he says.

I could continue giving examples, but space doesn't allow it. The book by Condon and Yousef, already cited, contains many examples of the faux pas that Americans are capable of committing when visiting other cultures. I would recommend you pack it in your suitcase along with your foreign language dictionary the next time you go abroad.

Some General Problems

One easy way to describe the general problems one is likely to encounter in intercultural communication is in terms of a game which is used a great deal in courses about intercultural communication. The players are divided into two groups, or "cultures," and sent to different rooms, where they learn the "rules" of their respective "cultures." Then they visit back and forth and, as visitors, try to adapt to the culture they are visiting. One of the cultures is set up so as to promote competitiveness; the members of this culture are engaged in a continuous card game in which *winning the game* by skillful trading of cards is of primary importance. The other culture is set up so as to emphasize social interaction; they too play a card game, but the game is part of the ritual which accompanies the social exchanges.

The first problem which quickly becomes obvious in this game is that *people are uncomfortable in cultures which operate by rules different from those of their own culture.* Visitors from the "competitive" culture are seldom comfortable in the "social" culture, and vice versa. They invariably express relief when they are allowed to return to their "own" cultures. What is so astonishing about this fact is that they may have spent as little as ten or fifteen minutes becoming familiar with the rules of their "own" culture; yet they identify with that culture so thoroughly that they reject the other. Imagine, then, what a *lifetime* spent learning the rules of one culture can do to your ability and willingness to adapt to another.

Second, *there is a strong tendency to describe another culture in terms of your own.* That is evident when those who have visited the "social" culture return to their own "competitive" culture. The others crowd around them and ask questions such as: "How do you win their game?"

and "Which are the high cards?" They simply don't consider the possibility that winning the card game may not be important in the other culture.

Third, *visitors generally fail to notice what is relevant and valuable in another culture.* Thus those from the "social" culture frequently fail to notice that the cards used in the "competitive" culture are *numbered,* or at least that those numbers are important. On the other hand, visitors from the "competitive" culture spend so much time watching the *cards* when they visit the "social" culture that they never see the importance of the *conversation.*

Fourth, *visitors tend to misinterpret the actions of the members of other cultures because of their own cultural assumptions.* When members of the "social" culture visit the "competitive" culture they are given certain cards which are valuable in their "new" culture. Since the "competitors" know that, they flock around the visitors as soon as they arrive, *trying to get their valuable cards.* Not knowing this, the "social" visitors generally describe the "competitive" culture as very "friendly," when in fact the visitors are being exploited. Conversely, when "competitive" visitors arrive in the "social" culture they see everyone else talking and laughing. But when they try to join the fun, not knowing the social rules, they almost invariably meet with rejection. Consequently, they generally describe the "social" culture as cold and unfriendly.

Finally, *visitors are likely to violate specific prescribed behavior patterns which they don't know about.* This is especially likely to happen when they try to mimic the behavior of those within the culture. The "competitive" visitors see all the happy socializing in the "social" culture, so they try to join it. However, they frequently approach someone of the opposite sex, and since there are carefully prescribed rules for approaching someone of the opposite sex in the "social" culture, they are frequently escorted out of the room in disgrace. Similarly, "social" visitors to the "competitive" culture see others writing numbers on the board. The numbers represent points that have been earned but the visitors don't know that, so they write their own numbers on the board and put their names beside them. That is a lot like writing a check when you don't have money in the bank, so the "visitors" are viewed as dishonest when in fact *they just don't know.*

Interracial Communication

Most of what has been said about intercultural communication applies
equally well to interracial communication. The difference is that interracial communication occurs among people of different racial, ethnic,
and cultural *backgrounds* who nevertheless live near one another and
are to some extent part of the same general culture. Thus they are
forced to deal with one another to some extent, whereas people usually
engage in intercultural communication because they *want* to. In fact,
visiting another *culture* is usually a privilege for which one pays; interacting with another *racial group* within one's own country is not usually
highly valued. The intercultural differences are considered exotic;
the interracial differences are at best common and at worst irritating.

Further, different racial groups within a culture naturally share many of the same assumptions, behaviors, symbols, and the like, which only serves to emphasize the differences. In fact, a given cultural assumption or behavior may seem perfectly reasonable in its home culture, but not when transplanted into and maintained in another culture.

The existence of different racial and ethnic characteristics, including different skin colors, accents, and customs, provides a variety of cues for group formation. Then the usual phenomena of group identification, which I talked about in Chapter Eight, begin to assert themselves: the members of one's own group tend to be seen as more productive, intelligent, likeable, and so forth, whereas the members of out-groups are disparaged.

All of this is complicated by the fact that these "groups" inevitably compete for limited jobs, money, and other resources. Theoretically, the *groups* don't compete; *individuals* compete with one another. But in fact, for the reasons just cited, those in power are likely to give preference to those of their own ethnic or racial groups. Frequently, they do not realize they are doing so; it is just that those of their own groups also coincidentally have many characteristics they consider valuable.

Which leads to the primary difference between these two types of communication: there is likely to be a much higher level of tension — even anger — associated with interracial communication.

Interracial Beliefs: Stereotyping

We have to generalize in order to get along in the world. If we could not generalize, we could not learn; we would be destined to repeat our mistakes forever. Stereotyping is a form of generalization. As I am using the term here, "stereotyping" is generalization applied to people.

Stereotyping is not *necessarily* nor *always* an undesirable practice. I may help a child cross a busy street because I can predict fairly accurately on the basis of my general stereotype of children that *this* child probably needs help when confronted with this sort of traffic.

Nor are stereotypes *necessarily* derogatory. Some of my best friends are stereotypes. If I say "I think you are *the kind of person* I would like to know," I am identifying you with a stereotype, but I hope you would not be insulted.

But stereotyping can become pathological when it is overused, when one begins to react to people as stereotypes rather than as individuals. If a stereotype is used as a very tentative "theory" as to what a stranger may be like and then discarded quickly as soon as the stranger becomes an acquaintance, it may be useful. Stereotyping is a means of reducing uncertainty, and it provides *some* basis on which to proceed. But among people who fear uncertainty, stereotyping can become a crutch which prevents the healthy development of social sensitivity.

Racial stereotypes are especially dangerous because they are so likely to be used to justify exploitation of other races. If one believes all blacks are strong, athletic, happy, and satisfied with low-paying menial jobs, it is much easier to justify "keeping them in their place" as low-paid laborers or somewhat higher-paid but nonthreatening entertainers. Notice that to identify someone as strong, athletic, happy, and easily satisfied is not derogatory *per se;* what is objectionable about this set of beliefs is that it has been used as justification for an exploitative social system.

Interracial Values: Prejudice

But beliefs always involve values, and beliefs about other races too frequently involve *negative* values. While "prejudice" in general can be favorable or unfavorable, the term *"racial* prejudice" invariably means *unfavorable* evaluation of an individual on the basis of his race. It is easy enough to see that believing those of another race to be lazy, dirty, and dishonest is evaluating that race negatively, since those are obvious negative values for most white Americans. But other races just can't win, for some races which white Americans believe to be clean and industrious are *still* negatively evaluated: they are so clean and industrious they must be hatching a plot to control the American economy and political structure.

A survey I conducted in the late 1960s among white residents of a small town in central Illinois provides an example of the ways racial beliefs and values can be organized to maintain prejudice in subtle ways.[3] Even in such an isolated community several years ago the respondents had learned the "right" answers to most of the questions. They did not indicate they believed blacks in general to be intellectually inferior, dishonest, prone to violence, or sexually promiscuous as per the older stereotype. But they were generally negative toward all aspects of civil rights movements and very negative toward interracial marriage. Further, these people believed that blacks were or should be satisfied with their status in the community, since they were believed to receive equal treatment in the schools, courts, and stores in the town. What few racial disturbances had occurred were attributed to the presence of outsiders stirring up trouble.

Interracial Plans and Policies: Discrimination

With the exception of the beliefs about interracial marriage, the picture one would get from looking at these beliefs and values is that of a group of fairly liberal townspeople who believed blacks and whites to be equal, who were willing to treat them alike, and who only wanted to preserve the serenity of their little community.

But there was a third part of the questionnaire which asked them what kinds of *behaviors* they were willing to perform with specific people. They were asked to indicate how likely it was that they would do such things as "admit this person to my neighborhood," "date this person," "be a partner in an intellectual game with this person," or "work for this person." The "persons" referred to were described in terms of age, sex, occupation, and race. But for every white person described there was a black who was identical in every respect except race. That fact was not called to the attention of the respondents, of course.

The payoff was this: *Almost nineteen out of every twenty respondents indicated they would treat the whites more favorably than the blacks.* Thus although the respondents' professed beliefs and values revealed little *stereotyping* or *prejudice*, their plans and policies indicated most of them would *discriminate* against blacks.

Interracial Communication Plans and Policies

Numerous studies have demonstrated how people base their perceptual plans on racial beliefs and values. One of the best known is that of Allport and Postman in which a picture of a white man holding a

razor and facing a black man is shown briefly to one person, who then describes the picture to another person, who describes it to another, and so on. The razor soon ends up in the hand of the black man.[4]

I have seen something similar happen in a communication class for white policemen. The policemen heard an audiotape which was supposed to be a recording of the radio communication of two policemen and the dispatcher. The policemen report they are investigating a black man and a white woman they see leaving a building at night. A scuffle ensues and the black man is arrested. Two of the more interesting responses are: (1) several of the students agreed that the car the couple were getting into was a *Cadillac,* when in fact it was described as a Corvette, and (2) they provided descriptions of the woman's provocative dress, when in fact her dress was not described on the tape.

There is no way to describe all the ways stereotyped beliefs and prejudiced values are reflected in communication plans. Andrea Rich, however, conducted a study in which she asked members of various racial and ethnic groups to compose lists of statements they particularly resented from members of other racial and ethnic groups.[5] She then classified these statements into five categories: (1) stereotypic statements, such as "blacks have natural soul," "Mexicans are loyal and will work for little money," and "Japanese are very hard-working"; (2) statements lacking sympathy with antiestablishment complaints, such as "You have the same opportunities as anyone else," "Nothing happens overnight," and "What do you people want?" (3) condescending statements including words such as "boy," "culturally deprived," and "minority"; (4) statements regarding sexual attributes or interracial sex, such as statements about the promiscuity of the women of the group or the sexual desire of the men for white women; and (5) statements trying to cross the ethnic line, such as those containing the terms "soul brother," "right on," and "amigo."

Such lists will never be complete, since the *specific* problems of interracial communication will be different by the time this book is published. Similarly, it is impossible to describe everything which might go awry in intercultural communication. What is more important is the development of sensitivity, empathy, and awareness with respect to interracial communication. That may be enhanced by some consideration of the functions racial discrimination may serve for an individual.

Functions of Stereotyping, Prejudice, and Discrimination

Like other opinions and policies, the racial stereotyping, prejudice, and discrimination too often expressed in interracial communication develop in order to serve certain functions. If you will recall the functions of opinions and policies in general, then I can simply discuss how those functions relate to racial opinions and policies.

Social Learning
We learn to express those racial opinions and adopt those interracial communication patterns and manners which are socially rewarded. Children whose parents use words such as "nigger," "honky," "kike," "wop," and "spik" are likely to follow suit. More subtly, children whose parents give nonverbal indications of anxiety or disdain in the presence of people of other races are likely to develop similar nonverbal mannerisms. If your group of friends or the people in the office where you work are given to telling ethnic jokes, the social pressure to laugh and to tell them yourself can be difficult to resist.

Consistency
There are many ways interracial opinions and communication policies operate to maintain consistency. Probably the most pervasive way is this: We observe people of other races cast in certain social roles and economic circumstances, and we use our opinions and policies to justify or explain to ourselves and others *why* they are there. I have said several times in this book that there is a strong tendency to believe fate is just, and if fate isn't, then the American system of democracy certainly is. Consequently, if a given racial group lives in poverty, there is a strong tendency to believe (a) they are lazy, (b) they cannot be trained for or trusted in higher paying jobs, and (c) they like to live that way.

Ego-Maintenance
Frequently, one's self-concept includes expressing certain racial opinions and policies. Members of racial groups with emerging identity and self-awareness are especially prone to this. If one thinks of himself as a militant black or Chicano, it is naturally difficult to express that identity without expressing hostility toward the "Anglo oppressor." On the other hand, the white who sees himself as a liberal is equally

likely to produce condescending statements which other racial groups will see as objectionable.

The ego-defense mechanisms are especially likely to be used against other racial groups, since fear and guilt seem to be major components of racial prejudice. Thus we frequently see white pseudoliberals *denying* and *repressing* racial prejudice, or professing unusually strong attraction to those of other races (reaction formation). When the Black Power movement was strongest and most threatening to Anglos, we saw them buying African art work, using the Black Power handshake, and wearing African garb in droves (identification with the aggressor). But as "equal opportunity employment" and "affirmative action" became more widespread, we saw every unemployed white blaming his troubles on racial quota systems (scapegoating). The scapegoating, of course, was not confined to whites; "whitey" is a ready-made scapegoat to which blacks and Chicanos can attribute any of their troubles, sometimes with justification and sometimes not.

Finally, ego-involvement plays a part in racial prejudice. Remember that *central, extreme* opinions are those most difficult to change and those which are most likely to lead to rejection of anyone who tries to change them. For a majority of white Americans, the opinion that the American system of democracy and free enterprise is basically fair and American foreign policy basically "right" has been both central and extreme. And who were the first to seriously challenge those opinions? You guessed it. Blacks, Chicanos, and their freaky white friends. The rejection was indeed violent, psychologically and physically.

Summary

Intercultural communication provides an opportunity to become aware of the beliefs, values, and policies which are characteristic of one's own culture and to determine to what extent one's own opinions and policies reflect those of his or her culture. Further, the study of intercultural communication can alert one to potential problems which may arise when visiting another culture or encountering a visitor from another culture. Some general types of problems which frequently arise are that the visitor (1) becomes uncomfortable when forced to operate by unfamiliar cultural rules; (2) tends to view and evaluate the new culture on the basis of his own cultural assumptions; (3) may fail to notice what is valued in the new culture; (4) may misinterpret the actions of members of the new culture because of his own cultural assumptions; and (5) the visitor may violate specific prescribed behavior patterns because he or she doesn't know about them.

Interracial communication differs from intercultural communication in that it occurs among groups which are *forced* to deal with one another because they operate within the same culture; they share many of the same cultural assumptions so that those they do not share are emphasized; the racial differences serve as cues for group formation and the resulting discrimination against out-groups; and these "groups" compete for limited jobs, money, and other resources. Thus we form interracial beliefs or *stereotypes,* interracial values or *prejudice,* and on the basis of these we practice interracial policies or *discrimination.* These interracial opinions and policies are reflected in the ways we perceive messages and in the messages we produce, and they serve the functions of social learning, consistency, and ego-maintenance.

Suggestions for Developing Awareness

1. Have you encountered persons from other cultures whose behavior was *inconsistent* with the stereotypes you have of those cultures? If so, give examples.

2. Conduct your own survey of interracial stereotypes. Ask people to write short descriptions or list characteristics they attribute to another race. Are the descriptions or characteristics similar? Can you detect whether they feel favorably or unfavorably toward another race by closely examining the language they used to describe that race?

    You might want to use this format to investigate how your classmates and friends stereotype people of other cultures.

References

1. Some of these examples are taken from the excellent treatment of this area by John C. Condon and Fathi Yousef, *An Introduction to Intercultural Communication* (Indianapolis: Bobbs-Merrill, 1975). The framework of American beliefs and values is also adapted from Condon and Yousef, who in turn adapted it from Florence Kluckholn and Fred L. Strodtbeck, *Variations in Value Orientations* (Evanston, Ill.: Row Peterson, 1961).

2. Sharon Ruhly, personal conversation, May 1975.

3. I reported these results in part in a paper entitled "The Behavioral Syndrome Approach: An Alternative to the Attitude Myth," delivered at the Central States Speech Association Convention in Chicago in April 1970, and also in "Syndromes of Symbolic Interracial Behavior" at the Conference on Symbolic Behavior in Akron, Ohio in October 1970. If you would like more information, write me in care of the publisher.

4. Gordon W. Allport and Leo Postman, *The Psychology of Rumor* (New York: Holt, Rinehart and Winston, 1947).

5. Andrea Rich, "Some Problems in Interracial Communication: An Interracial Group Case Study," *Central States Speech Journal* 22 (1971): 228-235.

Epilogue

My purpose throughout this book has been to emphasize how important it is to be aware of what is happening in communication encounters. I have tried to make the point that, in order that our communication will serve its major functions of information-gathering, facilitating cooperation, and maximizing self-actualization, we must learn to listen critically, cooperatively, and sensitively not only to others but also to ourselves.

To help you develop that sort of awareness, I first described what I consider to be some important aspects of the communication process in general: its role in the development and survival of the human species, how it may be defined in terms of response to symbols, what its major functions are, how it relates to human perception and cognition, what some of its essential characteristics are, and how some of its most important concepts can be represented in models.

Next I described how one can understand oneself and empathize with others during communication: how interpersonal demographic and personality differences can be recognized and bridged; how personal opinions and policies develop so as to maximize consistency, social reward, and ego-maintenance; and how reference groups and reference persons affect communication through commitment, consensus, and credibility.

Then I turned to a description of how messages operate: how they appeal to a variety of motives by means of various types of reasoning, how we express them in language and how language in turn affects us, and how extraverbal messages sometimes complement and sometimes contradict verbal messages.

Finally, I discussed some special problems imposed by certain communication contexts: problems involved in organizing speeches and papers; problems of communication flow in social structures such as small groups, formal organizations, and mass society; and problems which arise when one encounters the unfamiliar beliefs, values, and behavior patterns of other cultures and races.

But I have a few reservations at this point. First, I may have left the impression that communication problems are all that stand between humanity and Utopia. As another writer has put it:

In this day and age one of the most popular forms of piety has to do with communication, somewhat narrowly defined. An ailment called "lack of communication" has taken the place of original sin as an explanation for the ills of the world, while "better communication" is trotted out on every occasion as a universal panacea.[1]

Not all problems are communication problems, and not all disagreements between people are due to inadequate communication. As a simple illustration, imagine two starving cave men fighting over a piece of meat. The problem is not a lack of communication, it is a lack of food. Nor is their disagreement due to a lack of communication. They probably understand each other perfectly. They *may* be able to use communication to solve the problem—by devising cooperative strategies for hunting, for example—but if one succeeds in killing the other, it would be strange to say that poor communication was the cause. Further, *"successful" communication can sometimes create problems where none existed.* Remember that massive wars and massive traffic jams would be impossible if they were not carefully coordinated by means of communication. Communication is a powerful tool, and you can severely hurt yourself with a powerful tool.

Second, by promoting the worship of "awareness" I may have left the impression that analytic thinking is always better than intuitive thinking. Hammond and Brehmer make that sort of distinction:

> The analytic end of the continuum is characterized by a form of thinking that is *explicit, sequential,* and *recoverable.* . . . Intuitive thinking, on the other hand, is *implicit, nonsequential,* and *nonrecoverable.*[2]

Making a decision analytically in response to communication has an advantage in that one can explicitly retrace the process by which one arrived at that decision, can test one's own inferential leaps, and can ask others to check them. But analytic decisions can be dull, plodding affairs, void of creativity. Frequently, intuitive thinking runs on ahead to find imaginative solutions to a problem while the lumbering analyst is still trying to decide whether to take the first step.

So there are two kinds of awareness involved in communication: *analytic* awareness and *intuitive* awareness. Both have a place. For example, one can empathize analytically to some extent by enumerating the probable beliefs, feelings, and motives of another person, but real empathy is going to require some intuition as well. And one can study verbal and extraverbal messages analytically, but intuitive judgments about the meaning or sincerity of the author or speaker certainly shouldn't be disregarded.

Probably it is best to think of the decision process as consisting of two phases. First, one gives one's intuition freedom to rush about producing creative, imaginative alternative solutions or interpretations, and then subjects those alternatives to critical analysis before making a choice.

Third, I may have left the impression that "complete" awareness will produce "correct" decisions. Of course there is no such thing as "complete" awareness, and in most real situations there is no such thing as a "correct" decision. *The best one can hope for is to be aware of the reasons for his choices.* Suppose I discover that a friend is about to spend fifteen dollars to have a stylist work on his hair, and in talking to him I discover he fully recognizes his reason for doing it is purely a matter of ego-maintenance. Now who am I to question his values, so long as he knows what he is doing? Fifteen dollars is probably damned cheap ego-maintenance, as a matter of fact. I'm sure there have been many times I've spent more and profited less.

Which leads to my final reservation: *Amateur communicologists can be just as obnoxious as amateur psychologists.* What friends one can make at a party with some of the following quips:

"You're just saying that because you're middle-aged and insecure."

"That's a very dogmatic position; are you low in self-esteem, too?"

"How terribly Machiavellian!"

"I used to believe that, too, before I realized it was just reaction-formation."

"You're just trying to reduce dissonance."

"Oh, you're trying to appeal to my need for gestalt closure."

"Putting that in the form of a conditional syllogism makes it obviously invalid."

"You're just looking for social reinforcement."

"Oh, you read *Cosmopolitan*? You *know,* of course, what that says about your self-concept."

"Do you know why you just crossed your legs?"

That is the sort of communication awareness the world can probably do without. Still, the temptation to use it as a put-down can be very strong. But enough of that. If I have done my job well that sort of admonition really isn't necessary.

I have honestly enjoyed writing this book, and I feel I have learned a great deal in the process. I hope you have also profited from reading it. I also hope that you will continue to profit—that your developing awareness of communication processes will not stop at this point. *Communication behavior is a set of deeply ingrained habits.* Communication awareness can become a habit, too, but not in the short space of one academic term. A book such as this and a course such as this can produce a surface scratch which can either serve as a guide for deeper etching to follow, or it can be quickly eroded by the abrasion of business as usual.

Communication is a social disease for which there is no known cure. But communication is also the second most pleasant form of social intercourse. Since you can't cure it, enjoy it at a high level of awareness.

Suggestions for Developing Awareness

1. At the beginning of this book the author asked you to be thinking about your own model of communication. Now it is time to ask you to articulate your own working model of communication. What do you see as the essential elements? Discuss why your model is useful and important to you.

2. The goal of this test is to increase awareness of your own communication behavior and that of other people. Plan your own communication course or text with this goal of "communication awareness" in mind. What content and activities would you cover? How would you present them?

References

1. Charlotte Olmstead Kursh, "The Benefits of Poor Communication," *Psychoanalytic Review* 58 (1971): 189-208.
2. Kenneth R. Hammond and Berndt Brehmer, "Quasi-Rationality and Distrust: Implications for International Conflict," in *Human Judgment and Social Interaction,* eds. Leon Rappaport and David A. Summer (New York: Holt, Rinehart and Winston, 1973).

Index

DATE DUE

OCT 20 '80		
NOV 3 '80		
NOV 17 '80		
NOV 28 '80		
NOV 30 '81		
NOV 12 '90		
MAR 16 '92		
APR 6 '92		
APR 27 '92		

GAYLORD   PRINTED IN U.S.A.